# TURNING
# DOWN
# THE
# NOISE

# TURNING

## THE QUIET POWER OF

# DOWN

## SILENCE

# THE

## IN A BUSY WORLD

# NOISE

## Christine Jackman

murdoch books
Sydney | London

Published in 2020 by Murdoch Books, an imprint of Allen & Unwin

Murdoch Books Australia
83 Alexander Street, Crows Nest NSW 2065
Phone: +61 (0)2 8425 0100
murdochbooks.com.au
info@murdochbooks.com.au

Murdoch Books UK
Ormond House, 26–27 Boswell Street, London WC1N 3JZ
Phone: +44 (0) 20 8785 5995
murdochbooks.co.uk
info@murdochbooks.co.uk

A catalogue record for this book is available from the National Library of Australia

ISBN 978 1 76052 589 7 Australia
ISBN 978 1 91163 293 1 UK

Cover design by Sandy Cull, sandycull.com
Illustration by Roman Sotola, Shutterstock
Text design by Megan Ellis

Typeset by Midland Typesetters, Australia
Printed and bound in Australia by Griffin Press

10 9 8 7 6 5 4 3 2 1

*For Dad*

*'Silence at the proper season is wisdom, and better than any speech.'*
PLUTARCH (c. 45–120 CE)

# CONTENTS

# PROLOGUE

I fell in love with silence long before I could name it.

Perhaps we all do. Perhaps it is there, that human attraction to silence, gently imprinted on our genes as uniquely and as indelibly as our own fingerprints, from the time we bob like little satellites in the soft, dark universe of our mother's womb.

But once we enter this noisy and colourful world, the power of silence is eclipsed. There are so many exciting things to discover, not least the impact that our own noises—crying and cooing, screaming and babbling, and finally words and sentences—have on the people around us.

Eclipsed, then, but not erased. I believe the memory of silence lingers somewhere, like a first love, in our unconsciousness. Sometimes it might give us a nudge, like a deja vu, a familiar chord resonating somewhere deep in our souls. The question is whether we turn to it again—whether we choose to reignite this ancient human love story amid all the babble, the pings, the alerts, the alarms of daily life.

The first time I felt a pull towards something bigger than me, some-thing that felt like a welcoming space without being physically tangible, something as soothing as a parent's whisper and yet not audible, was in the early 1970s. It was a time when a generation of young hippies were ditching relatively privileged lives in the West to immerse themselves in the esoteric practices of yoga, chanting and meditation found in places like India, Tibet and Nepal. But nothing quite that exotic was happening in Brisbane, Queensland. And besides, I was just four years old.

The high-water mark of progressivism in Brisbane at that time may have been a decision by the Brisbane Kindergarten Teachers College to accept male students, establishing it as the first such institution in Australia to do so. A record 392 students enrolled at the college in 1973, perhaps also attracted by the completion of a state-of-the-art demonstration kindergarten equipped with the latest 'observation technology', including a narrow viewing room hidden behind a one-way mirror. This was my kindy, nestled into the curve of the hill just below the college in Kelvin Grove, on the fringe of the city.

Early childhood education was still a relatively new concept then, and plenty of children started 'big school' with no experience of regular days playing away from home, let alone a formal schedule. But for those whose parents were progressive—or desperate—enough to hand their offspring into the care of others, there were plenty of novelties that couldn't be had in your average lounge room or backyard.

Like the big bottles of thick paint, which would glug out in such fat, bright sausages that there would always be at least one child who succumbed to the temptation to taste it. And a real potter's wheel and kiln—plenty of kids tried eating the clay, too. And a carpenter's bench where, if you weren't paying attention, you could smack your thumb with a real hammer or jam a finger inside the vice.

But it was outside where the real delights were to be found. Beside the sandpit and swings was a cubbyhouse of such remarkable dimensions that it seemed, at least to a child, that a Kansas tornado had caught up the palace of the Wizard of Oz himself and deposited it in Kelvin Grove. Granted, there were no glittering emeralds or horses of a different colour; the cubbyhouse was, in fact, built of stodgy brown plywood. But it boasted a maze of levels that could be explored via ladders and tiny crawl spaces, until you emerged out the top and slid back to earth on a fireman's pole, or skittered down on a slide which, as it too was made of wood, barely deserved the name. A fishing net of chunky knotted rope hung down one wall, which meant that, most playtimes, a staff member would have to rescue a wailing child who, having lost its nerve halfway up, had become stuck like a starfish caught in a fisherman's haul.

That cubbyhouse breathed stories. Its unlikely presence here, in an otherwise nondescript town that spent much of the year in soupy, subtropical torpor, was welcome evidence that magic might exist after all. It was easy to become a pirate clambering up the nets, a princess calling from a window, or a unicorn stamping on the thick, tangy pine bark below. And inside, in the dim, protected spaces, there was room just to sit and be.

But, like everything else at the kindergarten, access to the cubbyhouse was ruled by a very strict schedule. And that schedule demanded that after an hour or so of outdoor play each morning, children were required to come in for 'rug time'. Once we had queued in a manner that was sufficiently subdued and ordered—and therefore deemed 'grown up'—we were ushered inside to remove our shoes and socks, before assembling on a bright-green shag pile rug to chant nursery rhymes and sing educational songs.

On the day a routine headcount revealed one child missing from the throng on the itchy rug, it was entirely possible the group was being observed by a class of student teachers behind the one-way glass. Perhaps, then, when a kindy teacher was dispatched to check the playground, a ripple of excitement ran through the viewing group, like tourists on an African safari sensing a disturbance among a herd of grazing gazelle. And imagine the furious speculation and note-taking that broke out when another, more senior staff member joined the first outside, and assumed a position not unlike that of a hostage negotiator, addressing the tall brown walls of the cubbyhouse in a calm but assertive—and, of course, age-appropriate—manner.

How did the young would-be teachers resist surging outside to get a better vantage point when the first staffer finally heaved her way up the cubby's ladder, squeezing through a child-sized trapdoor to the second floor? And what were the pedagogic insights—the 'key learnings', to use today's equally clunky management jargon—when she re-emerged, her fingers clasping the wrist of a decidedly unimpressed little girl? Did any of them speculate as to why one small child had opted to remain alone in the shadows of the cubbyhouse, rather than join her classmates on the shag pile for a few rowdy choruses of 'Incy Wincy Spider' and 'Hickory Dickory Dock'?

That little girl was me.

This memory is like a Kodachrome snapshot of the day I fell in love with silence. But I didn't know what to call it back then—so when those teachers came to haul me out of the cubby, I couldn't explain why I so desperately wanted to stay. At just four years old, I didn't have the words to describe the serenity I felt in that dark, cool space once the chaos of outdoor play had faded, or the confidence to argue that my remaining in the cubby wasn't affecting anybody else anyway.

Instead, I remember feeling acutely embarrassed that I had been caught doing something that was apparently so wrong. The teacher who dragged me inside was visibly annoyed as she insisted I remove my sandals, then shepherded me onto the rug. In turn, I stifled a ripple of irritation when I noted she was standing over me on the shag pile rug *still wearing her shoes.*

I was normally a compliant kid. Just months before, when my Styrofoam angel's wings had disintegrated on the morning of the kindy Christmas concert, I had accepted without complaint my mother's suggestion that I surrender my place in the heavenly choir—and went on stage as a sheep instead, tended by a grubby boy with a beach towel knotted around his head.

Had there been a staff and student teacher 'learning opportunity' after the Cubby House Incident, I suspect the participants may have surmised that I was sickening for something. Or feeling shy. Or perhaps that I was just a bit slow on the uptake. In fact, I was beginning to work out a few things for myself.

The first was that the people in charge often make rules they don't follow themselves. The second was that this process of 'growing up' seemed to involve doing a lot of things over and over for no apparent gain—just like Incy Wincy Spider. And finally, I learned that day that silence—the precious, then unnameable space in which one was free to think and breathe and simply *be*—was not to be trusted. Indeed, it must be avoided assiduously. It took me more than four decades, and a heck of a lot of unnecessary noise and disturbance, to unlearn those rules.

This is my story of unravelling into silence. And I think my four-year-old self, imagining the future from the sanctuary of her cubbyhouse, would have liked the idea of sharing it very much.

# 1

# RUSH

My instinct for silence was reawakened when my father became unwell.

It was January 2017 and he had fallen. On his way to meet a mate for their weekly lunch, Dad had missed a step outside the local football club and crashed to the ground.

His friend, a doctor, told me later that he had been parking his car nearby when he heard Dad scream. Before retiring, Ron had served for many years as the director of the emergency department at one of Brisbane's biggest public hospitals; perhaps as a result, he seemed almost congenitally unflappable. 'I heard that and thought, *Oh no, that's not good*,' he told me in his understated way.

It wasn't good.

Falls for folks in their late seventies seldom are, but they're unfortunately a pretty common occurrence for people like Dad, who was 78 years old and still recovering from a stroke the year before.

Ron had been with him on the day of the stroke as well. They were regular bridge partners and were playing together at a competition on the Gold Coast when Ron noticed Dad reach for a glass on the table, only to miss. He tried again and knocked the glass off the table. Then Dad shuddered as he tried to stand up. Before he'd hit the floor, Ron was on the phone calling for an ambulance, correctly suspecting a stroke in progress. Now those warning bells were going off again, followed by another ambulance.

About 730 kilometres away in Sydney, the piercing shriek of one of my phones signalled that my already busy day was about to kick it up a notch.

That's right—one of my phones.

After more than two decades as a journalist, I had worked as a strategic communications consultant for a few years, and then moved in-house to give communications advice to the Business Council of Australia, a peak body representing the CEOs of Australia's largest companies.

That's the official version. Back when I was a journalist, I may have put it another way:

### Working Single Mum Sells Out to Pay Bills

'I loved journalism but corporate communications just pays so much more,' said mother-of-two Christine Jackman, from her office overlooking Martin Place in Sydney's CBD. 'And with two phones, I can keep the important priorities of the BCA—advancing the policy agenda of Australia's biggest employers within the 24/7 political news cycle— separate from the equally important needs of my friends and family.'

My journalist self would have been particularly cynical about those two phones. My mates in the newsroom would all have agreed that owning two phones was irrefutable proof that you had crossed over to the dark side of PR spivs and spin doctors, and were in danger of becoming something that, in Australian parlance, rhymes with 'banker'. Which was perhaps appropriate, given Australia's biggest banks were among the BCA's most influential members. But I really did want to keep my work life and my home life separate.

It worked for precisely . . . Okay, it didn't work. A lot of people— my family, my friends, and my media and political contacts who had known me previously as a journalist—had both numbers. So when they couldn't reach me immediately on one, they would simply try the other.

Double the noise. Double the pressure. On that day in early 2017, however, it was a blessing.

I was preparing for a business trip—to Brisbane, coincidentally, where my CEO had finally landed a meeting with Senator Pauline Hanson, whose support would be critical if proposed legislation to reduce company tax rates was to pass into law—when I noticed a barrage of missed calls on both my phones from my parents' landline, my mother's mobile and my brother.

When I returned my mother's call, she told me that Dad had fallen. He had been taken to hospital with a suspected break of the hip or femur, either of which would require surgery. But they were yet to locate an orthopaedic surgeon to operate during the post-Christmas holiday period, and couldn't guarantee Dad would have that surgery in the next 48 hours. Apparently, all the orthopaedic surgeons go skiing overseas in January.

*You've got this*, I told myself. I'd tackled more confronting situations as a journalist, and untangled more complex problems. I'd been in the world's largest brothel—a sprawling Bangladeshi village on the Padma River—on the morning a jealous john opened fire on a beautiful young sex worker, sparking a panic that swept like a virus through the crowded, scum-ridden laneways. I'd waded neck-deep through filthy water during the fatal Brisbane floods of 2011, with a man desperate to confirm whether or not his family home had been inundated. I'd tracked teenage people smugglers to their poverty-stricken fishing village on the shores of Lombok, and had witnessed a boy drown there in the harbour, as if fate wanted to illustrate just how cheap life could be in those parts of the world that people would do anything to escape.

As I stood and talked to my mother on the phone that day, what I felt was a familiar surge of adrenaline. My journalist's instincts took over: I was the problem-solver dropped into a drama, charged with imposing some coherence on chaos. As long as you don't get personally involved, a job can always be wrapped up neatly to deadline.

Briefly, I even allowed myself a moment of black newsroom humour: surely there was something funny about every orthopaedic surgeon in Brisbane fleeing the post-Christmas rush of kids falling off new skateboards, bikes and trampolines, and heading to the ski fields of Japan, where instead they would watch a bunch of people fall off skis and snowboards and end up being some other surgeon's problem? I made a mental note to write about it someday.

Within minutes, I'd pulled my flight to Brisbane forward, alerted my chief of staff to the change of plans via text message, and called my communications team to run through the day's tasks. On my way to the airport I would call Peter, my partner, and rearrange the boys' schedules, and once in the air I'd crack on with any briefs and emails, before heading straight to the hospital at the other end.

What seemed like a cacophony of competing demands could be turned into a symphony if I just worked hard enough. That's what I told myself. *Just keep moving.*

Hearing the Uber arrive outside our townhouse on Sydney's Lower North Shore, I *click-click-clicked* down our steep, tiled stairs in my work heels, congratulating myself for remembering to hurry but not to rush. A few months earlier, racing to catch another flight, I had slipped on the same stairs with my arms full of briefing papers, an overnight bag and a laptop case. Unable to break my fall, I'd landed squarely on my lower back, cracking my coccyx.

(I still made the flight. And stayed in those heels all day, skittering at breakneck speed alongside my boss, until I checked into my hotel room that night—and finally dropped to my knees to crawl across the floor to the bed, sobbing in pain. The agony was matched perhaps only by the indignity of having to carry and sit on a special cushion, otherwise intended for men recovering from prostate surgery, for several weeks afterwards.)

I was on one of my phones when I arrived at Sydney Airport and checked in at Virgin's Premium Lounge, where some of the security staff had come to know me by name. I'd already called my best friend in Brisbane to ask whether she could meet me at the airport in Brisbane and drop me at the hospital. We'd been planning to catch up for a coffee while I was in town anyway; we'd have to settle for being in the same car together for the half-hour or so it would take to get to the hospital.

We met up but didn't really get to talk: as soon as I'd landed, my phone had erupted in an insistent chorus of pings and alerts, like a hungry chick whose mother had strayed from the nest too long. I wanted to ask Alexis how her son was doing at school; I wanted to hear about the books she was reading and what it was like to be a mature-age university student studying law; I wanted to sing along to the *Moana* soundtrack with her curly-haired daughter in the back seat. But there was no time for any of that. Every one of those things might have unfurled into a discussion or an experience, and I knew that they would contribute precisely nothing to the action items on my phone screeching for my attention. I had to maintain my focus and concentrate my energy. So I checked my email again instead.

Alexis shot me a look of concern as I climbed out of the car at the Prince Charles Hospital. 'I've got this,' I assured her, but I saw a shadow of suspicion flicker across her face; it's hard to fool a friend who has known you since the first day of school. So I turned on my heel and *click-click-clicked* away to the entrance before she could tell me she didn't believe me.

Years ago, when I was in high school, I had a casual job at one of the busiest McDonald's stores in Australia.

McDonald's Regent spanned an entire city block. Most customers entered it by descending a large tiled staircase from the Queen Street Mall, which was then the bustling centre of Brisbane's CBD, but there was another, smaller entrance on the next street, at the end of a dim and unprepossessing arcade. The massive 'dining room', which could seat a few hundred customers at a time, sprawled between the two.

Back then, there were limited options for a quick bite in Brisbane, which really did fit the tired cliché of a large country town. If you were too young to qualify for a counter meal at one of the many CBD pubs, and too poor—or poorly dressed—to take high tea in the refined mahogany booths of cafes like the Shingle Inn, then you had to scramble to find a sandwich at a greasy spoon or milk bar.

Partly as a result, when the World Expo attracted a flood of tourists to its site across the Brisbane River in 1988, Regent became Australia's highest-grossing McDonald's store. Customers would queue six or eight deep at lunchtime to be served at one of twelve cash registers.

Much of the store was underground, although there was a bank of windows at one end that offered a rather unedifying view of a grey, dead-end alleyway. Fortunately, those windows didn't open. If they had, the diners would have been treated to aromas of urine, vomit, rotting garbage or even an evocative blend of all three, depending on which of the city's roaming night creatures had most recently taken shelter there.

Inside the restaurant, customers and staff marinated instead in recycled air infused with a mixture of deep-fryer fat, grilling meat, cigarette smoke and a bleach-like chemical known simply as 'sanitiser'. The latter was used on the cleaning cloths of the unfortunate staff charged with maintaining hygiene in the dining room. I wondered about the cleaning power of a cloth dipped for the twentieth or even the fiftieth time in a plastic bucket full of increasingly greasy, lukewarm water and food detritus. But as the skin flaked away from between my fingers after the third hour of my dining room shift, I understood that few things survived extended exposure to the Macca's sanitiser.

Shifts in the cavernous dining room were not only physically draining but often mind-numbingly dull as well. Conversations with customers or other staff members were actively discouraged by the managers, who would chant, 'Time to lean, time to clean,' with all the ardour of Orwell's Thought Police. Mopping floors, clearing and cleaning tables, and collecting bulging garbage bags from enormous bins, the dining room staff had to make do with what entertainment could be gleaned from the fizz and crackle of the commercial radio blaring from the sound system.

Of course, the closer you got to the counter and the kitchen, the less likely you were to hear anything at all over the babble of timers and alarms. Toasters, grills, deep-fryers and cash registers all added their piercing shrieks to an urgent electronic chorus that assured customers that we were busily committed to producing the perfect meal on a tray. It was full sensory overload, with a side of French fries.

My first few shifts at McDonald's Regent left me drained of energy but mentally jittery. Too naive to recognise this as a symptom of over-stimulation, I instead beat myself up for being a loser who didn't know how to fit in with all the cool kids, who would bounce into the crew room before a shift, wisecracking and flirting and throwing pickles. Nobody else seemed bothered by the noise. Not the crew, not the managers, and certainly not the hundreds of customers who formed a fleshy gridlock in front of the cash registers each day between midday and 2 p.m. and between 6 p.m. and 8 p.m., the lunch and dinner 'rushes'.

It was a moot point anyway; I needed the job. Dad had investi-gated the Queensland industrial laws and discovered that, from the age of fourteen years and nine months, my siblings and I could legally work. Thereafter, we were told, all pocket money would cease. So I sucked it up and kept clocking on for my shifts—and took refuge in people watching.

I'd always been intrigued, and not infrequently mystified, by human behaviour. And at Macca's I quickly discovered that wielding a mop or a cleaning cloth somehow rendered you magically invisible, in the same way that the steering wheel of a cab or Uber apparently renders the driver deaf, particularly after 10 p.m. when we are fighting with our partners or gossiping with our sozzled girlfriends. There, beneath the blazing lights on that vast, tiled urban savannah, I became the David Attenborough of the odd species *Homo burgerectus*.

Few places provide a better opportunity for observing the crazy spectrum of human antics up close and personal than a fast food restaurant in the inner city. Stay there long enough and you'll see all types pass through the doors, from the homeless and mentally unstable to harried mums cursing the school holidays, to boozy business suits on the prowl after work, to the suits' tipsy, trilling prey, many of whom are barely older than the crew who take their orders for Diet Coke (the prey never eat). But it was the babies that fascinated me the most.

I will never forget the first one I noticed. It was so tiny it seemed entirely possible its parents had stopped for a Happy Meal on the way home from the maternity ward. As they headed for the counter, pushing a pram in which their tiny bundle snuggled quietly, their faces were glazed with an odd mix of shell shock and contentment (much later, I would learn this is a unique marker of all new parents).

But not for long. As the couple joined a long queue to order, a series of high-pitched but potent wails exploded from the pram. Soon, a little red fist popped up, jabbing jerkily at the air. It was quickly joined by another, as the enraged occupant broke free from its bunny wrap. The parents did what most new parents do: they rocked the pram faster.

No luck. If anything, the shrieks increased in volume, as if in an auditory arms race with the grills, the deep-fryers, the cash registers and the idiot on the sound system promising to play another long block of nonstop rock from your nonstop rock shop.

One of the first things I noted, in my capacity as undercover anthropologist, was that a screaming baby is like a rock thrown into the pond of humanity. At the epicentre, panicked looks are exchanged between parents. Travelling outwards from the nappy-clad Ground Zero, there are distinct ripples of aggravation, irritation, concern and curiosity.

So it was that day. With her infant now howling urgently, as if to alert everyone in the store that THESE PEOPLE ARE NOT

MY PARENTS! THEY MIGHT EVEN BE ALIENS! SO PLEASE, FOR THE LOVE OF GOD, PUT DOWN YOUR BURGERS AND SAVE ME!, the new mum eventually extracted the writhing creature, which no longer bore any resemblance to her beautiful baby, and cuddled it against her shoulder. Then Dad had a go. The screams continued.

My attention was torn away at that point. Possibly some idiot was sticking his pickles on the mural wall to create a large, green phallus for Ronald or the Hamburglar. Or maybe somebody had set a napkin on fire in the smoking section, and thrown it into one of those really big bins. Or handed their five-year-old a large Coke, which, predictably, was now an icy brown puddle on the floor.

But later, I noticed the parents gingerly juggling their burgers and fries while rocking the pram outside in the grimy—but much darker and quieter—arcade, while their furious mini-terrorist appeared to be shape-shifting back into a drowsy and adorable baby.

And so the Jackman Theory of Inverse Stimulatory Overload was born. My shifts in the dining room—and, later, on front counter—became opportunities to catalogue how other small humans reacted when exposed to the fast food environment. The younger the baby, the less time it took for them to protest being in the store. It's not scientific, of course. But it made some sense. The more recently one had been snuggled in the comforting, dark clutch of the womb, the more violently one might take offence at the sensory overload that McDonald's Regent presented. By the time babies had become toddlers, however, most seemed to have overcome their acute aversion to that environment. Perhaps the lure of fat and sugar eventually trumped the pain of a full-frontal stimulatory assault.

Sometimes, when I felt twitchy and irritable after a shift, I wondered whether I had somehow missed that developmental milestone. I wasn't sure, but there were plenty of days when those squalling babies struck me as the most discerning people in the entire restaurant—and I had to

fight the desire to throw myself to the ground in a tantrum of solidarity
against the affront of noise.

*Why am I thinking of those babies*, I wondered as I slumped in the corner
of the hospital elevator. *Is there a maternity ward nearby?* The door
chimed as it opened onto the surgical ward, and I stepped out into the
glare of fluorescent lighting and shiny surfaces, all ideal for amplifying a
barrage of pings, bings and alarms. *Welcome to McHospital—may I find
your orderly?* Fleetingly, I wanted to cry. Or scream. Or run away.

It is odd that when human beings are injured or sick, when they are
in greatest need of rest and recuperation, we send them to places like
this. Is all the noise necessary? Surely, in this age of high tech, when so
many of us carry digital devices that can be individualised to communicate through a variety of hums, vibrations, muted tones and colours, it
would be possible for the modern hospital to do the same, leaving the
loud trills and alarms for the true emergencies?

Or is all the general noise maintained specifically to engender a
sense of controlled urgency? At a time when patients and their families
may be otherwise tempted to succumb to despair, anger or outright
hysteria, perhaps all those officious sounds are intended to encourage
us to put our faith in some power that is monitoring, measuring and
controlling us in ways we cannot really understand?

Four strong cappuccinos, one intense peak-hour commute and
an interstate flight into my day, I was tempted to pursue this wave of
paranoia—or at least indulge in a rant against the public hospital
system. But there was no time. I turned into a small ward and came to
an abrupt halt next to a bed on which an old man was lying, his eyes
closed and his face drained of colour, his knuckles white as his hands
gripped the safety rails. My confounded brain sent a signal to my feet
to turn around and leave: *You are not needed here; this is not where you*

*are supposed to be.* But even as that reflexive twitch reached the balls of my feet, the weight of recognition hit me, rocking me back on my heels.

This was my father—my hero, the strapping man who used to bodysurf in the wildest seas at Sunshine Beach. To Dad, enormous waves simply represented an opportunity for a better ride; one moment he would be staring the monster in the face, and then, with a lunge and a few strokes, he would merge with this force of nature as it hurtled towards the shore. Often he would disappear in the froth and roil of the breakers, only to emerge near the shore like a killer whale rearing up to snatch an unsuspecting seal.

*Is he dying?* The thought popped into my head, unbidden and unwelcome, like the bubble of acid panic that had surged up my throat.

But there was no room for emotion—at least, that was what I told myself. It was safer to revert to the familiar hustle and bustle of problem-solving than to be still in this disconcerting moment. It was easier—far easier—to begin a to-do list and take action: find a doctor or someone in charge, ask questions, make phone calls, alert relatives, ask more questions, check emails, text my team, anything. *Just keep moving—inaction is the enemy.*

Mentally, I did the maths. Actually, it was more like a giant jigsaw puzzle. I needed to find places for all the pieces of information I had, to link them up in a neat and controlled manner. First, I needed to find an orthopaedic surgeon who was on duty somewhere in Brisbane. Then I needed to convince him or her to add Dad to his theatre list as soon as possible. Then I would need to convince whichever hospital was nominated by the yet-to-be identified surgeon to admit Dad immediately. I'd be damned if I let him miss out on the surgery he needed because the paper-pushers failed to admit him in time.

War-gaming further, I knew I'd need to identify and quickly befriend whoever was rostered on the admissions desk at the hospital that was yet to be named by the yet-to-be-identified surgeon. By the end of the day, we were going to be best friends; I'd know the names of his or her kids, and he or she was going to be personally invested in finding Dad a bed. (If there was one thing I'd learned from years of seeking access to the offices of political, business and creative leaders, it was this: underestimate the executive assistant, diary manager or switchboard operator at your peril. They could be your best friend or your worst enemy—or you could be utterly irrelevant to them, which was almost as bad as the latter.)

Once I landed Dad a surgeon and a hospital bed, I would need to find him an ambulance to move him. And to do that, I would need to hustle the staff of the current hospital to discharge him. There was an unnerving number of variables on this list. But at least I had a plan of attack.

Meanwhile, I also needed to update my mother and the rest of the family on Dad's progress; make sure the meeting with Pauline Hanson was still on track; check in with my team in Sydney about other media inquiries; locate both my boys, who were on school holidays; work out where the hell I was staying that night in Brisbane; and confirm whether I was going to attend a series of focus groups we had organised.

But hey, it was all going to be fixed because I had two phones!

As my panic receded, one of them chirped with a new text message: 'You've got this.' It was supposed to be a supportive statement. The sort of positive stuff your #squad posts when you hint that you might be feeling a little overwhelmed. The stuff of a hundred thousand inspirational GIFs and memes that bloomed across the internet every day.

*You've got this.* Cute toddler pumping determined fist.

*You've got this.* Kitten hanging off a tree branch while looking adorable.

*You've got this.* Ryan Gosling smiling (#heygirl) without a shirt on.

It never occurred to me that there can't always be a neat and controlled outcome. Contemplating that was just too big, too scary a thought. Besides, there were no shareable social media posts for failure. No pictures of that toddler tripping, the kitten falling, Ryan Gosling getting paunchy in middle age. So I kept moving. And I fixed it.

Or I thought I did.

With the help of Dad's brother-in-law, who was also his GP, I managed to locate a surgeon who was working and had space on his theatre list. And with the help of my new friend Kate, who had only just come back to work in the admissions office after an overseas holiday with her fiancé, and who *totally* understood how tricky it could be to find a doctor at that time of year, a bed was found for Dad at the right hospital. Meanwhile, the discharge process had begun at the current hospital and an ambulance was on its way.

Dad had relaxed a bit, now that he knew he'd have had the necessary surgery and be in recovery by the end of the day, rather than in medical limbo. The X-rays had confirmed that his femur, the largest bone in the human body, was broken badly in two places, which explained why even the slightest movement triggered waves of agony.

It seemed outrageous that the default plan had been to leave him like this, a hostage frozen in the claws of a savage injury, for up to two days before surgery. Sitting beside him in the ward, I allowed myself a brief flush of self-congratulation for extracting my father from the insidious quicksand of an overburdened and under-resourced public health system.

Then, suddenly, we were on the move, down to the ambulance bay. Dad's pale-blue eyes were open and focused, but as we whizzed through the hospital hallways I thought I caught a flicker of fear, too. Or was it just the reflection of those ubiquitous fluorescent lights overhead?

The ambulance officers were lovely. They explained to Dad that they had to lift him from the hospital trolley onto their gurney. There was no way to avoid it: it was going to hurt. They explained that they would give him a countdown and then he would have to brace with his good leg while they lifted him. Then they disappeared outside to prepare a gurney while the discharge paperwork was finalised.

As Dad and I waited, I felt the noise close in around me again. The beeping of a monitor; a phone ringing; someone querying how long they would have to wait; another patient moaning. And there was a TV on somewhere nearby, with high-pitched American voices hurling insults. Finally, the paperwork was done. The ambos came back. 'Are you ready, Tony?' one asked.

Noise. One of my phones began to ring. I flicked it to silent and tried to ignore the reproachful vibration that continued to emanate from my bag.

'Three, two, one . . .'

Noise. Dad's hand reached out to me as an animal-like sound erupted from his lips.

'And lift!'

He screamed and I stifled another sudden urge to run, to flee to a place where my father was still invincible, incapable of fear or pain. It was over quickly, but the colour had left Dad's face again. Now his eyes stayed shut.

Somewhere inside me there was a faint but insistent whisper. I struggled to focus, to screen out enough of the surrounding noise to hear what it was saying. There was a brief pause as the ambulance doors closed and the hubbub outside was muffled. In the sudden quiet I caught the whisper that was circling in my mind.

*I'm not ready for this. I haven't got this.*

Dad didn't die. He had surgery late in the evening, while I sat bleary-eyed, observing focus groups and eating lukewarm slices of pizza in a nondescript meeting room. The next morning I set up my laptop on the windowsill in his hospital room and tapped away while he fretted and twitched through his fentanyl. If I had to take a call, I'd do laps of the ward, glimpsing a series of grey, lined faces and sagging bodies through open doors as I strode past, until they began to morph into one giant collage of ageing decrepitude.

Dad was uncomfortable and confused, but in no immediate danger. A stream of doctors, therapists and nurses were speaking brightly about rehabilitation routines and recovery exercises. They were positive in a fiercely pragmatic way. The golden rule, if unspoken, seemed to be that recovery would be tough and sometimes painful, but it was infinitely preferable to the alternative, so it was best not to worry about that.

All of this busy-ness was reassuringly familiar to me. Secretly, I felt stupid, even ashamed, for being spooked by thoughts of death. And relieved, also, that I could defer to experts who were confident Dad's problems could be solved if he adhered to a crammed schedule of therapists' appointments, drug protocols and exercise programs.

Outside, the city was shimmering in the bright summer heat. I booked a cab to meet my boss and colleagues for lunch at a swank CBD brasserie. Taking my place at a table that overlooked the wide, brown snake of the Brisbane River, I brushed aside their concerned queries, preferring to focus on tactics and political gossip ahead of our meeting.

The next morning, I kissed Dad goodbye, promising him I would help Mum manage all the financial and administrative paperwork while he was incapacitated. My brother had started a WhatsApp group to keep everyone updated, and my sister was working on a spreadsheet of tasks to be allocated between us, to ensure Mum wasn't overwhelmed. It all felt very grown-up; just another cluster of responsibilities to be managed.

As my plane flew south, Sydney Harbour put on a show to welcome me home, the light bouncing off the sapphire water like a thousand glittering sequins. It was a clear blue day, and with the Opera House flashing its toothy grin, it would have been easy to surrender to a warm glow—if not from the sun itself, then from a smug sense that I had successfully managed a difficult situation. But, soon enough, I had to admit to myself that something had changed.

I was reminded of a time, years before, when I ran out of petrol. In the early 1990s, while I was still living at home with my parents, I would sometimes borrow their Mazda 626 to drive to university or the gym, blithely ignoring their warnings about the dodgy fuel gauge, which would sometimes get stuck on about a quarter of a tank. One morning I was at the head of a queue of cars waiting in peak-hour traffic at an inner-city intersection. When the lights changed, I shifted from the brake to the accelerator—and nothing happened. Well, almost nothing. We were on a slight hill, so the old green Mazda did roll forward half-heartedly. It's possible the angry wave of sound created by a dozen or so blaring horns also helped push the car on to a final, kerbside surrender.

I have long forgotten the details of that day: where I was heading, what I was wearing, whether I had to find a payphone to call for assistance. But the experience left a distinct emotional footprint: I can clearly recall the feeling of utter incomprehension that surged through me as my panicked jabs at the accelerator failed to summon the anticipated response from the engine.

Fast-forward a few decades and I was jabbing at my own internal accelerator—the one that would lift me to meet any challenge—but nothing was happening. And I was completely bewildered. Each morning, as I made my way up Martin Place to the 'dream job' that had doubled my journalist's income overnight—and unlocked opportunities many journos dream about, including the chance to pick the brains of some of the country's most influential decision-makers and thought leaders—I felt like I was wading through molasses. Why couldn't I accelerate? This disorienting heaviness, as if I was stalled at a busy, cacophonous intersection, was unfamiliar.

Ever since I first left Brisbane in the late 1990s, when I was posted to New York as a foreign correspondent for News Corp, I'd been running, learning, hustling and running some more. Not out of ambition, but spurred on by what I now call the Carrot–Stick Curse.

The Carrot is that tantalising suggestion that somewhere out there, just beyond your grasp, is happiness, and that just one more important assignment, one more big job, one more kilogram lost or one more pay rise won will deliver it. Alternately, the Stick is the gnawing terror that if you stop for a breather or withdraw from the ongoing conversation, the whole world will notice you're a big fat imposter and the entire charade will collapse around your ears.

The Stick plagued me in the form of frantic nightmares, in which I would discover that I hadn't actually finished high school or university and would have to rush to a final exam with no time to study. The Carrot gave me nightmares too, but they were different: I'd be assigned an important, high-profile interview, or even land a glamorous new posting, but somehow, on the way to the new gig, I would become hopelessly lost amid the twists and turns of a massive airport as I rushed to make the flight.

Rushing—that was the common theme, asleep and awake. Rushing to get to work, rushing to get home. Rushing to answer emails, answer the phone, answer my colleagues and my boys. Rushing to get lunch to eat at the desk. Rushing to the ladies' room because I'd been ignoring the call of nature for the last three hours of back-to-back meetings. Rushing to make dinner and, after I met my gorgeous partner, Peter, rushing to make love before rushing to catch some sleep before the whole darn thing started again.

Of course, I knew the dangers of this sort of accelerated lifestyle. As a social affairs writer for many years, I had written numerous articles about 'work/life balance', or the lack thereof, when it was a hot topic in the early 2000s. Even then it used to strike me as supremely ironic that the stories that got the best run for me as a journalist were the ones that made me feel worse as a woman—the ones that generated headlines like 'Working Mothers Average 3½ Minutes a Day on Self-Care'.

A piece like that would usually trigger an intense debate among female colleagues about whether three and a half minutes shaving your legs while supervising your toddler on the potty next to you in the bathroom should be categorised as self-care or child care, or perhaps be put in a separate category altogether: multitasking. We would usually decide the last option was the most appropriate—and yet it was also the least useful, as surely everything in a working mother's life could be listed there.

Even before I had children, multitasking had been my default setting. But something had happened that day when I heard my father cry out in agony. The multitasking setting, previously so comfortable and familiar, was now distorted and full of white noise.

In the months that followed, I had some optimistic Monday mornings when I committed to finding a good yoga class or joining a walking group or taking up meditation. But by the Friday afternoon I would look at those commitments and feel exhausted, settling instead for listening to a podcast about wellness on my commute home.

'I have no time,' I shrieked at Peter when he gently suggested that I needed to find ways to replenish myself.

'There's no time,' I snapped when one of the boys asked for help to find a tennis racket, a music folder or a homework sheet as we were walking out the door in the morning.

'When I've got time,' I murmured as I scrolled past Facebook friends' posts about dinner parties, and invitations to concerts, and happy snaps from weddings and weekend adventures.

Sometimes, in disconsolate moments when I couldn't sleep, I worried that these friends and family members must think I was disinterested or antisocial or simply didn't care about them. I thought of ways to assure them that I wanted to join in—oh, how desperately I wanted to join in! But I was stuck on this express train called my successful life, and the best I could do was catch glimpses of their faces as I rushed past their social media platforms: 'Facebook, Instagram . . . next stop Twitter.'

## 2

# INTO SILENCE

I'd love to say that I had a light-bulb moment as the noise peaked, when I finally understood that what I needed was silence. It would be great to describe a blinding flash of clarity in which I recognised that my growing distress was a manifestation of a thwarted need to be more present for those I cared about most: my ailing father, my sons, Peter and the rest of my family and friends. Even better if it involved an unexpected encounter with a wise old monk, who whispered something profound to me that changed my life.

Like: 'Maybe you are searching among the branches for what only appears in the roots.'

Or: 'Like this cup, you are full of your own opinions and speculations. How can I show you Zen until you first empty your cup?'

Or: 'If no mistake have you made, yet losing you are . . . a different game you should play.'

But the first line is actually from the thirteenth-century Persian poet Rumi. The cup story is ascribed to Nan-in, a Japanese Zen master from the Meiji Era, during the turn of the last century. The final one is Yoda. And watching old *Star Wars* movies with my sons was probably the closest I was getting to any insight at this point. When you think about it, Yoda does look and sound like an old Buddhist monk.

There were no light-bulb moments or blinding flashes of clarity.

Unfortunately, enlightenment tends to be a messier and blurrier process than that bright, crisp word *enlighten* suggests. And 'the getting of wisdom' is only a straightforward linear narrative in the book by Henry Handel Richardson. In real life, it's more like a game of snakes and ladders: we try our best and advance a few steps, but then we slip back into bad habits and have to start inching forward all over again.

To complicate matters, most of us are much better at articulating what we don't want than what we do, which is how we come to spend an awful lot of time avoiding things we don't like while remaining incapable of recognising the things we actually need.

A few months after my father's fall, I certainly knew what I didn't want: I didn't want to keep talking. As someone who had built a career in communications—who had even, for a while, been paid generously by the word for tapping out her opinions in a weekly newspaper column—this came as quite a surprise.

But after many years in media, in consulting and then in corporate communications, talking had come to encapsulate everything that was exhausting about my busy life: decision-making, organising, problem-solving, getting things done. All the things that made my mind so full, so tired and so very, very irritable.

That's why, when the opportunity arose for me to take some time off over Easter 2017, while my sons were spending time with their father, I became obsessed with the idea of finding a place that didn't require me to speak. But not a silent retreat: I wasn't ready to choose silence, I just knew I didn't want to talk. To my mind, these were two very different things.

I wasn't completely ignorant of silent retreats. I'd even been an innocent bystander at one in India a couple of years before. In 2015 I'd travelled to Shreyas, a luxury ashram and yoga retreat outside of the southern Indian megacity of Bangalore, on the advice of Sarah 'I Quit Sugar' Wilson. After attending a month-long Ayurvedic clinic to tackle her auto-immune disease, Sarah had written a detailed blog post about the experience, which I had found both startling and compelling. (How startling? Well, the headline read: 'One Month Without Exercise, Soap and Loo Paper . . .'. I rest my case, Your Honour.)[1]

Despite Sarah's clear conviction, and her pithy and heartfelt writing, I had zero interest in living for a month without toilet paper, or cleaning myself with mung bean powder, or consuming only the water used for boiling rice (I'm not making this stuff up). I didn't even want to live off the rice that had been boiled in the water that was consumed by the Ayurvedic fasters. That clinic was not for me. But at the end of her blog post, Sarah had recommended Shreyas as an excellent 'Ayurvedic-lite' stopover for those looking for some gentle yoga and meditation.

The Shreyas website looked more like an exotic destination for honeymooners, with tented pavilions and a frangipani-fringed pool, places where guests could practise yoga several times a day while enjoying organic vegetarian meals sourced from the ashram's own garden.

I was in. Within hours of reading about Shreyas for the first time, I had booked tickets to Bangalore and signed up for a five-day yoga retreat, during which I would finally fulfil a lifelong ambition to perform *Adho Mukha Vrksasana*. In short, I wanted to learn to do a handstand, a skill that had eluded me through years of on-again, off-again yoga practice. I didn't want to be purified or achieve enlightenment; I just wanted to be able to maintain my balance on my hands. And have access to a full supply of toilet paper. It didn't seem like much to ask.

Three months or so later, when I arrived at Shreyas, I may have even written that on my questionnaire as I waited for my admission interview with one of the resident Ayurvedic doctors. But he was more interested in identifying my *doshas*, or unique biological energies, which would determine the types of food that would best suit me, as well as the exercise and spa therapies that would be most effective for me during my stay.

The doctor explained that all meals would be served in a communal dining room or, on clear nights, on tables around the pool. But because it was the off-peak season, he said, I would likely have the pick of where to sit because there were only a few other guests, two of whom were conducting silent retreats for the first few days of their stay.

'You will be speaking to them, but they will not be speaking to you,' he told me earnestly.

This did not make any sense. I figured I'd misunderstood his accent and asked him to explain again.

'You will be speaking to them,' he said, more slowly. 'But they will not be speaking to you. They . . . will . . . be . . . silent.'

Right. Given that they'd signed up for a silent retreat, it seemed fair enough that they wouldn't be speaking to me. But I didn't see why I would be speaking to them. Perhaps Shreyas encouraged its other guests to take the opportunity to unburden their souls to what was a captive and effectively gagged audience? But I didn't want to unburden my soul to anybody; I just wanted to do a darn handstand. I nodded, making a mental note that I would actually *not* be speaking to them.

But, as the ancient masters teach, we are kidding ourselves if we think we can control how our path unfolds. In my case, this was demonstrated a couple of days later, not by one of Shreyas' meditation teachers but by one of my fellow guests as we lay by the pool after a morning of yoga, chanting and *Jalaneti*, a particularly confronting practice in which you pour warm salt water into one nostril with a tiny watering can, while tilting your head to let it trickle out the other.

'Do you know where the sunscreen is?' the guest asked me.

When you have nothing else to do but wonder what's for lunch (and assess whether you really want to participate in *Jalaneti* tomorrow), it is surprising how quickly the simplest question can become a great conundrum. Here I was, under a gloriously blue Indian sky, with nothing to do but browse Pema Chödrön's *Start Where You Are* by the pool while being lulled by the distant *tock-tock* of village kids defending their stumps on a makeshift cricket pitch, and now suddenly I had to pick my way through an ethical dilemma.

The Shreyas staff had made it quite clear: *They will not be speaking to you*. And yet she was. And not for any dramatically important reason. I could understand breaking your silent retreat if you were suffering an allergic reaction to the soya fritters served at breakfast, or had collapsed during your fifth shambolic attempt at *Adho Mukha Vrksasana*, or had fallen into the pool when you didn't know how to swim. But this was a need for SPF, not CPR. And I'd already observed that the silent retreatants were each given little notebooks to carry, should they have any requests to make of the staff.

Should I tell her to *shh*? Should I assume this was a slip on her part, and pretend I hadn't heard her? Should I dob her in? Was this all some weird Ayurvedic test? I glanced around to check whether we were under surveillance. But the staff were, as always, keeping their distance and focusing on their tasks, moving to their own neatly choreographed rhythm of serenity and discretion. So I did what any native of Brisbane, the melanoma capital of the world, would do in such a situation: I offered her my sunscreen.

We did not speak of it again, even a few days later, when the silent part of these retreatants' stays ended. With their voices liberated, they joined the rest of our small, multicultural band at a larger table in the dining room. I doubt I was the only one secretly hoping that they would reveal some special jolt of wisdom they'd received during their silence. But it was not to be. The young woman who had asked me for sunscreen confided that she'd been hungry an awful lot of the time because she had chosen to do a juice cleanse as well, and that she had been mortified when her stomach growled in protest during one session of *Pranayama*, when we were being taught to breathe through alternate—and freshly cleansed—nostrils.

The other woman turned out to be a Saudi businesswoman who had formed the view that all Westerners thought women in her country were subjugated because, at the time, their government prohibited them from driving. She was determined to set us straight; indeed, it seemed entirely possible that she had spent her days of silence collecting all the words she wasn't allowed to speak, mentally constructing one long, detailed and defensive lecture.

Suffice it to say I was left unconvinced about the usefulness of choosing silence. It wasn't that I had anything against the practice. It just seemed like a venture that demanded a considerable amount of sitting still, a great deal of focus and only a tiny chance that you'd come out with anything remotely useful. A bit like macramé. Or decoupage.

Meanwhile, I still hadn't mastered a handstand. Instead, I had submitted to the gentle suggestion of my young yoga instructor that perhaps my obsession with *Adho Mukha Vrksasana* was running counter to my practice of yoga. In other words (mine, not his), if you keep smashing your head into the floor, perhaps it's time to sort out what's going on in your head, rather than keep trying to avoid the floor.

It was a lesson that, I would later discover, applied just as power-fully to silence.

A little more than two years later, as that Easter holiday approached, I was no longer smashing into the floor. But I was still smashing into noise and busyness, with roughly the same effect on my head.

As I grew more tired and overwhelmed, I sought to remedy— or at least identify—the problem by adding even more things to my schedule: more yoga, and sometimes running as well; blood and saliva tests to rule out any pathological reasons for my pervasive exhaustion; sinus scans; naturopathic appointments; even a sleep assessment, which required me, somewhat counterintuitively, to stick wires all over my body before I went to bed to assess overnight why I wasn't sleeping well.

The medical tests did not detect any serious physical problems. The sleep assessment confirmed what I already knew—that I didn't sleep well—but ruled out sleep apnoea or any other breathing issue as the cause. I was enjoying yoga more now that I had let go of my hand-stand obsession, and running was what it had always been for me: an opportunity to sweat profusely for an extended period of time while wondering if it would ever feel better.

But none of this was a salve for the hyperstimulation of my over-scheduled life. It was a little like strolling out into the garden with a watering can as a roaring bushfire bore down on my house. Or, as my naturopath, Janella Purcell, put it with trademark tough love: 'Christine, you can swallow all the herbs and green smoothies you want, but your body won't know what to do with them while you're this stressed.'

When a person who sells herbal brews and recipe books full of smoothie recipes for a living hits you with raw honesty like this, it tends to have an impact. It also helps when that person boasts the dewy skin and clear-eyed sparkle of a woodland sprite. I figured Janella was onto something.

But what could I do? I wasn't going to become a naturopath and embrace a tree change, trading my house in the bustling city for a haven in the Byron Bay hinterland like Janella had done. Maddeningly—both for me and for many of those around me—trying to figure out how I could soothe my disquiet had become just one more task on my onerous and ever-present to-do list.

One morning, as I followed the soft curves of Sydney Harbour's northern shore home on my lumbering run, I glanced up from the path and stopped dead. There, across the bright blue quilt of water, was the Opera House. She was always there, of course, at precisely this point of the run (it's hard to look at the Opera House in all its regal glory and not personify it, to transform it from a collection of concrete and tiles to a living, breathing presence, a 'he' or 'she' rather than an 'it'), but this was the first time I had seen her sails bathed in such a delicate shade of pastel pink. She was the same as ever, and yet this morning she was different, simply because of the light.

Almost immediately, images of another Australian icon sprang to mind. Uluru, too, changes moods with the intensity and pitch of light throughout the day and throughout the seasons, which means you can be in the brooding presence of this monolithic rock, knowing it has endured for millennia in the desert, and yet simultaneously feel as though you are engaged in an animated conversation.

Even in those few moments of thought, the Opera House's colours had changed again. Was it possible, I wondered, that Jørn Utzon, all those decades ago, had been trying to evoke a similar interplay with light, drawing inspiration from Australia's most distinctive landmass as he designed what would become Australia's most distinctive building? I knew almost nothing about the history of the Opera House—and I still don't, really—but the thought captivated me, at least enough to distract me from the sweat pouring down my temples as I slogged my way home to Neutral Bay. By the time I arrived, I had made a decision about what I would do at Easter.

I had been searching for radical transformation—a way to create something big and distinctive and enduring, to counter my unhappiness. But perhaps all I had to do was make little shifts, to adjust and respond to the changes all around me, while recognising also that everything would change again; indeed, was already changing. Like light itself, nothing was really solid, so perhaps all I needed to do was play with how things were in the moment.

These words here on the page seem too solid, too weighty, for an idea that was, that morning, only shimmering in my mind like heat over sand. But it was enough for me to make a decision about what to do with my few days of holiday leave. I booked myself into Gwinganna, a health retreat that sits on the crown of a lush hill in the Gold Coast hinterland, for four days. And I asked, for reasons I couldn't really explain, if it was okay for me not to speak while I was there.

*Not to speak.* Again, it's important here to be clear about what I was asking for, and what I was not.

I was not seeking enlightenment, or a guru, or any sort of religious conversion. A professional life covering politics had taught me to be very wary of blokes claiming to have all the answers (and they're almost always blokes, aren't they?)—and, before that, a childhood growing up Catholic had endowed me with a reflexive suspicion of formalised religion. Nor was I seeking to meditate all day, or engage exclusively in any other sort of activity normally associated with a vow of silence. Had I wanted that, I would have enrolled in a meditation retreat. I wasn't even intending to cut out all communication. I was very happy to carry a notebook and pen, just as I'd seen done at Shreyas, so I could communicate with staff—and with other guests, should they want to.

I just wanted to be relieved of the burden of talking. I was too exhausted to really know why—although I would quickly begin to find out. At the time, I simply knew I was not just burnt out, I was *talked out*.

The staff at Gwinganna, bless them, did not skip a beat when I made my request. I suppose when you work in an award-winning spa that offers everything from massage, facials and acupuncture to colonic hydrotherapy, chakra balancing and equine meditation, a guest who simply wants not to talk might seem refreshingly straightforward, even a little plain. They assigned me a badge to wear alongside the name badge all guests received. It read: *Shhhh! In silence.* And just like that my wish was granted. For four days, while we were all abstaining from caffeine and alcohol, sugar and meat, I would forgo speech as well.

I stepped out of the Gwinganna reception and into the gentle autumnal sunlight, drawing a deep lungful of oxygen infused with the tang of eucalyptus. Bubbles of excited chatter floated on the air as other guests arrived and were shown to their rooms. There was something liberating about allowing it to flow around me, with no obligation to join the social swirl. I tentatively began practising a response for situations where others might attempt to initiate conversation: a polite, slightly apologetic smile while gesturing towards my *Shhhh!* badge.

Thus relieved of the burden of finding the right words and forming the appropriate responses, I was certain I could feel all the organs and other body parts that were usually on high alert—my brain, my jaw, my throat and lungs—beginning, ever so slowly, to relax as I settled into my room, which overlooked an orchard.

The feeling of peace lasted until dinner.

Communal dining tables and vows of silence (even steadfastly non-religious, non-meditative, not-searching-for-enlightenment ones) do not coexist happily. As we took our seats for our first meal together, my fellow retreatants introduced themselves and quickly moved into the small talk that establishes comfortable coexistence. It was like Swedish flatpack furniture: nothing too quirky or unconventional, quick and easy enough to put together, but not intended to endure for all that long.

'Where are you from?'

'Do you have children?'

'Is this your first time here?'

'What do you think of the food?'

Simple questions, contrived to avoid points of contention. But I could answer none of them. I tried my serene smile and pointed towards my *Shhhh!* badge, and to the first page on my notebook, on which I'd written: 'I'm doing a silent retreat but happy to write answers or questions here.' Even so, I was conscious that I was breaking the rules of social engagement. The notebook slowed things down, so that little more than yes/no questions was possible. My mute presence was a conversational stumbling block, requiring an unfamiliar style of engagement. Or none at all.

Eventually, the froth and bubble of conversation simply ebbed around me, like a river flowing past the stolid surfaces of a rock protruding from its bed. As elements, the other guests and I could coexist, and perhaps there was no more judgement of me than there is when water encounters stone. But it was plainly, incontrovertibly evident that we were different.

And I really didn't like being different. I never have. Somewhere in my subconscious, the shy kid from conservative Brisbane was stirring, unsettled and anxious.

Dinner was a delicious carrot and amaranth gnocchi with lemon cream and beetroot sauce, prompting delighted exclamations and feigned swoons around the table. But I may as well have been consuming Vegemite sandwiches, warm and limp from a lunchbox stored in the midday heat. Alone in the crowd, I was back at school, the awkward girl with smudged glasses and a livid red birthmark across one cheek, who almost always knew the right answers in the classroom but could never find them in the playground.

*They probably think you're a pretentious git.*

*Those women are rolling their eyes and laughing—it's probably about you.*

*You're making everyone feel uncomfortable.*

*Maybe you should sit by yourself in the future.*

*But if you sit by yourself, they'll definitely think you're a pretentious git.*

And so it went, a vicious inner chorus of criticism and self-loathing, escalating in volume to occupy the void normally filled by social interaction.

I'd dabbled previously in meditation to help me sleep, so I recognised this as the notorious 'Monkey Mind', the internal chatter that fills our heads in a particularly maddening way when we are trying to still our thoughts. But I'd always envisioned Monkey Mind as one of those cute capuchins, or perhaps a pygmy marmoset. The petulant baboon that was currently stomping through my psyche was another thing entirely.

The only thing that saved me that night—and I can imagine now that this admission would elicit some very Dalai Lama-esque chortles from your average Buddhist—was my ego. For it was my ego that determined that while this silent social limbo was painful, the humiliation of backing down, of speaking again so soon after taking my public vows of *Shhhh!*, would feel infinitely worse.

*Are you kidding? You can't even make it through the first night?*

*Suck it up, princess. That which doesn't kill you makes you stronger. And nobody's ever died of not speaking at a luxe health retreat on the Gold Coast.*

*Why would anyone care what you're doing anyway? You're not that important. Why do you always assume you're so important?*

*I wonder if they'll give us dessert?*

And so it went. Baboon, pygmy marmoset or just plain ego, my Monkey Mind had plenty to say.

Thankfully, nobody lingers for long after dinner on health retreats. All that extra exercise in the fresh air, as well as the looming prospect of qi gong at dawn, makes an early bedtime much more attractive. That and the absence of alcohol. I've never met a person whose instinct to party hard is ignited by a cup of chamomile tea.

Stepping out of the dining room, I surrendered to the embrace of a soft darkness tinged with salt drifting in from the coastline. Reduced to a shadow along a dimly lit path, I no longer had to justify my separateness to myself or anyone else. I could breathe out again.

As my anxieties settled, it occurred to me how outrageously naive I had been to assume I could strip away something as fundamental as speech and expect to find tranquillity waiting patiently for me on the other side. Human beings are social animals. And if, as the saying goes, nature abhors a vacuum, then human nature resents it particularly acutely, rushing to fill it with . . . anything, really. (If you think this is too sweeping a statement, stop and consider the sorts of apps that captivate phone users today: Candy Crush Saga, Roblox, Clash of Clans. And let's not forget the fun to be had embellishing your selfies with rabbit ears or puppy noses. Or simply scrolling mindlessly through your newsfeed. More about that later.)

Because most of us live in tribes, albeit the modern-day ones that bind together family, friends and work colleagues, the act of choosing silence—or choosing not to talk—will always be infused with meaning beyond the individual. But who gets to assign that meaning? At the dinner table, I had been preoccupied by what my fellow guests might be thinking about me and my choice. But that frenzied inner monologue masked a far more important, and more confronting, question: how comfortable was *I*, sitting alone in silence, with myself? Stripped of the ability to curate and present myself to others, who really was I?

This much I knew: I'd been a shy but smart kid who had spent an awful lot of her childhood and youth watching others closely, working out what words and behaviours were safest and would win greatest approval. A love of words and reading had led to a love of writing, and that love had eventually led me, almost by accident, to print journalism.

As a newspaper journalist, I had discovered the wonderful liberty that was the act of interviewing. It meant being able to engage with others, to ask questions and delve into their stories, while retaining a 'safe' distance, both socially and emotionally. It didn't matter whether they liked me or didn't like me; as long as I got their story and told it well, I could win approval on all sides. It was human connection without the awkwardness, emotional risks and potential for misunderstanding that was inevitably part of friendships and other relationships.

For a shy kid, it was bliss—and still is. Put me in front of a Hollywood star or a grieving mum, a triumphant sports hero or a disgraced politician, and I'll know what to say. Drop me at a barbecue with new neighbours or a morning tea with other school parents and I'll struggle, stricken by the possibility of rejection. Fortunately, the art of the interview applies in these situations as well—everybody likes to answer questions about themselves.

I stood for a while on the verandah outside my room, listening to the orchard trees rustle and sway. A possum skittered across the roof. The night felt laden with expectation. Perhaps I was on the verge of some deeper insight, or perhaps it was merely the time of evening when the breeze swings around, and instinctively I was bracing for a cool change. It was late and I was tired after a day travelling from Sydney. Insights could wait.

Stepping into my room, I luxuriated in the sheer spaciousness of having no social or familial obligations, nothing to do and nobody to check as bedtime approached. I had already locked my phones in the small safe in the cupboard, having told Peter and the boys I would only check in with them once a day. I'd also decided, somewhat tentatively, to leave my book in my room during the day, rather than carry it with me as a distraction and a refuge, in a bid to truly empty my mind. But for now I decided to lie on my bed and drift in and out of sleep.

It was quiet. It was peaceful.

It was . . . *agony!*

The first smudges of morning light were seeping around the blinds. I had dozed off and slept unusually deeply through the night—but now I was immediately, fully awake to a pain so intense that it felt like someone had broken into my room and buried an axe deep in my skull.

I don't suffer headaches often, and rarely intensely enough to seek anything more than a Panadol or two. But this savage screaming behind my eyes, accompanied by waves of nausea if I dared move, was instantly familiar from the two occasions I'd previously experienced it. *Caffeine withdrawal!*

As suggested by Gwinganna in its pre-arrival paperwork, I had cut my coffee intake a couple of days earlier. As I was only averaging two double shots a day by then anyway, I considered myself a pinnacle of virtue. I was confident I'd dodge the outraged protests my body had unleased on me when I'd gone cold turkey before. Back then it had been a noxious stream of four or five coffees daily, supplemented by a couple of diet soft drinks, which had sustained me through two university degrees, juggled with a part-time job and then a graduate cadetship at a newspaper.

But if the pain was less acute this time, it was only by a fraction. And here I was, in the middle of hippie heaven, with not so much as an aspirin to fight it off. I would have kicked myself if I wasn't terrified of the spasms that would be triggered by such a swift move.

*Argh! How could you be so stupid? How could you underestimate this pain?*

I've always been particularly good at self-recrimination when I'm suffering. Indeed, as I lay on my bed, convinced I could feel each individual ray of dawning sunlight piercing my face like a poison-tipped arrow, I had already reached into my mental archive and pulled out a familiar script.

*You've ruined this trip. It'll be a waste of time and money now. Because you didn't think ahead, because you were so self-indulgent, because you didn't plan . . . How the hell could you have forgotten what this pain was like?*

Like an incantation, that last question conjured up another memory, unclear and incongruous at first, like something shiny on the bottom of a pond that comes into focus only when the ripples above it begin to settle.

*The Pacific Highway. The turn onto the freeway, and ahead the lights of the Sydney CBD. I am in the passenger's seat of the car, in the throes of a contraction.*

The memory took form and suddenly made sense. On my way to hospital, in the last stages of labour, I'd decided—emphatically, forcefully, with the most clarity I'd experienced in the preceding few hours, and possibly in my entire life—that it had been a dreadful mistake to commit to having a second child, and I needed to stop the whole process immediately.

Roughly 30 minutes later, my son Luke rushed into the world—the midwife's notes recorded me entering at the delivery suite at 9.10 p.m. and Luke arriving six minutes later. And instantly, I thought he was perfect.

What had changed in those 30 minutes, from fear and resistance to delivery and love? I remembered how I had turned to face the pain, visualising the contractions as waves rolling in from the sea. There was no point fighting the ocean. If you were out in the surf, you had to work with it, not against it. Dad had taught me this when we bodysurfed together at Sunshine Beach. *Face the waves—don't try to flee or fight. Read them, and decide which you can catch and which you must dive under, but accept that they will just keep rolling in around you, regardless.*

It's funny how angry we humans get when things don't go the way we expect them to. And how self-pitying. How much energy we waste in our fury and our recriminations when we encounter yet another reminder of the limited control we wield over our world. I could work with this pain, I decided. It wasn't how I'd envisioned spending my second day at Gwinganna, but it was here on this hill with me anyway.

*Something good may come out of this*, I thought. *Not a baby, but . . . something.*

I got out of bed.

*Step.*

*Breathe in.*

*Step.*

*Breathe out.*

*Step.*

*Breathe in.*

*Step.*

*Breathe out.*

The pain came first. The meditation came later. But the result was the same. By lunchtime I had accidentally embraced the practice of walking meditation.

Esteemed Buddhist teachers like Thich Nhat Hanh, who was nominated for a Nobel Peace Prize by none other than Martin Luther King Jr, advocate walking meditation as a way of being grounded in the body, connected with the earth and present in the moment.

Videos abound online of crowds of devotees, ranging from elderly nuns to children barely out of nappies, accompanying the Vietnamese-born Zen master as he walks the hills and fields surrounding Plum Village, the monastic community he founded in south-western France in the early 1980s—the first of many around the world. What is immediately striking is how such a diverse group of people can move together, slowly and quietly, with no apparent impatience or distraction.

I was just trying to walk without throwing up.

Still, there was something humbling about having to move so slowly and deliberately in a community full of bright, energetic folks who were hustling between the morning's stretch and boxing classes, enthusing to one another about the deliciousness of the pumpkin brown rice porridge at breakfast, and discussing whether they should sit by the infinity-edge lap pool this afternoon or sign up for some Hawaiian bodywork or Reiki healing at the spa.

Perhaps 'humbling' is too understated a word. Humility was being forced upon me, and I wasn't accepting it all that graciously. Wary of the pain in my head, I trundled along the paths of gravel and crackling grass like a grumpy wombat that's been woken too early from a nap.

I'd learned in yoga classes about the importance of working with the breath, of drawing oxygen in to release muscles taut with the stress of the day or panicked by an unfamiliar posture. So it felt natural to slip into a rhythm: *Breathing in, I calm my body. Breathing out, I release the pain.* Or something like that. It didn't really matter what the words were; they blurred and wafted like a child's nursery rhyme chanted in time with her garden swing. And eventually, perhaps bored by the repetition as the hours passed, pain unhooked its claws from my skull and queasy stomach, peeling back one bony finger at a time.

Meanwhile, I was peeling off a few layers of my own. First to go: the hyper-vigilance of the night before, my panicked focus on everyone else and how they might be scrutinising me. By morning tea, I had accepted that my fellow guests were far more interested in their own schedules; most acknowledged my presence on the sunlit communal deck with the benign, passing attention one might accord the family labrador in the corner of the lounge: a wave here, a smile there.

Having relinquished my fretfulness, my attention moved to the second layer, the place where my inner monologue replaced the conversations I would otherwise be joining over the tahini balls at morning tea. Not all of these were as excoriating or judgemental as the one I'd had with myself at dinner the night before: *What sort of weirdo hippie freak are you, thinking this is a good idea?* Indeed, for much of my life, that inner place of secret stories had been my comfort zone. The kid in the kindy cubbyhouse did it, the girl who always had her nose stuck in a library book did it, and as an adult I was still drawn to it: building stories and creating characters, constructing arguments and analysing issues in my head, to explain or illustrate the weirdness of the world.

There was nothing inherently wrong with this, of course. But I had to confess that losing myself in my thoughts—to daydream, or create and impose a narrative, or re-prosecute an old argument—was occasionally easier than being present in the world around me. Specifically, it could be easier than being completely present to the *people* around me.

Becoming a mother was what had exposed my secret. Nobody will call you out faster on your habitual distractedness, your lack of presence, than a needy toddler or a fractious teen. So often I'd resented being called to account by those who loved me most. Yes, I loved them too, but that didn't mean I didn't regularly want to escape. I suppose it's one of those double-edged mysteries of love, this discovery of an intimacy that can be both excruciating and exquisite.

But that morning at Gwinganna, with the pangs of caffeine withdrawal still playing havoc with my brain, losing myself in my thoughts was not an option. So I was forced to sit—and just sit. Or walk—and just walk. Without active thought or even daydreams. And that was how, in some moments of clarity that gleamed like shards of glass in the sun, I uncovered a third layer.

It was deeper, quieter, but not wholly unfamiliar. It was a state that existed beneath those times when I was focusing on others' opinions or preoccupied with framing and voicing my own—which for me, as for most of us, was most of the time. Put simply, it was a state of presence, of bearing witness without adding commentary or conversation or making judgements about what was going on around me.

A cloud passing across the sun. A myna tormenting a magpie. Voices tumbling from the yoga pavilion. A waft of frying garlic from the kitchen. In those moments, fleeting at first, my senses became acute, as if I could trace an outline around each smell, each sound, even the touch of wind on my skin, as it materialised.

Then it would pass. With a habitual glance at my watch, a niggling thought, frets about not wanting to be late for my massage or whether I was wearing the right clothes. It would dissipate and I would be left breathless, as if I'd just stepped back from a lover's embrace. Off-balance, I'd instinctively reach out for more, and then, realising I had no idea what 'it' actually was, let alone how to get it back, I would be stricken with consternation.

Cynicism is the journalist's refuge, and I wondered: was I breaking the first rule of news reporting and letting my feelings get in the way? Was this thing I was sensing a side-effect of my having too little to do and being overly pampered? The privileged flipside of a #firstworldproblem—a #firstworldindulgence, perhaps?

But it didn't feel like whimsy, privilege or indulgence. I couldn't imagine myself flitting off to the gift shop and decking myself in neutral layers of hemp, bamboo and other natural fibres. Or crystal necklaces and feathered earrings. Or any of the other designer clichés preferred by born-again New Age matrons who insist on saying hello with prayer hands and an earnest 'Namaste'. I simply wanted to know what this thing was, this calm awareness that was flitting across my consciousness like a bird of rare and beautiful strangeness, one that takes flight whenever you turn to look at it directly.

Did I want to catch it? Did I want to tame it? At first, I simply wanted to *know* it.

When I woke the next morning, my caffeine withdrawals were gone. My brain, my head, my whole body felt scrubbed bare, as if the pain, like a wildfire, had consumed vast swathes of my mental undergrowth before burning itself out.

After breakfast, I played drums in the gym. It would be difficult to find two words less likely than 'drums' and 'gym' to feature on my list of preferred activities at a health retreat. 'Smoking crack' would probably be up there. But the option of drumming, when it was put to us after our quinoa bircher muesli, was so unexpected, so utterly outrageous here in the serenity of a hinterland health retreat, that I almost laughed aloud when it was proffered.

Less than 48 hours ago, it had felt like a radical act to choose not to speak, the social opprobrium potentially so great that I had almost surrendered that choice as soon as I'd begun. But my time in silence—and particularly my discovery of something mysterious and breathtaking there—had shone a light on the complete arbitrariness of what is considered 'normal' human behaviour. On the horizon, the Pacific sparkled seductively, and the air was so clear with promise that I felt it might almost be possible to step off this bluff and glide in a long, slow arc to the faraway waves.

If I could choose not to speak, then I could choose to drum. *Of course I would drum!*

The drums turned out to be large exercise balls, held in place by square plastic frames. We were a motley group ranging in age from twenty-somethings to seniors—although what the standard profile for a 'health retreat–based drum enthusiast' was, I didn't know—and drumsticks were distributed to us as we filed into the gym. Our hyper-energetic fitness leader urged us to position ourselves behind balls, and it became quickly evident that it was impossible to take yourself too seriously when paired with something that looks like a giant primary coloured all-day sucker.

The rules were pretty straightforward: our leader would play music, and we would follow her shouted instructions for drumming patterns and steps around our gym balls.

*Steps* . . . The word unearthed a memory in me that explained why the plastic frames holding the balls seemed so familiar: they were actually the bases used in step aerobics classes. This, in turn, unleashed a nasty flashback from an overcrowded class in the early 1990s, when a collision with another step enthusiast during a particularly frenetic sequence choreographed to Madonna's 'Vogue' had left me with a twisted knee—and my aforementioned apprehension for gyms.

A furtive glance to my left revealed a doughy colossus of a man, already sweating so profusely that his T-shirt had blossomed in wet floral patterns. To my right, a brunette with the hindquarters of a panther was bouncing in lycra mesh cutaways.

*What was I thinking?*

Too late. The instructor hit a remote control and an urgent rhythm flooded the room.

Suddenly we were drumming to an international hit my kids loved, Sheppard's rousing earworm 'Geronimo'. Drumming in ways we didn't know we could. Miss Lycra, the Damp Colossus, the Fit Nanna in front of me, and the Macho Bloke (possibly Miss Lycra's boyfriend) behind—we were all pounding, beating, whacking those gym balls like we were born to drum.

The music rose in a euphoric crescendo, the leader shouting instructions and we, her willing followers, leaping to execute her commands, as focused and eager as if we were storming some enemy's battlements. Or competing in Battle of the Bands. We were powerful. Surging. United.

And that was when I noticed it. For the first time, I felt connected to my fellow guests. We were creating this bold, throbbing roar together, the loudest noise I had heard since the Gwinganna bus had gunned its engine to climb the steep, winding driveway to reception. And yet nobody was speaking. I had joined them—and they were just like me.

None of this was profound. I knew that. But it was such pure, adrenaline-soaked fun that for weeks afterwards the tune would pop into my head unexpectedly and make me grin. Occasionally I'd even break into a bit of air drumming. Eventually, I googled the band and the song, curious to find out why a group of young Brisbane musicians would choose to write a pop song about a legendary Apache warrior.

'You say "Geronimo" when you want to take a leap of faith or a leap of defiance, and I think that's what the song is about,' one of the Sheppard members explained in an interview. 'Just taking a leap of faith and doing something that may not work but having the courage to give it a try anyway.'[2]

I couldn't have nominated a better anthem for my leap into silence.

As I pulled my sneakers back on after the drumming session, I fretted briefly about whether I had done something to upset my new equilibrium, something that would permanently frighten off the strange, quiet presence I had encountered yesterday.

Surging out of the gym, my fellow drummers were alive with the energy of primary school children on a summer excursion to the zoo. As they traded jokes about their drumming talents or otherwise, gusts of laughter rolled through the crowd and over my head as I bent over my laces. The energy fizzed—but, just as quickly, it dissipated, the guests hurrying away to their next activities.

I had already decided to walk one of Gwinganna's bush trails alone, eager to bear witness to one of those brilliant April mornings that Queensland mounts in spirited defence against the impending winter, as fleeting as it is in the Sunshine State. This time, rather than having the pace forced on me by a throbbing pain, I chose it freely: as slow as yesterday, timing my breaths with my footsteps, trying to keep my attention from drifting to daydreams or any inner monologue, but resisting the urge to criticise myself when it did.

In spite of my fears, the cloak of silence settled back on my shoulders easily. If I had any aim at all, beyond following the trail up through the orchard and along a ridge line away from the cabins and villas, it was to hold a soft focus on my senses and what they were presenting to me. I reassured my cynical journalist self that there was nothing much else to do anyway.

The dry grass crackled beneath my feet. Moving through the orchard, I discovered a small mob of wallabies grazing in the morning sun. They seemed relatively unfazed by me—or perhaps they were just greedy for grass after a dry season—so I was able to enjoy the choreography of their attention as they registered my passage: head up, freeze, hold focus, flick one ear, flick another ear, drop down, swing hindquarters forward in a slow hop, head down, snatch a new mouthful of grass. As I moved past the mob, each wallaby picked up the pattern, in a gentle marsupial Mexican wave.

On the other side of the orchard, at the beginning of a trail up the side of the hill through light bush, the familiar smells of the Australian scrub hit me. Although I didn't know enough to match each aroma with a particular plant or tree, the cloud of sharp eucalyptus, underscored by the richer notes of undergrowth, borne by the sea breeze, brought back memories of childhood, holidays, *home*. But I tried not to chase the memories. I wanted to stay in the present, to savour what was here, now.

*Step . . . breathe in . . . step . . . breathe out . . .*

Eventually, the bush on the trail's downhill side gave way to a panorama, a vast picnic blanket spreading from forest across farmland to the ocean. From the valley below I could hear farm machinery complaining as it rumbled into action, a dog barking encouragement. There were birds calling, the sharp rustle of lizards and other reptiles fleeing from warm rocks ahead of my footsteps—and insects, always insects, providing the whining, buzzing chorus that creates the backing track for the Australian bush.

It wasn't silent. And yet it felt stripped of extraneous noise. And this time, when I felt the arrival of the ethereal presence I'd noticed yesterday, I stopped. Resisting the urge to move, to fidget, to add anything to what was here already, I simply stood. Every cell in my skin seemed to expand slightly, to reach out to greet the air and everything else that was present here on the hill. I felt the breeze shift slightly, and the precise moment a cloud drifted past the sun, my face cool and then warm again. Had the world around me, I wondered, always been capable of provoking this sensory play, so acute that I could stand still in its thrall and know that this was *enough*?

I wasn't doing anything. I wasn't buying anything or reading anything; I wasn't testing or analysing or rushing somewhere or meeting someone. I just *was*. And I was happy. Peacefully, solidly happy—for what felt like the first time I could remember.

That was the moment I realised that, in coming to Gwinganna, I had done something more than choose not to talk. As I tried to avoid all the obstacles and things I knew I didn't like, I had somehow found the space I needed—a space in which I could finally stop. That's right: I reverse-parked into silence.

# 3

# THE RULE

I sat alone for my last meal at Gwinganna, savouring the sense of crystalline clarity that had settled around me since my walk. But when I saw the retreat's general manager, Sharon Kolkka, I was compelled to reclaim my voice, to thank her and acknowledge the support of the staff, who had never questioned my mute participation in their activities.

Speaking for the first time in four days felt unfamiliar, like being asked to sort through a mouthful of gravel with a numb tongue. As I enthused about the difference my silent days had made, I noticed I had to consciously calibrate my voice against the chatter in the room. Things already felt loud, and I was reluctant to add to the volume. But I wanted Sharon to understand that, for the first time in many months, I not only felt physically healthy but also confident and optimistic about decisions that had previously felt so overwhelming. With the noise stripped away, I felt able to see what needed to be done for my own wellbeing, and for that of those closest to me.

(It didn't occur to me until much later how odd it is that we routinely use 'see' in this context—'I could see what needed to be done'—when we are referring to understanding something. This turn of phrase is typical, I think, of our society's bias toward the visual, the visible, the measurable and tangible. But during my stay at Gwinganna, I had discovered that when all the extraneous noise was reduced, I could 'hear' what needed to be done—I could hear my own voice, my instincts, and perhaps even something deeper than that. But all of this I was yet to explore.)

A few weeks after my stay, Sharon emailed me. She expressed the joy she felt at seeing guests have light-bulb moments during their visits, and wished me well. 'Silence is the gift you have had all your life that you finally opened,' she concluded.

The sentence sat on my computer screen, compact and unadorned. Fourteen words, delivered as casually as the many administrative messages I'd received from Gwinganna. But something in her words made me catch my breath. Here was someone else who had seen the unicorn. Sharon was acknowledging that what I had been simultaneously chasing and doubting was, indeed, real. I hadn't been crazy or self-indulgent or just flailing with exhaustion. We were fellow travellers: we both knew the secret handshake, the incantation that could weave straw into gold, the wardrobe door that could reveal Narnia. In the eloquent simplicity of Sharon's words, I detected a confidence that I would now know exactly what to do with this wonderful gift I had finally discovered.

Except I didn't. I didn't have a clue.

There was a time, predictably enough for a sixteen-year-old girl, when the greatest gift I could imagine was a horse. Back then, I was a regular volunteer at an equestrian centre operated by a rather euphemistically named 'country club' in which my parents had bought a timeshare. During our holidays there, I would get up and out before dawn and return home after dark, my skin thick with the smell of horse sweat and hay, to be lulled to sleep by the rhythmic muscle memory of cantering on mountain trails.

One summer, the centre's chief instructor offered to sell me a quarter horse I had grown fond of. She had decided he was too valuable and too challenging to be consigned to a life spent carting overweight tourists who sagged in the saddle like potato sacks in the midday sun. My parents vetoed the idea almost immediately. Their concerns were multiple: chief among them the belief that a horse would prove too onerous a financial burden, too great a distraction from my schoolwork and too physically risky.

On the last count they were proved correct almost immediately. On New Year's Eve I was rounding up the horses to move them to a grazing paddock for the next day's public holiday, when I was thrown by a strong young gelding unaccustomed to mustering his peers. My next memory was peering into a pool of thick blood. I remember how captivating it was, how ethereally beautiful, this rich magenta sea that was slowly submersing the dust and gravel so close to my nose. Then I realised the blood was mine. I was transferred to hospital in an ambulance with sirens blaring, my neck immobilised in a brace amid fears I had broken it.

I hadn't. But I did need multiple stitches in my forehead, my head and my hand, plaster to correct a broken thumb, and, eventually, minor surgery on one leg. Worse, most of this was required on one of the busiest hospital nights of the year. It all thoroughly disrupted my parents' plan to attend a beachside New Year's Eve party. My teenage dreams of owning a horse had died before the plaster set on my arm.

Now, more than three decades later, the idea of receiving silence as a gift was beginning to feel a bit like being handed the reins of a Melbourne Cup favourite at the starter's barrier, fully aware that beneath the horse's surface beauty hid a wilder force, waiting to burst forth. What would happen when it did? Could I tame it? Was I even meant to? Or was I simply supposed to cling on for the ride? And would it be safer, easier, to stay back behind the barrier or up in the stands, content to have a flashing glimpse of this magnificent force of nature?

At the very least, I had recognised that I was seeking something greater than simply refraining from speech. Choosing not to talk had been a key that had opened a door.

Indeed, my experiment at Gwinganna had demonstrated that silence—at least, the type of silence that delivered the calm state of awareness and equanimity that I had experienced—was not just about stripping away speech and other external noise. If it was just about the absence of auditory stimuli, then why had I been able to maintain the sense of balance and peace during that thunderous drumming session? And I knew that some of the greatest proponents of silence, peace campaigners like Thich Nhat Hanh and Mahatma Gandhi, had lived for significant parts of their lives in extremely noisy environments.

So while I guessed that reducing extraneous noise might help, along with the luxury of stepping away from domestic demands and professional obligations for a few days, these were clearly not the only variables involved in accessing the rich quality of silence I had experienced. Otherwise, anyone who could go to a quiet bedroom at home or an isolated meeting room at work—or an empty church or a park or a bush trail—would be guaranteed inner peace. If only it were that simple!

Similarly, if this was simply an exercise in reducing decibels, then I should be able to sit in any of those peaceful environments while scrolling—quietly—through my Twitter and Facebook feed or the news headlines and remain completely sanguine. I was beginning to suspect that turning down the volume of the *inner* noise—the self-talk and thinking and observing, the clicking and liking and sharing—was at least as important as tempering the external noise.

Back and forth my questions flew, occasionally prompting me to laugh at myself—and specifically at the sheer amount of internal noise I could create while pondering the value of silence.

Some days I felt philosophical and would write rambling thoughts in my morning journal about this special state called silence, something that must have predated life itself, and would continue afterwards:

We dance with the idea of Silence just as we dance with the idea of Truth. Or Love. These are things we seek instinctively, almost from birth; things almost all of us agree are good. But how do we know when we've found them? Would we even recognise them? Do they look the same to everybody?

And what if, like Truth and Love, I finally find Silence only to discover it reveals things about me that I don't want to know?

The next day, my newspaper reporter's cynicism would return.

Does anyone ever tell you if you're having a midlife crisis? Maybe I should just buy a red sports car. A lot less pompous and more fun than pontificating about bloody silence like a self-absorbed git.

I was always pithier when I was in journalistic mode.

Weeks after my return from Gwinganna, I was no closer to working out how to build silence into my daily life—or even whether it was worth the pursuit. Away from the tranquillity of that Gold Coast mountaintop, it felt incongruous and unattainable. Worse, it sometimes felt like an exercise in self-indulgent navel-gazing. So I did a deal with myself. I would continue wrestling with the question of silence—what it was, whether it had value and how I could achieve it—but I would do it like a journalist would. And that meant going to the experts.

It was a time of civic corruption and social disruption—a time when public anxieties were soaring, and public morality was skidding to new lows. The rich were getting richer. The poor and those in the middle, struggling simply to survive, were torn about whom to blame. Perhaps they would have been angrier at their own leaders had they not been distracted by the prospect of invaders from beyond their borders, terrified of odd-looking interlopers speaking in unfamiliar tongues and apparently threatening their way of life.

Could this be Australia in the early twenty-first century? Or the United States in the era of Trump? Perhaps—but it was also Rome around AD 500, when the son of a noble Christian family arrived there from his Umbrian home to further his studies. The once glorious Roman Empire was in rapid decline, but the imperial city still offered plenty of pleasures for a privileged youth like Benedict.

No doubt he tasted some of them; some reports have it he fell in love at least once. But ultimately Rome failed to seduce Benedict; instead, he grew disillusioned with his friends' debauched behaviour and his teachers' poor standards. So disillusioned, in fact, that he not only left the city but renounced all vestiges of wealth and sophistication, eventually making his home in the stillness of a cave about 60 kilometres east of Rome. That the cave existed close to a ruined villa complex that had once served as a 'pleasure palace' for the former emperor Nero was likely a coincidence, but in retrospect the metaphor is irresistible: a scathing statement about the corruption and degradation of ego-driven power contrasted with the tough but rewarding life of renunciation.

Benedict was not the first Christian to turn his back on the city. About two centuries earlier, an Egyptian who would become known as Saint Anthony the Great had also walked away from a comfortable existence, selling or giving away everything left to him by his wealthy parents in favour of a life of asceticism and solitude in the desert. The Romans' brutal persecution of Christians formally ended a few decades later, when Emperor Constantine I legalised the religion.

But even as it became substantially easier to embrace the faith— being a Christian no longer carried the threat of martyrdom, for a start—not all were happy with this mainstreaming. Some feared a blurring of the line between 'the things that are Caesar's and . . . the things that are God's' (Matthew 22:21), while others believed a true faith required commitment and sacrifice. Thousands ultimately followed Anthony into the wilderness, eventually becoming known as the Desert Fathers and Mothers.

Nor was Benedict the first Christian to pursue silence as a means of communing with something greater. Despite their numbers, a fundamental part of life as a Desert Father was solitude, with time devoted to *hesychasm*, a form of silent prayer that aimed to invoke inner stillness and emptiness. *The Sayings of the Desert Fathers*, a compendium of teachings recorded in the fourth century AD as *Apophthegmata Patrum*, outlines the approach thus: 'Take care to be silent. Empty your mind. Attend to your meditation in the fear of God, whether you are resting or at work. If you do this, you will not fear the attacks of the demons.'[1]

Unlike most of the Desert Fathers and Mothers, Benedict would ultimately emerge from his self-imposed exile, and eventually embrace communal life as the abbot of a nearby monastery. After three years living as a hermit, he brought with him a very deep appreciation of both silence and mutuality. While they might appear to be contradictory, Benedict was convinced that these two values, when lived in balance, could enhance the human journey towards something greater.

Ultimately, he established a number of monasteries, an achievement that would see him recognised as the founder of Western monasticism. But Benedict's real legacy extended far beyond the bricks and mortar of those communities, to a set of enduring principles and instructions for monastic life, recorded in a small book which came to be known as *The Rule of Saint Benedict*.

*The Rule* reflected Benedict's commitment to organisation and clear governance, fuelled by his vision for a contemplative lifestyle that bonded the most powerful features of silent practice with the strength of community. With a prologue and 73 short chapters, it combined practical advice about the clothes, meals and other concerns of communal living with very precise spiritual direction. Chapter 7 outlined twelve degrees of humility, for example.

Perhaps Benedict's expensive Roman education wasn't entirely wasted after all—his *Rule* has been in use for more than fifteen centuries, spread across every continent except Antarctica in hundreds of monasteries of varying orders, all of them broadly subscribing to

Benedictine principles. Most are found in quiet, even isolated, rural locations. Not only do such settings protect the peace which Benedictines see as fundamental to the contemplative life, but they also make possible the manual work that sustains the monastic communities, at least in part. Many monasteries run farming operations, while others engage in woodwork, baking, weaving, or—perhaps most famously—distilling liquor, brewing beer or making wine.

This work is not merely to pay the bills. Throughout *The Rule*, Benedict espoused balance in all things, and particularly recognised the value of physical activity as a complement to periods of quiet contemplation. 'Idleness is the enemy of the soul,' he wrote. 'Therefore the community should have specified periods for manual labour as well as for prayerful reading.'[2] Thus, the Benedictine motto emerged: *Ora et labora*—pray and work.

Underpinning all of this, of course, is the pre-eminence of silence. Not as a punishment to be borne—contrary to the common, somewhat Gothic stereotype, modern Benedictine monks do not creep around in dark hallways, forbidden to speak—but as a way of heightening one's awareness of the power of words and thoughts. Benedict himself put it best: 'Listen carefully . . . with the ear of your heart.' (*The ear of your heart!* With that single perfect phrase, an ancient cave-dweller won respect from this twenty-first-century journalist for knowing precisely how to grab your readers from the opening line.)

In a Benedictine monastery, the Great Silence occurs from the end of night prayers (the Office of Compline) to the following morning. Some meals are eaten in silence, but sometimes a book is read aloud; occasionally the monks are permitted to engage in quiet conversation. Again, balance is key.

Perhaps Benedict also had a wicked sense of humour, as he liked to set thorny challenges for his followers, lest they become too comfortable and smugly pious in their quiet, cloistered communities. Whatever his intention, chapter 53 of *The Rule* added warm-hearted hospitality

to the expectations placed on the monks: 'All guests who present themselves are to be received as Christ, who said, "I was a stranger and you
welcomed me."' Later, *The Rule* even directed a monastery's abbot to
nominate a 'porter' to attend the door at all times—'a sensible person
who knows how to take a message and deliver a reply'. Best of all, to
my jaded eyes, was the instruction that when the porter hears a knock,
he must respond, 'Thanks be to God!' or 'Your blessing, please!' A far
more personable approach than 'Please leave a message after the tone,'
or 'I rarely listen to voicemail; text me if it's urgent.'

And so it is that, some 1500 years later, Benedictine monasteries around the world continue to throw open their doors to visitors,
offering simple accommodation and meals to all who genuinely seek
refuge there. It may be gently suggested that guests pay what they can
afford (relatively few monasteries advertise a rate for accommodation),
but otherwise the only request is that they respect the monks' routine,
especially with regard to limiting noise.

It's tempting here to riff on the idea of a hitherto undiscov-
ered global network of PrayerBNBs . . . In fact, as incongruous as it
may seem, you can even find a few of these monasteries, abbeys and
hermitages rated on TripAdvisor. Indeed, my first encounter with
Benedictine hospitality was prompted by a glowing review by a travel
writer. I wasn't on a spiritual quest at the time. I was simply looking for
some creative inspiration in Google's rolling pastures of prose, having
left News Corp to 'go freelance' around 2012. The great Pico Iyer, who
has been published pretty much anywhere a longform journalist would
want to see his or her words—*The New York Times, Harpers, Time,
National Geographic, The New York Review of Books,* the *Times Literary
Supplement*—wrote in 2011:

> In 30 years of constant travel, I've never found anywhere more
> sensuous, luxurious and liberating than the monastery I visit several
> times a year. Even the most exciting places—Venice or Havana or

Easter Island—never leave me feeling clarified, stimulated and
refreshed as this retreat house does . . . I've been here when I'm tired,
jetlagged, sick and exultant, and every time, in any mood, I drive back
down into the world feeling like a new being, with a fresh sense of
direction and all the energy I could want. Ready, in fact, for a new life.[3]

It was catnip to the soul of a tired single working mother of two. I can
actually remember my breath catching in my throat as I absorbed
Iyer's description of New Camaldoli, a Benedictine hermitage on a
remote stretch of Californian coast known as Big Sur. It was clear
this was a man whose very being had been rocked to its core. Like the
woman near Meg Ryan in the famous scene in *When Harry Met Sally*,
I wanted to call this destination and tell them: 'I'll have what *he's* having.'

In a later feature, Iyer explained that while the Camaldolese—
one of the many orders borne of the Benedictine tradition—opened
their doors to anyone seeking specific spiritual guidance, there was
no proselytising or religious discrimination at their hermitage. 'The
monks—sometime scholars, psychologists, Coast Guard workers and
painters—are full of down-to-earth companionship and counsel if you
want it,' he wrote, 'but happy to let you roam and rest as you wish.'[4]
This aspect of Benedictine hospitality is frequently misunderstood or
misrepresented. Theirs is not a missionary vocation; they do not seek
to win converts or save souls—at least, not in any intrusive, zealous or
obnoxious way.

It took me several years, but eventually I made it to New Camaldoli, which perches like an eyrie above the ocean at the end of a steep
and winding drive. Periodically, the unsealed road is swept away in
muddy landslides, leaving the monks isolated for weeks or even months
on end. I immediately saw that Iyer hadn't exaggerated: every view was
spectacular from so high and isolated a spot. Somehow, the wild sweep
of the Pacific diminished everything, even the tree-lined mountain
ridge that hugged the coast. When I visited, the highway far below was

being repaired after another mudslide, and New Camaldoli's driveway was the last accessible turn-off before the road became unusable. The absence of traffic made the remoteness seem even more stark; on this windswept hillside, all markers of time, of civilisation, were erased. This could have been any era, and I could have been anyone.

While at New Camaldoli I attended the Liturgy of the Hours, the schedule of communal prayer that provides the gentle rhythm of the monastic day. It begins with the Office of Vigils in the inky black of pre-dawn, when the air was so still I could hear the hiss and sigh of the ocean far below. Then it was home again for a cup of tea, and perhaps a quick nap, before Lauds at 7 a.m. My reward for this routine of yawning and groping for clothes in chilly darkness came later, when I would emerge from the chapel into an infant day, with colours as vibrant as paint still wet on the mountain ridges beneath the porcelain arc of the sky.

One morning, I stumbled upon two rabbits playing on the grass outside my cabin. These were nothing like the invasive pests I'd occasionally seen in the Australian bush, sinewy and coarse-haired. With their fat haunches and fluffy tails, the Camaldolese rabbits were entirely Disney-worthy. I startled myself, and them, by crying out reflexively— a sound from a time years ago, when unfettered, wide-eyed joy was still permissible.

After breakfast each day, I was drawn to tramp the precipitous curves of the driveway back down to the road, before turning and climbing back up, shedding layers of fleece as I began to sweat, like some bizarre and protracted hitchhiker's striptease. Then I would hike the mountain trails behind the hermitage, averting my eyes when I came to a disconcerting sign that offered instructions about what one should do if approached by a mountain lion.

In the afternoons, I read. First, I fulfilled a longstanding ambition to read Henry David Thoreau's *Walden* from cover to cover, in the hope that I might expand my understanding beyond that oft-quoted insight that 'most men live lives of quiet desperation'. What I discovered was a more enlivening tale than that grim quote suggests, about existential questions that remain relevant more than 160 years later.

'I went to the woods because I wished to live deliberately,' Thoreau wrote, 'to front only the essential facts of life, and see if I could not learn what it had to teach, and not, when I came to die, discover that I had not lived.' He had such a distinctive and unashamedly curmudgeonly voice that Thoreau quickly became an almost tangible presence in my cabin as I read. I nicknamed him 'HD', and sometimes laughed aloud as he shared what was essentially a quest to discover the meaning of life. He had 'gone to the woods' because he was convinced that much of what was considered modern or civilised was simply extraneous noise—HD was particularly irritated by gossip, railroads, current affairs and newspapers—that served only to distract people from the important question of how to live well.

Next I buried myself in *The Seven Storey Mountain*, the autobiography of the American Trappist monk Thomas Merton, probably the best-known monastic writer of modern times, and certainly of the Benedictine tradition. Published in 1948, the book became an international bestseller, with some even comparing Merton to Saint Augustine himself. But something about Merton's zeal—he had converted to Catholicism in New York as a young man in the late 1930s, after a period of beer-soaked hellraising and womanising at Cambridge University—not to mention his strident pre–Vatican II pronouncements, jarred with me. When I was raised Catholic in 1970s and '80s Queensland, there had been no suggestion that we could sin freely and often while we were in our teens and early twenties, comfortable in the knowledge that we would be forgiven and welcomed back into the fold—much less rewarded with a spot in the literary canon!

In the evenings I meditated with the monks and other retreatants for an hour after Vespers. It all felt good, in a slightly exotic way that was both rigorous and mysterious. Was this the rejuvenation that Iyer had extolled? Yet as achingly beautiful as New Camaldoli was, something in me still felt unsettled. The serene feelings swirled but didn't stick. Had anything fundamental in me changed? My head demanded evidence. If I was becoming a 'new being', with new energy and direction, how could I know it would last? What must I do to cement it in place, so I could take it with me when I left?

Sometimes, I had the sense of experiencing something both familiar and foreign. It confounded me, just as bathing in warm, golden light every afternoon did; having spent my life on the east coast of Australia, seeing the sun *sink* over the Pacific Ocean was unsettling. My favourite childhood holidays had been spent at the beach, and witnessing the sun rising over the water was a certainty I knew in my bones—and yet here, something marvellous was making me acknowledge the possibility of another reality, one that was equally valid, if seemingly contradictory.

One afternoon, as I waited for that gorgeous sunset moment when the ocean itself seemed to catch fire, I thumbed through the pages of a paperback I'd picked up at the hermitage bookshop. I'd been looking for a guide to the fundamentals of Benedictine life, and the author of this one was, according to the back cover, 'one of the world's experts on monastic spirituality'. To be honest, though, I think I was mainly attracted by the cover: a stunning photo of a Polish monastery, its reflection caught in soft pastel light in the river below.

As the pages flitted by, the word 'mindfulness' at the top of one of them made me stop. It seemed utterly incongruous. What was one of the buzzwords of the current zeitgeist doing in a book about the Rule of Saint Benedict? Indeed, what was a Catholic monk doing writing about a concept that (I'd always assumed) sprang from Buddhist teachings?

Page 29 grew brighter as the sun drew lower.

'Benedict's monastery is a place of leisure because those who live there are committed to a life of mindfulness,' the author of the book, *Strangers to the City*, wrote. 'Being attentive requires, first of all, that we renounce the desire to control what happens around us, to manipulate reality, to impose our will on events or on other people.' The writer warned that 'control freaks' would have the most difficulty with this life, because, behind their bluster, they were often very fearful people. '[T]hey are driven mercilessly by their own insecurity. Their life is a constant battle to prevent reality from asserting its independence. Their inner voices are shouting so loudly that they can hear nothing else.'

Ouch. Momentarily, I considered hoisting that pretty little paperback hard into the air, hoping it would make it to the heaving sea below. I could take this sort of hard talk from Dr Phil, but from . . . what was his name? I checked the front cover. 'Michael Casey. Monk of Tarrawarra.' I decided to give Michael Casey of Tarrawarra until the end of the page to convince me. Otherwise, his book was going for a swim.

'We all need to learn the art of silence, to still the clamour that comes from within as well as securing for ourselves a zone where outward noise is sometimes hushed,' he continued. 'In a world where communication is huge, it takes a fair amount of resolution to create for oneself a sphere of silence, in which external urgencies are put on hold and words are weighed.'[5]

*Damn.* I took a breath. Michael Casey made sense. For a cloistered monk, he seemed to have considerable insight into what it was like to be a crazy-busy working mother, struggling to hear herself think over the demands of her children, her boss and, loudest of all, her inner control freak. Or perhaps it was hard-won wisdom about the universal human condition. Either way, I decided that if the rest of his writing was anything like page 29, then this might be a helpful, even sympathetic guidebook for life after the peace and seclusion of New Camaldoli.

The sun seemed to flare larger as it kissed the horizon. I scanned the book for some biographical details about its straight-talking author. And . . . *Damn* (again). Michael Casey was an Australian. I had journeyed to the other side of the world, to an ethereal place where the sun seemed to rise and set in reverse, to find a new direction for myself, and it turned out I could have discovered it about 90 minutes from Melbourne.

I put the book down and waited in silence as the world caught fire.

# CONTEMPLATION

Driving towards Tarrawarra Abbey a little more than a year later, I wondered what Pico Iyer might say about it. The globe-trotting travel writer would find no dramatic vistas here, although the rolling hills of Victorian wine country are pleasant enough. The driveway to the abbey itself was an unassuming kilometre and a half of gravel; it was muddy in spots, but nothing like the heart-stopping goat track that challenges the resolve of pilgrims to New Camaldoli.

Another difference: as I arrived, in the brisk chill of an autumn twilight, I noticed that the thrumming of the ocean by Big Sur had been replaced by the lowing and stamping of cattle. To support themselves, the monks of Tarrawarra raise beef cattle—Charolais and Red Angus, to be precise—as well as baking eucharistic bread, and with the calving season recently ended, there were plenty of restless and protective bovine mothers nearby.

Overlooking 400 hectares of farmland bought by the monks in 1954 was a rambling house, typical of those built by cattle barons during the Federation era. Their homes sought to replicate what they must have considered the more civilised aesthetics and culture of 'Mother England'; just by looking at the façade I could tell that, inside, there would be high ceilings, multiple fireplaces, long, draughty hallways and plenty of dark wood.

However, while many modern Federation homes tend to be decorated in a cluttered, overtly luxe style that nods to the traditionalists, monastic asceticism had clearly guided the interior design here. My bedroom was large and airy, but sparsely furnished with a single bed, a wooden desk and chair, an armchair for reading and a bedside table and lamp. Exploring the numerous cupboards and nooks, I also discovered what appeared to be a drop-down bench and kneeling stool, which I assumed was intended for personal prayer.

From the large windows, I could gaze out to the mountains of the Kinglake National Park. Ten years earlier, they had been crisscrossed by livid red veins during the cataclysmic Black Saturday bushfires, which ultimately claimed 173 lives.[1] But now there was rain coming; the vista smudged like a watercolour as mist and cloud puckered around the ridges. Directly beneath my window was a collection of modest, low-set buildings—the secluded area where the monks lived and worked—as well as the covered walkways that connected them to the guesthouse and the church, which they had built themselves.

Within a day of settling into my room, with no wi-fi and severely limited phone range, I was struck by how easily my brain had embraced that window and the view beyond as entertainment. Two birds hunting for insects amid the lichened roof tiles; the patterns of sun and shadow across the hills as the afternoon waned; the swish and swing of the monks' habits as they made their way to prayer, like yachts tacking on Sydney Harbour, swift but unhurried. All held me mesmerised for minutes on end.

Silence, I learned, breeds an appreciation of small scenes like these—at least, when it isn't stoking a burning need to burst into song, something that I find hard to resist when presented with high walls and large, bare spaces—like my bedroom at the abbey. Aware there was a priest visiting from England in an adjacent room, my early days were spent catching myself a few bars into a song, and frantically slapping my hand over my mouth. But once the visitor had departed (or fled, depending on the sharpness of his hearing and his appreciation of random bars of Beyoncé), I was informed I would be the lone guest for a few days. Thus, I was free to roam the dim, panelled hallways and creaking staircase like a tuneless Miss Havisham.

If my visit to New Camaldoli had unfolded like a mesmerising out-of-body experience, Tarrawarra Abbey was more like a trip to see your nanna: it was homey and welcoming, but you knew you were expected to mind your manners, especially when company was coming.

That stripped-back, Australian style wasn't the only thing that distinguished it from the hermitage on Big Sur. The monks at Tarrawarra belong to a different order to the Camaldolese, borne of a breakaway movement in the eleventh century, when a group of their forebears decided the mainstream Benedictines had become lax in their practices and spiritually torpid. A few centuries later, after the Black Death had cut a swathe through their monasteries, another group of monks, committed to even stricter observance, emerged, based around the monastery of La Trappe. The Trappists—or, as they are more formally called, the Order of Cistercians of the Strict Observance—are thus a bit like the Top Guns of the monastic world: the strictest of the strict.

That's my analogy, obviously; given their limited exposure to television (a little goes a long way at Tarrawarra Abbey, and only on Sunday nights), I'm not sure many Trappists will have seen *Top Gun*, much less be prepared to equate Tom Cruise's strutting machismo with their own rigorous faith. That said, at Tarrawarra I discovered what seemed like a hardcore version of the already disciplined Rule of Saint Benedict. For example, the Trappists' Liturgy of the Hours extends to seven offices, or sessions of prayer, throughout the day, compared to the four observed at New Camaldoli. Imagine my consternation when, suffused with a sense of my own virtue, I set my alarm to attend the office of Vigils at 5 a.m.—only to discover that the monks had already risen at 3.30 a.m., for a 4 a.m. start.

After that, there was Lauds and mass at 6 a.m., then the offices of Terce (8 a.m.) and Sext (11.15 a.m.), with the latter marking the end of the morning's work. After lunch, the Office of Nones at 1.40 p.m.

heralded the monks' return to work for the afternoon, before Vespers at 6 p.m. and the Office of Compline at 8 p.m., marking the beginning of the Great Silence until Vigils again the next morning.

It was tempting to assume that the schedule itself was infused with magic. Why else would anyone subject themselves to such a demanding routine—a detailed choreography which would govern their daily movements for the remaining weeks, months and years of their lives—if it wasn't guaranteed to deliver them peace?

But I wasn't convinced that the quantity of time dedicated to devotion was the key. Not on its own. Growing up, I had known ostensibly devout folks who took Holy Communion every morning and then scowled fearsomely at small children and animals on their way home. Ticking off another church service as if it earned frequent flyer points that could be redeemed for peace or grace didn't make a lot of sense. And some of the wisest and warmest-hearted people I'd met, back then and since, might only step inside a church at Christmas time, and then only for the carols.

The one thing I was certain of was that silence appeared to be a common factor in accessing something profound. I'd experienced it at Gwinganna and witnessed it at New Camaldoli, and I felt close to it again here at Tarrawarra. I clutched that idea like a compass. I knew I was lost, and I didn't know what direction was best. But I was sure this thing called silence was a valuable tool, if only I could train myself to use it.

One night when I arrived for dinner—served in an enormous mahogany-lined dining room, where I half-expected to discover Maggie Smith lighting a cigarette by the mantlepiece—a note had been left by my plate. 'Fr Michael will meet you tomorrow at 4 p.m.,' it read. Having been educated at a Catholic girls' school, I succumbed immediately to the predictable gut reaction: a wave of panic and pre-emptive guilt that I had been summonsed to the principal's office, probably because I was in trouble, and almost certainly for a discussion for which I was shockingly unprepared. I retired to my room that evening to swot up on the subject of monasticism and contemplation.

The next afternoon, Father Michael was waiting for me outside the door of what would have been a sitting room, had this remained a rambling farmhouse. He looked almost exactly as I had expected a monk in his eighties to look—bespectacled, receding hairline, immaculate robes—although I hadn't factored in his piercing gaze. What was it? Was he sceptical about my motivations? Surprised that I had found my way here in the first place? Or simply bemused by my curiosity? I couldn't tell what Father Michael was feeling—and I have a lifetime of 'reading' my professional subjects—but I sensed I was in the presence of an intellect that was both formidable and utterly grounded.

We sat across from each other at yet another bare wooden table, and once again I was unnerved by memories of school offices and stern nuns. I might even have come close to calling him Sister Elvira, had the memory of that redoubtable deputy headmistress glaring at me, and pronouncing 'Miss Jackman!' with her trademark icy disapproval, not shocked me back to reality. I unfolded my long list of questions.

To begin, I read out a quote from Tarrawarra Abbey's own constitution: 'This order is a monastic institute wholly ordered to contemplation. The monks . . . lead a monastic way of life in solitude and silence . . . thus rendering to the divine majesty a service that is at once humble and noble.'

I wanted to know precisely what that 'noble service' was. And why it had to be carried out in solitude and silence. And what it was about a life devoted to contemplation that made it worth turning away from almost everything the outside world had to offer. Did monasteries contribute to the community at large by praying for them? Or did they serve simply as an example of an alternative way of living, for those who might seek answers to such questions? Or did they not care at all about what was happening in the outside world and the people within it?

As I said, I had a *lot* of questions.

For a while, Father Michael listened patiently, answering some of my more straightforward queries in equally straightforward ways, and deflecting those that were more personal. (He told me, for example, that he was certain while still in early primary school that he would become a priest, but demurred when I asked how he'd come to that realisation.)

I wanted to know more. What was to be *gained* through contemplation? Was it the same as meditation? And was *that* the same as prayer? Could those of us in the noisy world beyond the monastery benefit by adopting some of these quiet practices? And did I need to go to church to practise them properly?

Eventually, he spoke up. Politely, still, but firmly. 'What's happening here—if you'll excuse me—is that you're selling out to thought, to mind. What you have to do is chop your head off.'

This advice came as a bit of a jolt. Especially from a priest. And especially when directed at someone like *me*, someone who had worked out early in life that the most reliable way to gain approval was to use her head—her *mind*—to think, and particularly to get good grades and do all the socially approved things that good girls were supposed to do.

Perhaps sensing my mortification, Father Michael assured me he was using 'you' in the general sense. Gesturing to his heart, he continued. 'It's at the level of feeling. It's not morals or metaphysics. One would hope not that it would prompt thoughts, but that it would prompt feelings.' Prayer, he continued, was a process of 'putting aside avoidances and denials and distractions and fantasies. What happens in prayer is that you meet the real person you are in a very simple way, just by putting aside everything else. And more often than not, that real person presents in its negative form. The first thing is you start airing your grievances, or getting angry, or humiliated. Memories come forth. The chronic laziness that you experience wants to make you doze off and sleep. The inattention makes you want to go and do something more useful, like putting the laundry on.'

So far, all of this sounded remarkably familiar. I almost confessed to the priest that I went through a similar process whenever I sat down at my desk to start a new writing project or assignment that I'd been putting off.

'But all of that is an excellent prayer,' he continued, 'because prayer is the intersection between faith and reality. Faith is something that is given us. Reality is something we spend a lot of time avoiding. Or denying, even worse. So what is being exposed here is the reality of who you are. Not who you would like to be, not who you wish you were, but who you are. And the capacity is that you're being asked to respond to that negativity, to respond to that person who is hopeless at meditation. You're being asked to accept that and respond to that and to *be* that person.'

This didn't sound very pleasant. I was beginning to wonder whether I had made a huge mistake, thinking a monk could teach me how to replicate the glorious sense of completeness that I had found in silence at Gwinganna.

But then Father Michael added: 'Just occasionally, we get glimmers of something that is the complement of the negativity. But no matter whether our prayer is predominantly negative or predominantly positive, we often depart from it with the sense of being fed, of being sustained.'

That seemed better, especially the promise of positive glimmers. But it also sounded a lot like meditation, and not at all like prayer. Somewhat tentatively, and aware I might still be 'selling out to my mind', I contended that definitions about these things were important. Because if what I thought was meditation was what Father Michael preferred to call prayer . . .

'Then it's not marketable,' he finished for me, with barely a raised eyebrow.

If I had been surprised earlier, now I was shocked. I hadn't expected an ageing Catholic priest to be quite so relaxed about acknowledging that prayer is, frankly, a pretty uncool thing to do these days.

For me, prayer had always been carefully scripted. Those scripts were often embroidered with arcane or incongruous phrases—for years as a child, I had imagined a palm tree replete with coconuts whenever I uttered the phrase 'blessed be the fruit of your womb' in the 'Hail Mary'—and regularly meted out as a 'punishment' by a priest during confession. Three 'Our Fathers' and a round of the Rosary and you were on your way, with a heart pure as fresh-fallen snow, until you began smearing it with more greasy black sins to be confessed again in another seven days.

It's a hard habit to shake, this guilt-and-confession stuff. But I wasn't sure I could hide much from this monk with the intense gaze. So I fessed up and told Father Michael that, as a fairly lapsed Catholic, I probably wouldn't have embraced silent practices as wholeheartedly as I had done at Gwinganna if they'd been identified as 'prayer'. I might even have rejected them altogether. But as 'meditations' they felt safe, albeit in an enticingly exotic way. At the very least, they were unfamiliar enough to incite my curiosity, the journalist's inner busybody.

I got the impression Father Michael had heard all this before. 'That's the perfectly normal trajectory in life,' he replied. 'As children, we need things to be dressed up because of our prejudices. But at some stage in our lives we need to kick the mother-in-law out. The church was very much a mother-in-law. I'm not allowed to tell mother-in-law jokes anymore, but it is a wonderful image: of a nagging, "you're not good enough" approach. That was the church. One of my shocking statements is that the first crisis we get in our spiritual journey is when we have to stop being "good" and start being ourselves. You've reached the halfway point in life—not the chronological halfway point—when you start being yourself, being your own person, rather than conforming to an internalised parental voice, whether it's your actual parents, or educators, or bosses, or the church.'

I was starting to like this monk, who was challenging everything I had previously understood to be essential to the practice of spiritual life. I've always liked a rebel—and one who applauded 'being oneself' as a step forward in the spiritual journey, rather than something to be ashamed of, was particularly welcome.

But, equally importantly, Father Michael wasn't doing this in a loud or egotistical manner. Indeed, if I hadn't tracked him down in the Victorian countryside, he would doubtless have continued writing books and praying the Liturgy of the Hours in the stillness of the Abbey, while occasionally travelling to give lectures, just as he had done for the past six decades or so. This wasn't a man driven to convert others or denounce them loudly or prove them wrong.

A few days later, I discovered with some embarrassment that Father Michael had addressed the issue of meditation and prayer in some detail in one of his earlier books. But he hadn't pointed out my ignorance when I posed my questions, nor had he mocked my fretfulness about whether or not there were differences between the two.

In his writing, his approach was down-to-earth, even witty. 'To remark airily that I spend time each day in meditation sounds more exclusive than confiding that I say my prayers,' he wrote in *Toward God: The ancient wisdom of Western prayer*—another book I would never have picked up, much less read, had my accidental encounter with silence not started me on this quest.[2] I found it funny, though, to think these words were written almost three decades ago—long before recorded meditations were among the top trending genres in the App Store, and before Madonna led a second wave of celebrities embracing mystical traditions.

Of course, when you consider that Benedictine monasticism has been practised for more than fifteen centuries, 30 years is not that long ago at all. It's just that the rest of us—exhausted, overwhelmed and utterly sick of the noise—are only now beginning to grapple with the same sorts of questions that troubled young Benedict as he observed his smug tutors and privileged, carousing friends in ancient Rome.

I asked Father Michael about the changes he had observed over his years as a monk.

'The fundamental questions people have remain pretty much the same,' he told me. 'They're the kinds of questions that are triggered usually by some kind of experience. Something has happened in their life . . . For some people it's an instantaneous thing that changes everything; for others it's cumulative, it stretches, goes drip by drip until it reaches a tipping point. If they belong to a religious tradition, they will have a language that will approximate what they've felt and what they've experienced. If they don't, depending on the intensity of the experience, they either become naysayers to everything . . . or they become eternal seekers, trying something new. I think that's the benefit of a religious tradition that doesn't become a tyranny. It becomes a way of understanding experience.'

Given he had already removed the distinction between prayer and meditation, I wondered how much else that was involved in understanding these experiences was just semantics. Enlightenment, the divine, stream-entry, eternal peace, heaven, *nirvana, Jannah, moksha* . . . Were we all seeking the same thing, I asked, but just branding it differently?

Father Michael thought for a moment. 'Yes, I think that's a good way of putting it.'

Once again, my mind was blown. Silently. But blown, nonetheless. In my experience, most religious leaders were a lot more dogmatic about their particular faith being the one and only path to eternal happiness.

I asked why it seemed so easy for him to respond that way.

'Well, there's nothing else to seek,' he replied simply.

He straightened his robes as he stood. It was almost time for Vespers. As I watched him disappear down the long hallway that connected the guesthouse to the monks' private quarters, I wasn't sure whether I felt irritated or grateful. It was as though the contents of my head—all those carefully formed ideas and hard-won arguments— had been tipped out and scattered before me. And I felt weary at the prospect of gathering them up and putting them back in their old places.

Was it possible that I wasn't being served at all by scrabbling through what was essentially a toybox of assumptions and prejudices, carried with me from childhood? Should I instead be making space for something completely different? Something that wasn't *thinking*? All my life I'd assumed that rational problem-solving was the key to unlocking any dilemma—and yet it had only served to make my head noisier, my life busier. Somehow, Father Michael had worked me out in a heartbeat. Perhaps since he was so at home in the silence, the old monk's listening skills were particularly acute.

I woke the next day with images of Sufis, the spinning dervishes of Islam, dancing in my head. I thought of Rumi, the thirteenth-century Persian poet and Islamic scholar. If thousands of Instagram posts, hipster tattoos and inspirational calendars are any measure, Rumi is most familiar in the West for these words: 'Out beyond ideas of wrongdoing and rightdoing there is a field. I'll meet you there.' (It's a shame most don't include the next line as well: 'When the soul lies down in that grass, the world is too full to talk about.')

But it was a line from one of Rumi's lesser-known poems that emerged from my dreams that morning: 'Your old life was a frantic running from silence.'[3] My conversation with Father Michael had certainly stopped me in my tracks. Among other things, he had challenged me to recognise that my racing thoughts and endless ruminations were my own form of 'frantic running', even when I was otherwise still. For the longest time I had assumed that if I simply stopped, something awful would transpire. Was it possible that the very opposite was true— that I might discover something astounding? At the very least, I wanted to know what was so remarkable about this quality called 'silence' that both a Persian poet and an Australian monk might dedicate their lives to it, albeit eight centuries apart.

I had of course long known, at an intellectual level, that Christianity was not the only religion in which silent practices featured. In fact, if you dig deep enough into the wisdom traditions underpinning any of the major religions of the world, you'll eventually find prophets and priests, sages and sisters, gurus and other teachers, all espousing and embracing practices that cultivate interior silence, to help the practitioner connect with something larger, something sacred and transformative.

The 'children of the Book'—Muslims, Christians and Jews—have their Sufis, contemplatives and the mysticism of Kabbalah, respectively. In the so-called East, it is common for those devoted to Buddhist or Hindu practice—teachers, monks and priests—to take regular retreats from the world, sometimes for years on end. Meditation is a staple too, as is quiet study and work. But somehow we are distracted by, even fixated upon, the *differences* between the religions. Evidence of the wrongheadedness of this approach is smeared across our history books: centuries of bloodshed fuelled by fear, prejudice and hostility. When we focus on those differences, even without violence or prejudice, we imbue those details with significance, and so we are almost bound to underestimate, or even completely ignore, the *similarities*—of which one significant example was an appreciation of the power of silence.

That morning, I realised that is what I had been doing. I had been thinking about silence as something to be achieved through a process of negation, by eliminating all distractions in order to create a blank slate. Only then could the 'magic' happen, by deliberately adding or superimposing something new: some scripted prayer, or predetermined mantra, or other special combination of symbols and ceremonies, as specified by this religion or that one.

But what if we don't have to add anything? What if, for once in our overscheduled, overburdened lives, we don't *do* anything at all, except remain present, aware and receptive?

I had done this on the hill at Gwinganna, if by accident. The peace I had felt was not something I had created or invoked by chanting a prayer or incantation. It had been there all along, and I had merely stripped away everything else—all the 'avoidances and denials and distractions and fantasies' described by Father Michael—and experienced it without embellishment. Into that space, a sense of profound peace and wellbeing had flowed. But not because of anything I had done. Instead, it was precisely because I had ceased *doing*, and *thinking*— something that is so counterintuitive in our modern society that it seems almost impossible to attempt.

I still couldn't explain that psychological state I had experienced, but I understood now why others might reach for the terms offered by the religions most familiar to them: encountering God, touching the divine, glimpsing enlightenment, entering the stream.

My next thought was probably prompted by the fact that I was particularly hungry that morning. (For those thinking of using PrayerBnB as a way of enjoying a cheap holiday with a lovely outlook, it's worth remembering that, in most monasteries and hermitages, you eat what the residents do—and these residents are *ascetics*. The choices are limited, often plain, and unapologetically so.) When I'm hungry, I usually obsess about carbs—and that morning the image of freshly baked scones popped into my head.

I recalled how, as a junior journalist assigned to report on the local annual show, I was once advised by an older writer that stories about the perfect scone recipe were guaranteed to generate reader interest. Having tasted a great scone, it seemed some people became obsessed with developing a foolproof recipe for cooking them. And once they believed they had done so, they became passionate advocates for their method—whether it be mixing in cream with a flat-bladed knife, double-sifting the flour, or using lemonade, for example—and often equally impassioned detractors of the alternatives.

Sitting in my room with my stomach rumbling, I wondered whether it was possible that the same human foibles might be detected in our universal search for peace and meaning. Each of the world's religions has its own recipe for the perfect 'scone'—but instead of enjoying the finished product, they have too often become distracted by vicious inner squabbles and violent external wars about the minutiae: who has the right to share or teach the recipe, who can be trusted to handle the instruments, what particular set of words should be said as you mix the ingredients, whether women should even be allowed in the kitchen . . . the list goes on. In the end, we're all drawn further away from the scones we intended to make—the peace we're trying to achieve—by a senseless brawl about the details.

When I arrived at Tarrawarra, I had been obsessed with the minutiae, convinced that I could find an infallible formula for achieving the state I had briefly experienced at Gwinganna. But Father Michael had nudged me towards the realisation that thinking more about it was not the answer. Nor was trying to live like a Benedictine monk—unless I was, in fact, planning to become a Benedictine monk.

On the latter point, it would be misleading, also, to suggest that the monks of Tarrawarra spend their days in silent meditation stripped of Christian texts or references. Indeed, the psalms provide the common thread in the Liturgy of the Hours, supplemented by prayers and hymns, while another key component of the monastic day is *lectio divina*, or 'sacred reading' of the Bible and other Christian writings. In *lectio*, a particular text is read and then quietly repeated until, as Father Michael himself wrote in the abbey's brochure for guests, 'we . . . become progressively attuned to its subtle echoes in the heart. The text thus serves as a mirror that brings inner realities to consciousness. This heightened awareness exposes our need for divine help and readily leads to prayer.'

But Father Michael must have been alert to the 'searchers' like me, people looking for the magic recipe for inner peace, for he added: 'The four steps are not a method to be followed since often the phases are spread throughout the day. Now we read, now we ponder, now we pray, and sometimes we are drawn to contemplative awareness.'

For the rest of my stay, I committed to stop looking for the method. I would stop asking about the words the monks were chanting, or the hymns they sang. I would stop searching for hidden meanings. Instead, I looked to the relative simplicity of Saint Benedict's Rule, and devised just a single rule of my own for my remaining days. Every time I caught myself thinking, I was to stop and be open to the experience around me. *Be, don't think.*

First, I walked to the front gate and back, without headphones to listen to podcasts or a to-do list to fill my head. The air at Tarrawarra smelled like caramel and smoke, and the light was softer and gentler than in Queensland, even if my hands quickly stung from the cold. Free of distractions, I noticed these things—and many more.

I noticed that, along with the church bells, the rhythm of the day could be measured by the sounds of the cattle, as they bellowed to be fed in the morning, stamped and settled in the midday sun, and called for their little ones at sundown. I noticed two calves—one a sandy beige, the other off-white—that played like large, joyful dogs. Chasing each other, leaping across gullies and galloping at full pace, as if the earth itself had whispered to them that, very soon, they would be too heavy and ungainly to run that fast ever again.

In the evenings, after Compline, I noticed that the sky above glittered with the clarity of a hundred distinct pinpricks, while closer to the horizon a blurred smudge of light indicated a clustered, heaving humanity in a town elsewhere.

I became fascinated by the faces of the monks. Was it the unusual light? Did the soft tones of dawn, the sun's rays filtered through stained glass, or the flickering candlelight at Vigil endow them with more character, lingering on their creases and folds, rejoicing as much in the angles as in the hollows? Or was it the human beings themselves, lit by a glow within? Perhaps it was simply that I was looking at the world with fresh eyes—and a refreshed mind and heart.

At mealtimes, I found myself captivated by a new guest. A Vietnamese-born priest on sabbatical from his parish in the United Kingdom, he was clearly relishing his freedom after fifteen years of devoted but exhausting service. He recounted in precise detail the story of his flight from the punitive communist regime in the wake of the Vietnam War: how he had spotted a well-connected former schoolmate packing her belongings one day and realised a refugee boat must be on its way; the moment he left his mother, working in a field, for the final time; how he watched helplessly as two people who missed the boat swam frantically in its wake; the unnerving experience of flagging down a cargo ship with no idea whether or not its crew would be sympathetic, or where they would be taken.

The priest told me that, over the years, he had been astounded by the miracles delivered through human connections. He described how he had travelled from Singapore to London, Switzerland and the United States, and now to Sydney, Melbourne and Adelaide, and in every location he could pick up threads of the Vietnamese diaspora, which would somehow lead him to friends and even extended family members.

I had heard stories like this before, as a journalist. But at Tarrawarra I was held spellbound, as much by the priest's inflections and gesticulations as by the details of his story. Perhaps it was nothing more than granting myself the time to *really* listen, with no purpose other than to truly pay attention to the other person. How often had I missed the nuances of one of my son's stories about school—or the other's concerns about a mate, or a fleeting expression on my partner's face—because I had been rushing on to the next domestic task, or back to my open laptop?

Listen, said Benedict, with the ear of the heart. Hearing the stories around us, the stories that are most important to our lives, is as simple as pausing in silence and opening our hearts.

I returned to Sydney from Tarrawarra Abbey newly impatient with myself for sheltering for so long in the comfort zone of the intellect. I realised I could spend many more years researching the contemplative traditions—and there was no doubt that many monks and nuns were eloquent, engaging writers—but that would simply be marking time. It would be like someone who wanted to learn to ride a bike subscribing to a cycling magazine, in the hope that simply reading more about the subject would prevent the stomach-churning wobbles and knee-grazing, ego-bruising falls.

Similarly, I reflected on how each of the serene Trappists at Tarrawarra had once been a young man, out in the everyday world. Perhaps some had enjoyed football with their mates, or going to dances with a girlfriend. They may have considered working in their father's business, or joining the army, or travelling overseas. But every one of them, at some point, had made a very distinct and unusual choice. They had stepped into the silent unknown.

'If you're going towards something, you don't look back,' Father Michael had told me. 'Every choice of something is a choice to let something else go.'

He had made it sound simple. But letting go could not have been easy for the youthful Michael Casey, who as a teenager had won a coveted Commonwealth scholarship. In the pre-Whitlam years, this was the only way anyone other than the wealthy could get a university education. The thought of relinquishing something significant like that, as Father Casey had done when he chose the monastery instead, unnerved me. When I began my quest for a life less frantic, less punitively loud, I had never seriously contemplated that I might have to let go of anything substantial. Until now, my life had been all about acquisition and addition.

But as I stretched to explore these new perspectives, pieces of me were beginning to crack. A cobweb of fine lines had spread across my carapace, a shell built on the substance of multiple expectations met and exceeded over the years. This thing that had once been smooth and strong was separating into a brittle mosaic. One hard prod, and it was possible the whole thing would fall away, leaving . . . what? That was the question. I had visions of translucent skin and pale pink flesh, exposed to the unyielding glare of the world. It didn't feel safe.

They say that, should you ignore its first gentle nudges, the universe will take things into its own hands by giving you an almighty shove to get you on your way. Less than a month after I had returned from my visit with the monks, word came from Brisbane. Dad had seen another doctor. This time, he'd been diagnosed with advanced melanoma. A large cancer had been cut from his dear old balding head, leaving a shallow crater. But it was not just melanoma. It was Grade IV.

I had written my share of summer newspaper stories about the risks of sun exposure in Queensland, which held the terrible distinction of being the world leader in skin cancer rates. I had listed the awful consequences of melanoma and interviewed the grim-faced specialists, so I didn't need Google to know that, every five hours, someone dies of melanoma in Australia.[4]

But I *did* need Google to check the prognosis for Grade IV melanoma. I went to hospital websites, research institutions and charity pages as well. I crosschecked against information from the United States. I didn't want to panic. But the numbers all came back the same. The survival rate for Grade IV melanoma was about 15 per cent after five years. Worse for people over 65. Worse for patients whose primary cancer was on the head.

Numbers like bullets, facts like mortars. Finally, the carapace shattered.

That night I sat down with Peter to discuss some prospects that had been buzzing around us. One was a high-profile academic position for which Peter had been interviewed. It sounded like a fantastic opportunity but the stumbling block had been that it was with the University of Queensland—and my job was in Sydney. Now, I felt as though Fate had thrown us a rare and serendipitous lifeline: I knew that few people in a similar situation—wrestling with the need to care for family interstate—would ever be given the chance to change their circumstances so seamlessly. I told him he should take the position, should it be offered. I would quit my job.

I did not know what I would do, not completely, but for the first time in my adult life I didn't care about the not-knowing, the lack of financial or professional security. I needed to be in Brisbane. I needed to be near my father. This was a knowing that came from somewhere beyond thought.

The fragments of my former life were already crunching like sand beneath my feet.

# 5

# VIPASSANA

Peter and I moved to Brisbane in early 2018, but months later I was still struggling to make connections and renew friendships and acquaintances. One good friend, Alexis, invited me to join her book club, which was due to discuss Liane Moriarty's bestseller *Nine Perfect Strangers*.

The book, which tells the story of nine people who attend a very unusual health retreat, had enjoyed plenty of buzz ahead of its release. The film rights had been snapped up by Nicole Kidman, who had starred in the hit Netflix version of Moriarty's earlier novel *Big Little Lies*. In *Nine Perfect Strangers*, Moriarty cast a satirical eye over the wellness industry, dreaming up a retreat led by a crazy Russian émigré who is determined to do absolutely anything to trigger her clients' transformational growth during their ten-day stay. Her increasingly bizarre tactics include—spoiler alert!—lacing their green smoothies with LSD and locking them in a pitch-black cellar, where she convinces them they are doomed to die in an inferno. But before any of these wild plot twists unfurl, the retreatants complete a five-day 'Noble Silence', in which all speaking and eye contact is prohibited.

As our book club debriefed about *Nine Perfect Strangers*, it quickly became apparent that several of the women present thought the imposition of silence was at least as awful as secretly drugging your guests with acid.

'I can't think of anything worse,' declared one.

'Five days? I'd be screaming after five hours,' another confessed, and she mimed pulling her hair out with one hand, while nursing her wine with the other. 'Why would *anyone* do a silent retreat?'

I stared at the floor. It was perhaps not the time to reveal that Peter and I had just been accepted into a ten-day meditation course, where we would be expected to surrender our laptops, phones and any books or writing materials on arrival. We would be committing to practise silence for the duration. Then again, I mentally debated, if I truly believed in the value of silence, surely it would be dishonest *not* to speak up in its defence? So I did.

'Actually . . .' I began tentatively, before sharing that we were booked to travel to Tasmania in a few months' time, where we would spend ten days learning Vipassana, a technique drawn from the oldest extant Buddhist tradition, the Theravada.

For the briefest of moments, silence of a different sort descended. The stunned, speechless sort, to be precise. I might as well have announced that I had plans to build my own backyard drug lab. Or take up jelly wrestling. Or learn how to crochet my own underwear out of horsehair harvested from the pristine hides of Snowy River brumbies. Anything, it seemed, would have been more socially acceptable than confessing I had freely chosen to spend ten days—240 hours! 14,400 minutes!—without speaking, and without mobile devices for communication with the outside world.

Were these women—all smart, well informed and otherwise friendly types—feeling sorry for me? Some seemed gripped by horrified fascination, the sort normally reserved for viral videos of pelicans eating live pigeons, or the moment when hundreds of spider's eggs begin to hatch under the skin of an unsuspecting human host.

'Do you know anyone who's been to one before?' asked one woman tentatively. I replied that Peter had sat his first Vipassana course several years earlier in South Africa.

Indeed, on our very first date, in a painfully loud and therefore very hip cocktail bar in Brisbane, I'd asked how he had coped with solitary confinement when he was falsely imprisoned in Egypt on trumped-up terrorism charges.

'I don't know if you've heard of this thing called Vipassana,' he had begun cautiously.

Bells went off in my mind. I had heard of it, and had tried to get to a course myself for a number of years. But as a working single mum, it had been difficult, and I had largely abandoned hope of finding retreat dates that aligned with times when I could secure extended care for my two young boys.

Peter told me he credited the skills and insights he had gained through Vipassana with sustaining him through some very tough times, particularly in those grim Cairo prison cells.

More than anything else about him—the rugged war correspondent's charm, the grin like a slice of summer watermelon, the sharp intellect and burning curiosity about current events—it was this revelation that convinced me I needed to get to know this man better.

Back at the book club, I added that I didn't personally know anyone else who had done a Vipassana retreat, but they seemed very popular. Most Australian states have at least one centre that hosts retreats several times a year—and many book out within hours.

'But what if it's just a rip-off?' another book club member asked. 'What happens if you pay and it doesn't work?'

If that proved to be the case, I told her, then all I had to lose was my dignity. And ten days of invaluable holiday time. Once your application is accepted, there is no charge for attending a Vipassana course, as they're run by volunteer staff. At the end of each retreat, participants are asked to donate according to their financial ability, in order to support others learning the skills they have just acquired.

There was a pause while the women pondered this information. If you looked hard enough, you might even have been able to detect the word 'cult' hanging in several thought bubbles in the air above us. I congratulated myself for omitting the fact that my retreat was beginning on 27 December, which meant I would be seeing in the New Year in a single room in a silent hut, cut off from the outside world, and segregated from my partner. All after days of being teetotal and eating only vegetarian food. The conversation shifted to other subjects, in the polite way that socially adept folk seamlessly adopt when they realise they're in the company of someone's batty old aunt.

Afterwards, I reassured Alexis—who had the good grace to hide any misgivings about introducing me to her book club—that I was not affronted by the reaction. I felt no pressure to convince those present about a meditation technique I was yet to learn myself. But as I drove home, I was perturbed by my inability to articulate why I was drawn to silent practice. When given the opportunity to explain exactly why someone might choose such an apparently unusual thing, I had failed to come up with a compelling, rational argument. Then again, maybe that was the point. Maybe silence—and what we uncover within it— defies conventional description.

Journalism is a vocation that not only allows you to serve as a witness to history, but also exposes you regularly to the very best and worst of the human condition, and to every beauty and madness in between. As a result, I already had a conviction that there are some experiences in life that take us far beyond what the brain is capable of rationalising. And sometimes meaning can only emerge within that gap, if we have the patience or the courage to acknowledge it.

Once, for example, I was assigned to write a magazine cover story about the importance of organ donation, and the lives saved by that generous act. While researching the story, I was offered the remarkable opportunity to 'scrub in' during a double lung transplant, which would be the last chance of survival for a young Sydney man suffering otherwise untreatable pulmonary fibrosis.

Once an enthusiastic surfer who lived close to the waves at Bondi, Nick was, quite literally, dying before my eyes when I met him briefly in pre-op at a prestigious Sydney hospital. He had spent three years on the transplant waiting list and was no longer capable of eating independently. Nick weighed just 45 kilograms by then; stripped down and lying on a gurney, the blades of his ribcage threatened to slice through his skin with every rasping breath. We spoke briefly, and I turned away and wrote 'Christ-like' in my notebook. I had only ever seen a man in his thirties look like this in the thirteenth Station of the Cross, when the body of the crucified Jesus is taken down and placed in his mother's arms.

Almost eight intense hours passed in the operating theatre before Nick's scarred lungs were removed, the new donor organs stitched into place, and the bypass machines turned off. Operating theatres are noisier than most people imagine, with music, occasional banter between nurses and doctors, and machines beeping and buzzing. But in that moment I remember only the silence. Perhaps appropriately, everyone present seemed to be holding their breath as Nick took his first unaided one.

It was like watching dawn break. Slowly, a rosy glow crept across the grey, flaccid bags that nestled within Nick's chest cavity. His new lungs swelled and blossomed into life. I knew then I was watching a miracle—and, later, cardiothoracic surgeon Michael Wilson confirmed as much. When I asked Wilson how he knew the lungs would start working on their own when the bypass machines were turned off, he smiled ruefully and said, 'We don't. And sometimes they don't.' Even as technology and science advances around us, those gaps exist, the mysteries that defy the rational understanding and control we human beings crave so much.

You don't have to be a doctor like Wilson, working daily at the fault lines of life and death, to understand that. Just ask anyone who has witnessed or experienced a baby being born. There's that same moment of wonder, of being humbled in the face of an unfolding miracle: the pause, and the mesmerising, slow blink of new eyes, the flushing of cheeks and jerking of fists, and, finally, sound taking flight for the first time from deep within this tiny new person who has just joined the human race.

Indeed, when it comes to grappling with mystery and miracles, few experiences beat raising children. Every day delivers a stream of utterly ordinary things, things that defy logic or any utility at all, and yet simultaneously feel profound and immeasurably valuable.

An example: one time I was feeling acutely sad and alone. I knelt in the dark beside my toddler son's bed, because I knew that just hearing him breathe would be a balm for my bruised soul. Through the shadows, I felt him reach out. A small, chubby hand came to rest on each of my cheeks, and he simply held my face there, in silence.

I don't know why he did that. I don't know how he knew it was precisely what I needed—I didn't even know myself. And of course the dishevelled teenager who has taken his place remembers none of it, and would be deeply embarrassed to have his mother remind him. But what such moments have taught me is that sometimes we simply have to accept that we are in the presence of something more powerful than our brains alone can grasp, whether that 'something' is uncovered in nature or in a hospital bed, in the cries of someone in the throes of a tragedy or in the gaze of someone we love. Some might choose to call this 'something' God, or Enlightenment, or the Divine.

For me, trying to label or define it feels impertinent, like saying you understand what it's like to walk on the moon because you've spent a night observing that one luminescent milk drop from your bedroom window. I am more confident describing what it's like to have those moments unfolding around me, and *not* have the time or the energy to behold them. It feels like a slow death, a suffocation of the soul.

My suspicion, driving home from book club that night, was that silence could somehow provide a gateway back to clarity and awareness, a way to ground me and allow me to be open to the mysteries and greater meanings of life. At the very least, practice in silence might help rein in that reflexive human need to control and impose our will on every situation, to rush through life without pausing, and to pollute every unfolding experience with our subjective interpretations.

But it's hard. And it's unfamiliar. In a world where being busy is considered a virtue, where our value is increasingly calculated by how 'productive' we are, how can we justify simply being still? In an era when we are pushed to express our opinions, loudly and often, and to showcase our identities for perusal in an online shopfront, where's the reward in simply watching our thoughts and reactions and the world around us, without inserting commentary or curation? But isn't that the essence of truly getting to know yourself? And what's the alternative? Surely it cannot be found in making more noise.

All this may have helped explain why I was drawn to silence. But I didn't say any of it that night at the book club. I was silent. And not in a good way.

Of course, I'd begun to cultivate a greater understanding of the power of silence through my time at New Camaldoli, and later at Tarrawarra Abbey. But despite my admiration for the monks I had met, and all I had gained from the writings and gentle guidance of those like Father Michael Casey, I still felt reticent about mainstream Christianity, and particularly Catholicism. Worshipping in an institutional church that had bred guilt, fear and shame among its children, and that denied (and continues to deny) women an equal voice, while also protecting and promoting so many predatory men, was too great a hurdle for me at the time.

It was true that the Christian contemplative orders existed and operated quite separately from that tainted mainstream, so perhaps it was unfair of me to tar them all with the same brush. But I could not deny the emotional baggage I carried. While I discerned much wisdom and beauty in the Bible and other Christian writings, I did not feel comfortable invoking those traditional scripts and prayers in Christian settings.

Having practised yoga sporadically for years, I had also been exposed to smatterings of Hindu and Buddhist teachings, and I'd even studied a foundational Buddhism course when we moved to Brisbane. But I was wary of replacing one set of icons and rituals with another, as I'd seen many relatively privileged young Westerners do, with their yin/yang tattoos, mala bead bracelets and prayer hands greetings. Call it a double-whammy of cynicism: my background as a disenchanted Catholic, and my training as a newspaper journalist.

Eventually, all of this led me to the work of neuroscientist, philosopher and author Sam Harris. His first book, *The End of Faith*, written in the wake of the 9/11 attacks, generated international controversy with its argument that organised religions, and the irrationality of the faith they demanded, lay at the core of such terrorism. A decade later, Harris had returned to questions of spirituality in a different way, in *Waking Up*. The subtitle of the book—*Searching for spirituality without religion*—probably explains best why it quickly became a *New York Times* bestseller. There are clearly a great many people like me, hungry for meaning that is free of dogma or hocus-pocus, in this frantically busy but spiritually empty secular age.

Early in *Waking Up*, Harris pithily (I suspect the man eats pith for breakfast) sums up the modern dilemma: 'We manage to avoid being happy while struggling to *become* happy, fulfilling one desire after the next, banishing our fears, grasping at pleasure, recoiling from pain—and thinking, interminably, about how best to keep the whole works up and running. As a consequence, we spend our lives being far less content than we might otherwise be. We often fail to appreciate what we have until we have lost it. We crave experiences, objects, relationships, only to grow bored with them. And yet the craving persists. I speak from experience, of course.'

An avowed atheist, Harris posits that many religions have evolved to address this problem of humanity. But too many 'ask us to entertain unfounded ideas about the nature of reality—or at the very least to develop a fondness for the iconography and rituals'. As an alternative, he recommended Vipassana, the meditation technique outlined by Gautama Buddha as a practical guide to achieving insight or 'clear awareness'.[1]

One of the key strengths of Vipassana, in Harris's view, is that the technique can be practised in an entirely secular way, despite the fact that it is drawn directly from the *Satipatthana Sutta*, a core work of Buddhism's Pali canon. Indeed, it is widely taught that the Buddha himself insisted nobody should embrace his teachings on blind faith, but only try the methods themselves with an open mind, to see if they worked. The best-known modern teachers of Vipassana comply with this instruction, holding retreats that make no inquiry as to the religious affiliation of attendees (although they do request that you suspend all other religious practices or rituals, including prayers, yoga or other forms of meditation, while learning Vipassana).

Perhaps as a result of this openness to scrutiny, Vipassana has become the meditation technique most closely analysed by Western scientists. In fact, some of the most rigorous scientific studies of meditation were launched with the active support and encouragement of the Dalai Lama himself, and the participation of other well-known monks, including Matthieu Ricard and Yongey Mingyur Rinpoche. (More about that later.)

'Like many Buddhist texts, the *Satipatthana Sutta* is highly repetitive and, for anything but an avid student of Buddhism, exceptionally boring to read,' Harris declares in *Waking Up*, demonstrating for new readers why he is so regularly at the centre of intellectual, philosophical and ideological stoushes. 'However, when one compares texts of this kind with the Bible or the Koran, the difference is unmistakeable: The *Satipatthana Sutta* is not a collection of ancient myths, superstitions, and taboos; it is a rigorously empirical guide to freeing the mind from suffering.'[2]

What more could I ask for? Here was a remedy for human suffering, offered for free and endorsed not just by my boyfriend, but also by an accomplished neuroscientist and witty opinion leader. I'd signed up faster than you can say '4 a.m. wake-up bell and only two shower cubicles for fifteen women'.

My enthusiasm for our upcoming Vipassana retreat was undented by the reaction of the book club members. Or by my mother's. Or by that of just about everyone else I told. Eventually I decided that, should anyone ask how Peter and I were spending our holidays, I would simply say we were going camping in Tasmania.

My excitement grew as we enjoyed our traditional family holiday at the beach in December, and celebrated our first Christmas in our new home. By the time we had packed on Boxing Day and I had delivered the cat to the local vet for boarding and the dog to my brother, before rushing to the airport to check the boys in for their flight to stay with their father, I was positively yearning for those first moments of serenity. Then Peter and I arrived at the retreat pick-up point in Hobart—and I realised it had all been a dreadful mistake.

It didn't help that we had left sweltering temperatures in Brisbane and arrived in a city swaddled by drizzling clouds. As we huddled on an exposed street corner, a sharp wind reminded us we were now almost as close to Antarctica as we were to our home town. The bright yellow cotton overalls I had thought were so cool when I discovered them at a coastal market a few weeks earlier, especially when teamed with a white ruched boob tube, now felt cool in an entirely different way. Freezing, in fact. And damp.

The other retreatants at the bus stop were dressed either in multiple layers of natural fibres (the women) or fleecy tracksuits (the men). In contrast, I looked like a slightly addled children's television presenter, the type who does interesting things with glue, toilet rolls and glitter, and occasionally climbs into a laundry basket to sing 'The Wheels on the Bus' while wearing a false moustache and gesticulating wildly.

There would be no singing or gesticulating, wild or otherwise, as the wheels on the retreat minibus went round and round all the way to Dhamma Pabha, the retreat centre nestled in the foothills of Mount Dromedary, about 30 kilometres north of Hobart. Instead, a thick and gloomy hush descended, as if we were prisoners being moved to death row.

As the bus rumbled past the gaudy fast food strips that are ubiquitous on highways leading out of cities all over the world, some may have been craving just one more hamburger or bucket of chicken before their ten days of enforced vegetarianism. And as the suburbs gave way to dry bushland, and the bars on our phones wavered and disappeared, others may have nursed regrets about cutting short that last call to lovers, kids or friends. Or perhaps, like me, they were just fretting about the contraband they had hidden in their bags.

I once attended a strict health retreat where a guest was expelled in shame after being caught in possession of a prohibited item. Not only had he smuggled in a mobile phone, he had used it to order an extra-large meat-lover's pizza, which he happily consumed after sneaking out of his cabin at night. He had argued vociferously against the accusation that he had broken an important rule forbidding guests from leaving the property during the retreat, insisting he had taken delivery of his pizza over the front fence. Nonetheless, it was generally agreed that his heart wasn't really in the whole health retreat experience, and he was sent packing the next morning.

I planned to tell this story, should I be busted at Dhamma Pabha for sneaking in ten blank index cards and a pen; writing was strictly prohibited during our stay. Surely my infraction would pale in comparison to ordering a meat-lover's pizza; actually, I thought I was exercising admirable restraint by rationing my compulsive note-taking to one six-by-four-inch card a day.

As it turned out, I didn't need all those cards. It's amazing how little energy and opportunity you have for writing when you are spending up to ten hours a day sitting on a cushion doing nothing. But since I broke the rules, here are the notes I took—and some of my thoughts as I look back on them:

### Day One

All about trying to stay awake. So tired!

Yes, that was all I wrote. As I completed the first day of my long-awaited journey towards blissful enlightenment, I could muster only eight words to capture the experience.

Everything I had read about Vipassana retreats before finally participating in one had warned that the first few days could be brutal. Denied all its usual toys and distractions, the mind often throws the cognitive equivalent of a toddler tantrum. The more you ask it to calm down and be quiet, the more it screams in rage and self-pity. And after the first half an hour or so of holding the same position on your meditation cushion or stool, various parts of the body will join the angry chorus of recrimination. So much for serenity.

But the path to humility is an individual one (and as I write that, I realise I'm at risk of sounding like the narrator in *Monkey*). I had been meditating for about 30 minutes a day for several months leading up to the retreat, and the practice seemed to pay off: my mind settled relatively quickly into the longer sessions. My body, too, was coping quite well, once I discovered that kneeling on my meditation stool suited me better than sitting cross-legged in a nest of cushions, as the majority of retreatants preferred.

I had dodged the most common pitfalls of a retreat's early days. But instead I was plagued with drowsiness. I had battled insomnia for much of my adult life, and now, it seemed, years of sleep deprivation were catching up with me in that quiet, dim meditation hall. As each session settled into stillness, I felt a familiar weight descend behind my eyelids, a fog spread through my mind, and then my head would begin to nod... nod... nod...

And snap! I would jerk awake, only to begin the wrestle with sleep all over again. It was frustrating to be spending my long-awaited meditation time focused instead on trying to stay awake. And potentially embarrassing, although nobody in the room apart from the teacher was supposed to have their eyes open. And, yes, exhausting: a vicious cycle in which the effort to resist fatigue only drained more mental and physical energy. But I was determined to carry on. This was Vipassana, after all. It wasn't meant to be easy, right?

Then I discovered we weren't even doing Vipassana yet.

Each evening, after spending up to eight hours in the meditation hall during the day, we gathered there again for another hour's meditation, followed by the latest instalment of *The Discourses* by S.N. Goenka, the Burmese-Indian teacher credited with reviving the Vipassana technique in the 1970s. Goenka died in 2013, but his *Discourses* had been filmed in the early 1990s; these recordings form the backbone of what is taught in more than 330 Vipassana meditation centres around the world.

On Day One, Goenka revealed that we were actually only doing *anapana*, an exercise that involves focusing exclusively on your breath as it flows through your nose. Specifically, he instructed us to concentrate our attention on any feelings we could detect in a small triangle from the edges of the nostrils down to the top of the upper lip. It's not a lot to focus on, which was entirely the point.

As we learned later, new students arrive at a retreat with their senses so dulled from constant noise and distraction that it is important to spend time sharpening their focus. Launching straight into the finer points of

Vipassana would otherwise be a bit like handing a surgeon an axe and asking them to do a triple-bypass. No matter how well intentioned or disciplined the doctor, you'd have some doubts about their chances of success. For me, the challenge was a bit different. I was a surgeon who kept dozing off just as her axe blade hovered above the main artery.

### Day Two

Better sleep. Still battling drowsiness in morning session, then . . . Enlightenment!?!?

If there is one thing about which all the traditions of Buddhism agree, it is that the aim is to achieve 'enlightenment', and thereafter *nibbana/nirvana*. (Some Buddhist scholars treat enlightenment and *nibbana* as the same thing; others argue that there are subtle differences.) It's a bit like all Christian denominations agreeing that the ultimate reward for life's efforts is entry to heaven.

But if there is a difference between heaven and enlightenment, it is that the latter can be like heaven on earth, because a Buddhist doesn't have to wait until he or she dies to achieve it. While Christians believe in a dualistic framework in which there is a God and then there is the rest of us, all aspiring to be closer to Him, Buddhism teaches that we all have a Buddha *within* us, just waiting to be realised.

That's the good news. The bad news is that Buddhism, in its traditional forms, also teaches rebirth, which means that if you muck up, you can be condemned to many more rounds on earth (or elsewhere), perhaps as an amoeba, a sea slug or some other less fortunate being, like the person who invented MySpace or the Betamax video recorder.

While not ruling out the possibility that one might achieve enlightenment during one's first ten-day retreat, Goenka made it clear in his *Discourses* that most of us should be strapping in for the long haul: this was a journey that required 'patience and diligence' over years, if not lifetimes.

Which is why I was so very pleased to achieve enlightenment shortly after breakfast on Day Two.

Maybe it was my decision to allow myself the luxury of lying in until 5 a.m., extending a night of relatively good sleep. Or my discovery at breakfast that porridge with lashings of natural yoghurt and hearty spoonfuls of brown sugar really was delicious. It was an indulgence I would never allow myself at home, despite Peter's urgings (he also recommends cream), but I rationalised that when one is spending the Christmas/New Year break on a teetotal, vegetarian, silent retreat, one is entitled to certain small luxuries.

When I resumed my place on my meditation stool at 8 a.m., it seemed like the dreaded nods were back. This time, however, I was determined to remain *equanimous*. This was one of Goenka's favourite words; we would hear it dozens of times over the next few days. It meant simply accepting things as they were in that moment, even if 'as they were' meant my head whiplashing back and forth every few breaths as sleep cast its stealthy net over my brain.

The day before, during my regular check-in interview with my teacher—the only time apart from emergencies when students are permitted to speak—she had suggested I try to focus specifically on the sensations around impending sleep. Now, kneeling on my stool, I recognised more than just the familiar heaviness in my eyelids. Paying closer attention, I identified a slight shift in where I could feel my breath in my throat, and a change in tension around my solar plexus. All of this occurred in the seconds before I began nodding. It also seemed to help to label the collective sensations 'sleep' as soon as I recognised them, although I was later told to avoid attaching names to any sensations detected during meditation.

Around and around we went, sleep and I, in a tug-of-war for my consciousness. Perhaps for ten minutes, perhaps twenty. Time blurred and lost meaning in that familiar, slightly stuffy hall. And then it happened: an almost audible crack, as if a pane of glass had smashed and fallen away.

At the same time, I had an experience that was like putting my head above water after a lifetime swimming beneath the surface. With the crack, my head broke the surface and all the sensations that had previously seemed so muffled and blurred by fatigue came into stunning focus.

Normally when battling drowsiness, I find it loosens its grip slowly, often only after a double-shot cappuccino. Or two. But today I felt immediately, intensely awake—more awake than I could remember being before. My hearing seemed to have sharpened too, because suddenly I could detect bird calls and even the shifts of the breeze in the eucalypts outside the hall with the same definition as I could the man in the third row who continuously sniffled.

It was, quite simply, blissful. What's more, not only was I able to sit perfectly still, I now felt a clear awareness of my body—a heavy, thick presence somewhere beneath my observation point—without feeling anchored to it. Obviously, I had achieved enlightenment. My only query, as I floated above my meditation stool, was what I would do with the remaining eight days of the retreat: would I be left to drift along in my bubble of joy, or would the teacher issue me with some sort of special Buddha accreditation to recognise that I'd attained this privileged status? I could barely wait to be called to my next check-in interview.

When the time came, I was prepared. I wanted to begin with humility, so I thanked the teacher for her earlier advice about combating sleepiness, reporting that it had wrought great benefits. Then I told her about putting my head above water, about the crack and the sound of wind in the gumleaves. I told her it had been beautiful. That I had full clarity. That it was profound.

Her reaction was not enthusiastic. If one of the aims of Vipassana is to achieve equanimity—that marvellous state in which you are neither swept up in happiness nor consumed with angst—then my teacher chose that moment to demonstrate maximum, full-force, straight-faced equanimity.

'It's important not to get swept up in the drama of the sensations,' she pronounced. 'Try not to follow them. Keep observing your breath and what you're feeling around your nostrils.'

Suffice it to say this was not the reaction one expects when one announces one is now a Buddha. Focus on my breath? My *nostrils*? I felt like Charlie, yanked out of Willy Wonka's chocolate factory right at the point where he believes he has done everything to inherit the whole operation, only to be told he will be eating porridge tomorrow morning as normal with his four co-sleeping grandparents.

It seemed I had fallen prey to another common trap for novice meditators on retreat. As we settle into full concentration and become more attuned to our senses, our sensations can become heightened and seem overwhelming, beguiling, even magical. I recalled the first time I watched a program on a colour television as a very small child. Until then, black-and-white TV had seemed perfectly adequate—but you can never go back.

Worse, I was now displaying all the symptoms of a full-blown craving for that experience. We would later learn, from Goenka's *Discourses*, that craving was one of the two greatest enemies of Vipassana, because it drives an endless pursuit of a pleasant experience, rather than remaining 'equanimous' (that word again) and recognising that all sensations come and go. This is the key to overcoming *dukkah*, or suffering, as described by the Buddha in the Four Noble Truths.

Craving's ugly sister, aversion, is the other big enemy. When not pursuing the things we crave, how often do we burn up energy avoiding or railing against the things we *don't* like, whether they be peak-hour traffic, goat's cheese or that over-friendly school mum who wants you to volunteer for tuckshop duty?

And so I returned to my stool, Goenka's voice ringing in my ears: 'Focus on your *respiration*. In your right nostril, or in your left nostril. Or sometimes in both nostrils simultaneously . . .'

### Day Three

Saw an ECHIDNA! . . . Looks like God took half a coconut and, not wanting to waste it, stuck four stumpy legs and a drinking straw on the front. Then he handed it the instruction manual for a Robovac and said: 'go your hardest, son'.

By Day Three I was almost crying with boredom. Focusing on a couple of square centimetres between your nostrils and your top lip for up to ten hours a day will do that to a person.

I was back to slogging my way through the meditation sessions, trying to remain equanimous, neither disliking or liking the random thoughts that distracted me, nor the drowsiness that still came and went. And not craving the blissful state I had achieved the day before. Goenka's words echoed hypnotically in my mind throughout the day: 'Work diligently, persistently, patiently. You are bound to be successful. Bound to be successful.'

I admired Goenka's faith—although I suppose when you're talking about a practice that may continue over several rebirths, the odds were in his favour. And if I was reborn as a slug, I was hardly going to be in a position to report him for false advertising.

During the day, we had scheduled rest periods, during which we could shower, do our laundry or nap. But I was keen to avoid the claustrophobic four walls of my bedroom after spending hours in the meditation hall, so I would often walk—slowly and mindfully, of course—a short bush track near our cabins.

It wasn't particularly pretty bushland: a rocky hillside replete with the type of eucalyptus trees that, were they human, would have mothers constantly nagging them to clean up their bedrooms. Shedding bark in the same way teenage boys abandon pungent socks and sweaty school uniforms, these trees flourish in some of Australia's most unforgiving environments, littering their surrounds with tangles of decaying wood and greying leaves. Still, it was outdoors and, more often than not, I was alone. After the close quarters of the meditation sessions and the shuffling queues in the dining hall, not to mention the unpredictable logistics of sharing three toilets and two showers between a dozen women, it felt like a liberation and a luxury.

The track meandered in a figure eight of sorts, and I would vary the direction to add some novelty. A difference of perspective is everything when your awareness is sharp: from one angle, the sunlight made the gumleaves shine bright silver, and from another you could spy on a clearing where the baby magpies liked to take noisy, bickering dust baths. I quickly came to love how the air changed throughout the day: at 7 a.m., after breakfast, it still carried the sharp rebuke of a night of temperatures in single digits, but by midday it sat on the skin as thick as custard on apple pie. And as I made my way to our 6 p.m. meditation, the trees felt like they were sighing with me as they surrendered another day.

On the afternoon of Day Three, however, I was experiencing wave after wave of melancholy. Apparently, like Monkey Mind and muscles indignant about the constant sitting, violent mood swings are quite common during a retreat. One young woman had erupted in shuddering sobs in the meditation hall earlier that day, and another young participant, who seemed barely out of her teens, had disappeared from the centre altogether. For me, this silent self-pity was almost a relief from the tedium of striving constantly for emotional equilibrium; I wondered as I walked whether my subconscious was making a valiant effort to liven things up a bit. You tend to have thoughts like that during Vipassana.

As I pondered whether misery was more bearable than boredom, I spotted a woman crouching on the path ahead of me. At first I suspected this might be another retreatant succumbing to sobs, and considered changing direction. One of the most challenging retreat rules was the edict that you must not do anything to encourage inter-action with other participants, including glancing in their direction, holding doors open or responding when they sneeze or even cry. However, a few more steps revealed that the prickly problem occupying this woman's attention was real, rather than emotional or metaphysical. A large echidna was demanding right of way on the track.

I squeaked. Not a noise I have ever made before—but if ever there's a moment that challenges your maintenance of silence in the bush, it is when you spy an elusive native animal. (Or when you walk into a massive spider's web on the way to the toilets in the dark, which also happened to one unfortunate woman.) The sheer surprise of this discovery impelled us to break the rules of eye contact and exchange smiles, before the other woman continued her walk.

Alone again, I followed the echidna as it shuffled through the scrub like a dishevelled old man on pension day, occasionally stopping to inspect this prospect or that, and to grumble to himself about the state of the world generally. By the time he disappeared beyond the retreat's boundary, my soggy self-pity had evaporated. In its place, I felt a bright joy for the simple pleasures life presents when we are slow enough and quiet enough to receive them.

# 6

# EQUANIMITY

*Day Four*

Someone saw a snake!

Woman next door coughed all night.

I'm cranky with boredom and with dinner. Melon and grapes!?

Taught myself to do a headstand in my room at rest time.

Is it worth confronting boredom to see what is on the other side?

Oh . . . Happy new year.

On the first day of 2019, we were introduced—finally—to Vipassana. And not a moment too soon. Had I been asked to focus on my top lip for one more day, I might have bitten it off. Equanimously, of course.

The technique of Vipassana was ostensibly simple. We were directed to widen our attention, moving our focus slowly and systematically through the parts of our bodies, from head to feet and back again. Along the way, we were to note sensations as they arose and passed. The point was to step back and recognise the impermanence of these sensations (including thoughts and emotions), and to remain unattached from all of them.

Sounds simple, right? And it is . . . until you have a bead of sweat forming on your chin, and all you can do is observe the detail of that sensation, as it slowly fills, clings to the skin, then trickles slowly to the bottom of your face, before dropping and rolling into your cleavage. Only to have another one take its place.

Or until the mosquito bite which you sustained during last night's late toilet dash begins to itch incessantly.

Or until saliva accumulates so quickly in your mouth that you wonder whether that mosquito was carrying some strange disease, and suspect you are doomed to die freakishly by drowning in your own spit. (Excessive saliva is another common Vipassana perception; certainly, there were times when the sounds of swallowing rolled around our otherwise quiet meditation hall like a soggy Mexican wave.)

My personal cross to bear—or, if that's too Christian a metaphor, my 'aversion to bear'—was my left shoulder, a part of my body that had never troubled me before. The pain began like a single firework fizzing up through my collarbone, where it hung fairly innocently for a short while, before exploding in the point of my shoulder and shooting bright, angry sparks in all directions, particularly down my left arm as far as my elbow. As Goenka had instructed, I focused. I noted. I observed.

I noted that the key difference between this pain and a firework was that the sparks did not fizzle out. And I observed that, instead, they seemed to morph into individual, burning Catherine wheels which burrowed into my flesh, where they emanated their own throbbing pain.

I had already noticed that Goenka rarely, if ever, used the word 'pain'. Instead, he preferred the descriptor 'gross, solid sensation'. Perhaps, wise man that he was, he was aware of the risk of triggering aversion in his students, should he tell them instead: 'Observe the searing agony that feels like your shoulder is being gnawed by a hungry bear. Work patiently, diligently, and you are bound to be successful, bound to be successful.' Or maybe he just didn't want to risk cushions, stools and even the big meditation gong being hurled at the television screen.

I had plenty of time to consider whether this was the worst pain I had ever experienced. I 'observed' one thought, as it arose and passed, which compared the pain as just short of the abdomen-rending contractions that finally stretch your poor, protesting cervix to a full

10 centimetres, ready for childbirth. Ultimately, I realised, it didn't really matter what I thought. The pain was here to stay, regardless of whether I resisted or welcomed it. But how much would I have to suffer?

This is an important distinction in Buddhism, one fundamental to understanding the Four Noble Truths. As we progress between our very first breath in this life to our very last, it is inevitable we will all experience pain—meaning negative physical sensations—at various points. But whether or not we *suffer*, and how much, depends on how we react to that experience. Do we fight it? Do we rant about the injustice of it? Or do we observe it for what it is, a stream of sensations, all of which are already changing, even as we acknowledge them?

My 'shouty' left shoulder became my regular companion from Day Four onwards. Sitting right next to my left ear, it often seemed like the loudest entity at Dhamma Pabha. But, just as Goenka had predicted, it was not as stable a presence as it had at first appeared. Under close scrutiny, the pain did wax and wane. Sometimes its epicentre would move from my shoulder to my pectoral muscle, and then to a point in my upper arm. Gradually, as I became more accepting of its presence, I discovered that I could continue sweeping the rest of my body, as Goenka instructed, and not be completely distracted by the pain. While I don't think I ever reached full equanimity—I would have preferred it if my shouty shoulder had permanently piped down—I did learn to live with it without struggling too much.

And here's the most intriguing thing: often, as soon as I stood up at the end of a meditation session, the agony would dissipate, or even disappear completely. How was that possible? Could I be *imagining* a pain so intense it felt like my ligaments and tendons were being torn from their moorings?

I don't know the answer to that. I *do* know that neuroscientists and pain specialists are beginning to recognise that pain doesn't always emanate from its apparent physical site in the body. Instead, it can be manufactured by the brain for a myriad of reasons, including as a protective device that may be hardwired in us for evolutionary reasons. The criticism that 'it's all in your head' may turn out to be true after all, but not in the unsympathetic way it's usually offered.

That's the theory. More important to me, however, was whether all those hours toughing it out on my meditation stool, staring into the angry teeth of Pain, would pay off once I returned to my normal life. About a month after our retreat ended, I had a chance to find out—at our family's regular dental check-up.

To my sons' acute embarrassment, I am notoriously hopeless in the dentist's chair. While they kick back during their check-ups and watch cable TV on the ceiling screen, mine is spent 'butt-dancing' up and down the chair in a reflexive bid to escape the drill. And that horrible sucky spit tube. After several appointments, the affable and patient Dr Tony had admitted defeat and wheeled out the nitrous oxide. With a tube of *that* up my nose, he was free to inspect my mouth.

This time, however, I declined the laughing gas. I was determined instead to experience the procedure as a dispassionate observer, simply noting the sensations as they arose and passed. It went something like this:

*'Flossing . . . Dr Tony wrenching floss back and forth . . . more flossing . . . floss feels like it's slicing through my gums . . . dental hook . . . hook being pushed HARD into my teeth . . . surely that thing does more damage than I've ever done . . . okay, that's aversion . . . sucky tube . . . sucky tube . . . sucky tube . . . dear god, please don't get the sucky tube stuck on my tongue . . . I'm sweating . . . taking deep breaths into my belly . . . fluoride goo on my teeth . . . goo through my mouth . . . sweet . . . sticky . . . sweetstickysweetstickysweetsticky . . . spit! Spitspitspitspit . . . droooooooool.'*

And we were done. Vipassana had not magically transformed the check-up into a pleasant experience, but the technique had allowed me to gain some distance from what was occurring—to observe it rather than be overwhelmed with panic. I'd even managed to note some of the day's news headlines on the overhead TV.

Goenka, may he rest in peace, had saved me from paying a steep bill for nitrous oxide. And he'd spared Dr Tony another awkward tussle with a butt-dancer.

### Day Five
Silence has turned us into cows.

In my memory, Day Five was the day I stepped over an invisible threshold and discovered how silence works to a rhythm—a sweet, slow song all of its own.

There was certainly something hypnotic about the quiet routines of the day. Stripped of distractions, I found myself noticing and revelling in the beauty of small things: a particularly sweet slice of rockmelon; the intensity of the stars when urban light pollution is non-existent; the point on the path to the meditation hall where all the ants crossed together, in a jostling formation only they understood. Like the ants, we retreatants had established our own distinct choreography, one that enabled us to coexist at close quarters—serving ourselves from the buffet, washing our dishes, laundering our clothes or brushing our teeth—without intruding into each other's space.

These rhythms were particularly evident at lunchtime. Served at 11 a.m., lunch was the main meal of the day on retreat: true to monastic traditions, experienced attendees ate nothing more after midday (although they were offered a sweetened lemon drink at 5 p.m.), while new students could choose to eat two pieces of fruit for dinner. Fortunately, our meals were the best type of vegetarian cuisine: fragrant curries, warming stir-fries and colourful salads. I had fretted about being hungry when I first learned of the 'fruit for dinner' rule. But the food at breakfast and lunch was so nutritious, I was never hungry. Plus, we were hardly burning up the calories sitting on our meditation cushions and stools all day.

At lunch, we lined up to serve ourselves at the buffet, and then the same handful of women would move outside the dining hall to take up positions in the sunshine: at the edge of the small deck, on a small bench, or on tree stumps that had been roughly fashioned into stools. We may not have been allowed to make eye contact, but we were all acutely aware of each other, and would time any trips back inside—to make a tea or coffee, or to choose one of the small 'dessert' treats—according to what others were doing, to avoid any bottlenecks or awkward jostling.

Eating had become a reverie in itself; each fork- or spoonful chosen carefully, each mouthful slowly savoured. I had read about 'mindful eating' previously—it's said to be a means of easing stress and aiding digestion—and it made sense, especially as I often ate lunch at my desk without even thinking about it. But I had never been able to do it for very long. To be honest, in the outside world of multitasking, to-do lists and 24/7 newsfeeds and social media updates, I often felt guilty for focusing on *anything* exclusively for an extended period.

But on retreat, mindfulness came naturally. We had nothing to distract us or demand our attention, so we simply appreciated things as they arose, just as we had been doing in the meditation hall. The only difference was that we were encouraged to be equanimous—neither clinging to the pleasurable nor avoiding discomfort—while meditating. I understood that the ultimate goal was to take that equanimity into the outside world too, but for now I was happy to bask in the sunshine; I would have clung shamelessly to every pleasurable beam if I could.

Several other women appeared to be doing the same at lunch on Day Five, when a stranger arrived. A maintenance man or perhaps a council worker, he was wearing a uniform of some kind—but it was the hurried, purposeful way he walked that really distinguished him from the rest of us. Absolutely *nobody* hurries on retreat, except perhaps when they have slept through the pre-dawn gong for early meditation.

In the outside world, the appearance of an anonymous tradesman would barely rate a flicker of interest. In fact, during my morning bus commute in Sydney, I had often laughed to myself that an alien could have boarded and nobody would have noticed, so intently focused were the passengers on their phones. However, had an alien landed in New York's Times Square at the same time, every commuter would have known immediately, because the news alerts on those same phones would have updated them about something significant happening on the other side of the world. But on Day Five of a Vipassana retreat, a fast-walking stranger was the most exciting thing since . . . well, for me, since seeing an echidna on Day Three. Our heads lifted from our lunch bowls almost in unison as he passed. We watched intently, still chewing on our vegetables, as he fumbled with a lock on the door of a shed, and checked something on a clipboard. The weight of our combined attention was almost palpable. Then the Stranger turned and disappeared back towards the retreat kitchen.

And that was it. That was the excitement for Day Five.

Our collective gaze held in the direction of the kitchen for a few moments longer in case the disturbance returned. Then, slowly, one by one, our heads dropped back over our bowls and chewing resumed.

I had to stifle a guffaw when I realised why this scene seemed so familiar—and yet so unusual—to me. I had seen contented dairy cows, grazing on good pasture, do exactly what we had just done when an unfamiliar person or vehicle trundled past their patch. I wondered whether it was insulting to compare my fellow retreatants (and myself) to cattle. But then I thought about the lives many of us had left behind, if only for ten days: lives spent locked away from natural light, force-fed a diet of news alerts, emails and social media updates, with the greatest value placed on how much you produced each day. That was a battery hen's life; I'd rather be a dairy cow any day.

### Day Six

I am a bubble chaser. I have to stop chasing bubbles.

When asked to describe the state of mindfulness or insight that may be achieved with Vipassana practice, veteran teacher Joseph Goldstein often draws an analogy to going to the cinema. 'Becoming aware of thought is like coming out of a movie theatre after being absorbed in the story,' says the man who is credited, along with friends Sharon Salzberg and Jack Kornfield, with bringing Vipassana to the West in the early 1970s. 'Through mindfulness, we gradually awaken from the movies of our minds.'[1]

Bestselling author and podcaster Tim Ferriss, of *The 4-Hour Workweek* fame, describes it slightly differently, but in equally accessible terms. In a conversation with Dan Harris, an American journalist who had embraced meditation after suffering a panic attack live on *Good Morning America*, Ferriss said of Vipassana: '[It gives you] the ability, if you are inside the washing machine, to become an observer and to step six inches to the other side of the glass . . . so that you can observe what is moving around.'[2]

The things 'moving around' in that personal washing machine are your thoughts, along with a hotchpotch of physical sensations. Recognising that we don't have to be part of this cerebral jumble—that we can exist separately to it rather than be defined by it—is a small step towards enlightenment, if you're a practising Buddhist. And, if you aren't, a big step towards everyday sanity.

Ferriss's description particularly appealed to me because by Day Six I had begun to perceive the various sensations that arose during my meditation sessions as bubbles. Perhaps this was due to my experience on Day Two, when I'd had the overwhelming feeling of emerging for the first time from underwater. Now, when I settled onto my meditation stool, I found I could sometimes observe my thoughts and other sensations as bubbles of oxygen or other gas emitted from a deep seabed, while I floated above. Out of the depths of my consciousness they would appear, before ascending—some slowly and deliberately, others in quick, beaded streams—to the surface. If I simply watched them dispassionately, as instructed by Goenka and his teachers, rather than chasing them or trying to control them, I discovered that, just like real bubbles, they would eventually disappear.

Why is an experience that sounds as exciting as watching a fish tank (or the washing machine) so valuable, even life-changing? It's a common saying among committed meditators that it's not what happens on the cushion (or stool) that matters most. Just like a regular cardio or weights session, those 30 to 60 minutes spent in silence can be frustrating, painful or just plain boring. But what a joy it is, after weeks of going to the gym, to notice that you can actually pick up your toddler without groaning, or power up two flights of stairs to the office faster than those colleagues catching the lift. Similarly, the benefits of meditating creep up on you.

Weeks after leaving Dhamma Pabha, I was back at my desk working on a writing assignment. Except that I wasn't working on it. Each time I began to focus, I noticed my brain would throw up some alternative to writing. Whether it was pursuing more research on an obscure angle related to the subject, or returning the emails piling up in my inbox, or checking newsfeeds, or booking my next physio appointment, there was always something that seemed more interesting or more urgent than the task at hand. These were bubbles, I realised. The same as the ones that would multiply in my head at the beginning of a meditation session, as my hyperactive Monkey Mind rebelled against the sudden stillness.

Once I called them out for what they were, the 'thinking/doing' bubbles were (usually) the easiest to dismiss. The 'feeling' bubbles were tougher—the ones that manifested as emotions rather than thoughts. In my case, these were normally related to anxiety: a sense of uneasiness or sometimes simmering panic, or occasionally guilt or shame. In my head, they translated to messages about being a lazy mum, or a hopeless writer, or an unattractive/unfit/fat woman, or any combination of the above.

Of course, I knew that these messages, and the underlying angst, were irrational, just as I knew that checking Facebook or replying to emails was a way of avoiding the hard grind of writing to a deadline. But those extended periods of meditating had allowed me to witness just how quickly my brain could produce them, and how little that process had to do with the rational 'me', who I had previously assumed was in control of my experiences.

For example, one morning on retreat I observed some unpleasant physical sensations—a surge in my pulse, a fluttering heart and a twinge in my stomach—as they arose after two strong coffees at breakfast. Then a couple of thought bubbles appeared as well. One labelled the physical sensations collectively as 'I feel anxious'; the other applied a narrative to that anxiety, a compelling story about how I was a bad mother for taking ten days away from my children, in a place where they couldn't contact me. All of this happened within seconds, possibly less. (Time becomes a bit rubbery during meditation.)

It dawned on me then, as I sat in a stillness that hung from me like a thick winter coat, that this subconscious labelling and meaning-making was going on *all the time*. But our day-to-day lives were usually too busy, too noisy and too full of distractions for most of us to notice. Meanwhile, the invisible bubbles drove our behaviour, tumbling us through our days just like the grubby laundry in that washing machine.

Of course, not all the material our brain throws up is sinister or intended to undermine us. I suspect the same mysterious process that generates bubbles of distraction or self-deprecation is responsible for firing off those glorious sparks of inspiration so highly prized by artists, musicians and other creative types, and is probably intertwined with the functioning of real genius in some people.

Other bubbles are simply random. During one meditation session around the time I was writing this chapter, a memory of my grandparents' chicken coop—particularly its musty-sweet smell of straw and feathers—coalesced in my mind. My grandmother had died more than twenty years ago, and my grandfather about fifteen years before that; I hadn't been to their home town in central Queensland for about four decades. But that memory had been tucked away in my consciousness like a forgotten earring hidden in the folds of a jewellery pouch. Why it chose that particular time to tumble into view is beyond me. Perhaps there was no reason.

Regardless, on Day Six of the retreat, I recognised that chasing bubbles—or at least allowing them to define the world and the person I was within it—was like navigating by the appearance of rainbows. At best, it was a diversion; at worst, you were likely to end up empty-handed, frustrated and hopelessly disorientated.

I recalled explaining something similar to my younger son years earlier, on a summer's afternoon while I used a soapy wand to create real bubbles in our courtyard. 'What do you want to do with them?' I asked as he snatched at the floating orbs, glinting and burnished by a fat setting sun.

'I want to keep them as pets,' the three-year-old replied—and right then I knew the whole exercise was going to end in tears.

On Day Six, I decided to stop taking notes on my index cards. I had begun to understand why writing, as well as reading, was banned during retreat. The act of recording my thoughts—or even *thinking* during the day about what I would scribble down later, in the seclusion of my room—was becoming a welcome escape when things got too boring or uncomfortable.

We had entered the phase of 'sitting with strong determination': hour-long meditation stretches where the aim was not to move at all, resisting even the smallest adjustments on your cushion or stool. Staying still wasn't too difficult for me. But my incorrigible Monkey Mind had worked out that I could be diverted from meditation by the mental challenge of finding a colourful description for our teacher, or one of the volunteer servers, or perhaps the retreatant who burped gutturally and incessantly throughout the course.

Since early childhood, creating stories in my head had been a comfort for me; now, on retreat, as the flat, open plains of meditation stretched to the horizon of my mind's eye, the habit kicked in with a vengeance, under the guise of keeping a record of activities. But hadn't I often scorned the clusters of people who grinned at selfie sticks and hunched over their phones at events like music festivals, or on holidays at spectacular locations? They were more focused on recording and reporting their experiences, I would sermonise to those around me, rather than actually having them. But here I was doing a very similar thing, I realised, albeit without the hashtags or photos with appealing filters.

So I put my pen and the tempting blank index cards away. It was time to shock the #monkeymind with some #realsilence.

Day Eight delivered the fires of hell. If this is an exaggeration, it is only slightly so. I certainly don't need notes to recall it vividly.

At 6.30 a.m., immediately after the recorded morning blessing and chant by Goenka, our teacher announced that the authorities had declared a day of extreme fire danger, with temperatures forecast to climb over 40 degrees, and gale-force winds expected to stoke several blazes that were already burning in the region. We had to evacuate. We were to collect our belongings immediately after breakfast; a bus would take us to a community hall in a country town, out of harm's way.

The kicker: despite what sounded like an impending apocalypse, we were expected to remain silent. We would continue our meditation sessions as normal once we arrived at the hall, our teacher explained, and there would be no need for us to speak in transit.

If it was possible to hear silence heaped upon silence—silence squared, if you will—that is what descended at this point. I imagined this was how a nocturnal animal might feel, frozen and blinking in a hunter's spotlight, as it struggles to comprehend what has just happened to its dim, familiar world.

Leaving the hall only heightened the confusion. Dawn had arrived while we were meditating inside, leaving another exquisite morning framed by dewy grass, a cloudless sky and gum trees ruffled by the softest of breezes. This was a day for a picnic, not a panic. But we ate breakfast obediently and gathered anything we might need for a day of meditating. Swathed in blankets and balancing cushions, most of us looked like unmade beds as we boarded the bus; I trailed behind, repeatedly dropping my water bottle.

Forty-five minutes or so later, things remained calm as we clambered mutely off the bus at a community hall wedged between two well-tended sporting ovals. Halls like this are as common as crows across Australia. Here was the memorial to fallen servicemen, there the plaque with the name of the dignitary who had cut the ribbon on the building decades earlier. Along one side ran a dining room with long communal tables, stackable chairs, metal urns for hot water and plastic barrels for cold drinks. On the other side, a rough asphalt car park stretched from the hall to the springy green turf bordering one of the ovals.

Tucked into the building's corners were 'facilities' for the ladies and gents, clearly built at a time when space and materials were no issue, for they opened off large, empty ante-rooms lined with lockers and cupboards that, judging from the dusty padlocks, were rarely used. The hall itself rose from polished floors made of the sort of unforgivingly hard wood intended to withstand generations of ladies' heels, as they attended school concerts, councillors' speeches and performances by ensembles visiting, perhaps, from the 'big smoke' of Hobart. Those who had eschewed their mats and cushions for our unscheduled road trip were destined to do it tough on these floorboards during meditation.

We settled into our first session, trying to ignore (or at least not develop an aversion to) an air-conditioning system that rumbled like a road train as it drove the temperatures down. Judging from the shuffling in the darkened hall, some were already feeling the chill, or their knees and ankles were protesting about the floorboards.

I was grappling with a craving. Surely Goenka would understand if I took my shoes off at the next break and jumped the fence onto that deliciously green oval? I could almost feel the cool, spongy grass beneath my bare feet. But at some point during the hour-long session, things changed. It began with a persistent rattling, irritating but not loud. Soon, however, the sound had intensified to an incessant, clattering roar that drowned out even the air conditioning. With my eyes shut, and my ears unaccustomed to noise after so many days in the bush, I was sure I wasn't the only one wondering what on earth was unfolding outside the hall. Had a road crew started work in the car park? Were builders upgrading one of the grandstands?

The gong sounded, marking the end of the session. Someone heaved opened the side door—and we discovered the world had changed.

While we were meditating, the forecast gale had arrived: a relentless blast that drove dust into every crevice and threatened to wrench the windows and doors from their moorings. In the distance, we could see massive clouds of smoke surging like enormous, foaming breakers over the mountains we had fled that morning. But far worse was the searing heat. It was as if the devil himself had thrown open hell's gates, and was releasing his pent-up fury on this corner of Tasmania.

For the past week, we had been living with deliberately limited options for respite or distraction. But now we had lost even the small luxuries—a stroll on the bush track, a nap on a single bed in the privacy of your small room—of Dhamma Pabha. If you wanted to escape the dark, artificially cool environs of the hall between meditation sessions, as I did, there were only two choices. Segregated as always, the women could brave the scorching conditions in the car park. Or we could sit or lie in the antechamber outside the toilets, although that meant sharing the space with dozens of flies that had been swept in by the gale—and were no doubt wondering, like we were, what the hell had happened to them.

Of course, it was a wonderful opportunity to practise equanimity, by accepting the conditions without resistance or craving for something different. Failing that, it could have been a beautiful lesson in humility, recognising that equanimity was more difficult than it may have appeared in the relative peace of the retreat. Instead, as the hours ticked by after lunch, I hurtled through something akin to the five stages of grief.

Wave after wave of anger broke over me. Anger that my long-awaited retreat had been disrupted. Anger that the teacher wasn't providing us with updates about the fire and whether we might leave before nightfall. Anger that the men had access to a small area of lawn on their side of the hall, while the women had only the baking bitumen or an adjoining patch of bare dirt, which was riddled with glass from shattered beer bottles. Anger that I couldn't operate the tap on the hot-water urn, and that I had dropped my water bottle for the umpteenth time. Oh—and anger at myself for being so very, very angry. There was a lot of that.

Eventually, my anger burned itself out, perhaps realising that its heat was no match for the scorching wind outside. Briefly, I wallowed in depression and self-pity. But then I hatched a plan: I was going to escape. When the gong went for the next meditation, and everyone was distracted as they set themselves up on their cushions, I would jump the fence and keep running.

That was the easy bit. After that, I acknowledged, it might get tricky, as I had no wallet, no phone and no idea where I was. However, a couple of hundred metres down the road, on the crest of a hill, I could see a Catholic church. I figured there was bound to be a presbytery there. That's where the bargaining would begin. If I confessed to the parish priest that my boyfriend had convinced me to go away on some cultish meditating retreat, but now I had come to my senses, surely he would let me use his phone? Perhaps he might even pay for an Uber back to Hobart? It certainly wouldn't be the first time someone had massaged the truth during confession.

Maybe it was the crazy-making wind. Or perhaps I was beginning to develop heatstroke. But the plan made perfect sense to me. I briefly considered trying to make secret contact with Peter and convincing him to join me in my dash for liberty. But almost as quickly, I ruled that out. Peter had survived worse than this; I was pretty certain he would only convince me to tough it out. Plus, who else could retrieve my phone, wallet and laptop at the end of the retreat?

I decided to do one more meditation to calm my nerves and then execute my plan. The sun was beginning to sink in the sky, and I was running out of time. As I settled onto my meditation stool, I felt peaceful for the first time in hours. Maybe it was just habit, but I quickly fell into the hypnotic routine of focusing on my breath, and observing things as they arose over the next hour.

*The rattling of the door on its hinges . . . the chill of the air on my neck . . . pangs in my left shoulder . . . the thrumming of the wind on the windows . . . a fluttering in my stomach . . . an itch on my ankle . . . the hum of the air conditioner . . . one more rattle of the door . . . quiet outside . . . quiet outside . . . Hang on—quiet outside?*

The gong sounded again. This time, the door did not have to be forced open against a gale. The wind had shifted direction and slowed; already the temperature felt like it had dropped five degrees or more. For the first time all day, we saw signs of life as people emerged to greet the cooling twilight. Two mums were trying to teach a clutch of small children how to kick a football through the goalposts. A man ambled past walking a fox terrier. The tempest had roared, but just as quickly it had evaporated. Goenka's ghost could not have arranged a more appropriate metaphor for the hurly-burly rhythms of our minds.

Finally, our teacher gave us an update. The crisis was over; we were going home.

The final days of the retreat slipped by like silk. After the disruption of Day Eight, nothing seemed as difficult; I felt a surge of gratitude just to be meditating again in the relative peace of a carpeted hall, with wallabies grazing outside and my private bedroom offering sanctuary during breaks.

The standard ten-day Vipassana retreat actually ends on the morning of Day Eleven, with the ban on speech lifted on the preceding afternoon to give retreatants an opportunity to recalibrate their minds to 'normal' life. That transition was gentle, but not gentle enough for me. After a few hours debriefing with the other women—many seemed intensely familiar, but I was only now able to learn their names—my head was crackling with static. Eventually, I slipped away for one final solitary bushwalk before sunset.

It wasn't until the next morning that the segregation rule was lifted and I could debrief with Peter as well. It still seemed quite surreal that we had spent our New Year's Eve in single beds in segregated cabins (where we were both asleep well before midnight), when the previous year we had welcomed the New Year from a tiny patch of bush on the edge of Sydney Harbour, surrounded by revellers tipsy on champagne, all bathed in the rainbow glow of fireworks.

Peter had been dying to confront me about my brazen ploy to catch his eye one day as he left the meditation hall. It was completely against the rules, which is why I'd been compelled to do it—just once. He had resisted nobly when he first noticed me staring as he walked up the centre aisle, but then eventually glanced back fleetingly, as I was betting he would. Just long enough for me to wink cheekily. The exchange took little more than a few seconds, but I was amused for days by the knowledge that he would have to wait days either to rebuke me, if playfully, or to pay me back.

More surprising was Peter's confession that he had really struggled in the first few days of the retreat. I had assumed that, as a Vipassana graduate, he would slip back into the routine with ease. 'So did I,' he admitted, rolling his eyes. But he told me he had struggled badly with cramps, particularly in the early days. I was particularly shocked because whenever I'd viewed him from a distance, he had seemed completely serene. Once again, Vipassana had highlighted that what we anticipate, and even what we see with our eyes, is only a fraction of what the world presents to us from one moment to the next.

We had arranged to spend a few days on our own in Hobart before flying back to Brisbane. A visit to MONA, Tasmania's world-class Museum of Old and New Art, seemed like an appropriate way to reacclimatise. After all, we had just participated in something that provoked almost as many extremes of opinion, from cultish adoration to smirking cynicism to barely contained outrage, as David Walsh's sprawling temple on the banks of the Derwent River.

Having probed the dark corners of our own inner worlds, picked over some artefacts of consciousness and watched our sensory phenomena rise and fall, there was a comfortable familiarity in MONA's deliberately disorienting halls and passages, and its often confronting curation: a machine steadily pumping out faeces here ('Professional Cloaca'), a wall of real-life vagina moulds there ('Cunts . . . and Other Conversations'). However, I fell instantly, immediately in love with the first exhibit I stood before: German artist Julius Popp's 'bit.fall'.

The work uses a computer, a pump and 320 magnetic valves to create a towering waterfall of words. And here's the magic: those words are not random, but selected by an algorithm that scans digital newsfeeds to identify those that are the most statistically significant. Letters are then created in droplets, like 'bits' or pixels, forming words that fall through the air, appearing and disappearing almost before your mind has grasped their meaning. It's a mesmerising reflection on how human beings are grappling with the constant, hypnotic flow of ideas and concepts that is the 24/7 digital news cycle.

'Human brains have a specific speed, and once you go beyond that, they get lost,' Popp told MONA's senior writer and research curator, Elizabeth Pearce, in an interview for the visitor guide. 'We are getting too much information, too quickly.' Pearce notes in the guide that Popp has expressed frustration with the popularity of 'bit.fall' wherever it is exhibited. It was his intention to challenge, not enchant.

But 'bit.fall' did both for me, particularly when the word 'silence' appeared—not once, but twice. The first time, it slipped out just as I was dragging my attention away, conscious that we had much to see. Had I imagined it? Had my subconscious, fresh from ten days immersed in silence, or my intellect, which had been obsessing about silence for even longer, somehow manifested the word?

I insisted we return a few hours later, telling Peter it was my favourite work regardless of the words it spat out. But secretly I harboured a hope that 'silence' would make another appearance. Other words came and went, beating down relentlessly, and I sighed at what seemed like my own neurosis. Then it appeared: 'silence' shimmered, as hundreds of separate entities caught the light simultaneously, coming together to create something whole and beautiful.

And already it was gone.

# 7

# NOISE

'Quiet please . . .' The electronic message flashed up on the fence encircling the Gabba's cricket field like a digital bracelet, a string of advertising gems glinting as they beckoned for our attention. The punchline followed: 'Just joking!'

No kidding. There was no escaping the din as we joined more than 26,000 other cricket fans for a Big Bash League match between struggling locals the Brisbane Heat and the dominant Sydney Thunder in mid-January 2019, a few weeks after Peter and I got home. Between deliveries, the stadium erupted with thumping pop music, coordinated clapping, stamping and chants. There were familiar audience participation activities too: members of the crowd were encouraged to kiss their partners, or hoist their youngest child in the air to the music of *The Lion King*, or demonstrate the latest dance craze—in our case the maddening 'Baby Shark'. All for the roaming cameras. And all accompanied by more blaring beats.

Of course, social media was an integral part of the experience. There were free tickets to win, and even admission to the coveted 'pool deck'—where body-confident fans could enjoy a premium viewing position from a swimming pool built on the boundary, provided they posted pictures with the requisite hashtags to Instagram and Twitter. And in case anyone was still missing the point, frequent announcements ordered spectators to 'make some noise!', with an artificial meter on the electronic scoreboard purporting to measure the commotion.

I didn't need the Gabba's pretend device. By then I had become so obsessed with noise and sound that I had downloaded a portable decibel meter app, recommended by audiologists, onto my phone. When the crowd erupted, the meter often climbed to about 90 decibels, the threshold beyond which prolonged exposure (eight hours or more) is likely to cause permanent damage. The needle swung even higher just once, when three small children sitting directly behind us combined to emit a piercing screech, a sound you might expect if the flying monkeys from *The Wizard of Oz* were fed through a giant blender.

In my teens and early twenties, I had often visited the Gabba to watch Test cricket, as well as the one-day international match that was routinely scheduled in Brisbane during the slow, heat-drenched weeks of early January. But those fond memories were from decades ago, back when the ground was fringed by quaint wooden stands and a cluster of Moreton Bay figs, as shaggy and drooping as many of the fans who tottered into the members' stand. The crowd back then was separated from the playing field by a broad, grassed track used for greyhound racing; it was rumoured that one of the best views of the play was from the roof of the toilet block at the neighbouring East Brisbane State School. With all its quirks, the old Gabba was as much a personality as the players who clashed there. It felt organic, alive: a white lotus spreading out and up to greet the bleaching Queensland sun.

The sleek stadium we sat in for the Big Bash game was better equipped for large crowds, with multiple entry and exit points, easily accessible toilets and, of course, a vast array of food and drink outlets. But it also felt like we had landed in a parallel universe; this wasn't the Gabba I remembered. To butcher a popular *Star Trek* phrase: 'It's cricket, Jim, but not as we know it.' The nonstop entertainment and crowd participation had clearly been borrowed from baseball, calling to mind raucous afternoons I'd spent drinking warm Budweiser at Yankee Stadium as a New York–based foreign correspondent. Either the entertainment had grown louder or I had grown older and less tolerant. Perhaps both.

Regardless, within minutes of us taking our seats, I developed a thumping headache and a fluttering nervous feeling in the back of my throat.

Still, the boys were having fun, especially when they were joined by their young cousins (including five-year-old Felix, a Brisbane Heat tragic, who had to be dissuaded by his dad from bringing a sign declaring 'Sydney Are Idiots'). My younger son was busy posing for selfies and urging me to post the results on Twitter, while the other maintained the fine Australian tradition of grumpy armchair commentary, ranting about those on the field who were *a joke*, and others who were worthy of Australian selection but had been *robbed* of that status by the clearly biased selectors.

But after a couple of hours, all the on-field action stalled: two of the massive banks of lights that crouched over the stadium like glowering sci-fi gargoyles had fallen dark. For the spectators in the stands, the change in playing conditions was barely perceptible. But out by the wicket, the captains were conferring with the umpires about whether it was now too dim to safely face a hardened sphere of leather hurled at up to 150 kilometres per hour.

For once, the incessant chatter of social media provided no additional information; nobody seemed to know why the lights had failed or how long it would take to repair them. As the minutes dragged on, and even the most enthusiastic fans became restless with the music and other distractions, we decided to 'up stumps' (as they say in cricket) and head home early. The Heat were already looking like they would be soundly beaten; why prolong the agony?

When we got outside, though, we discovered that the buses scheduled to provide free transport for ticket holders after the game were not due for another hour or so. We could either wait by a busy intersection in the smothering humidity or trudge the couple of kilometres back to where we had parked our car.

We walked. As we did, the crackling energy generated inside the stadium quickly fizzled and soured. One son grumbled and fretted about his ears ringing, while the other, still twitching with the adrenaline of the game, insisted on reciting, in rapid-fire succession, a list of the most gruesome scenes in a horror movie he wanted us to see.

My head throbbed. My feet ached. And as the hyperstimulation of the past few hours ebbed away, it seemed to be leaching all the clarity and calm I had cultivated so attentively at the Vipassana retreat. I tried focusing on my breathing. I tried observing without judgement what was going on around me. I tried—oh, how I tried!—consciously maintaining equanimity.

We came to a point in the busy three-lane road where we would either have to risk crossing or take a lengthy detour in the other direction, under a bridge and down a few extra blocks before we would be able to double back to the parked car. It was getting late. We were all tired. And hot. And I was sure I could almost see the car from where we stood. Looking back up the road, I could see a break in traffic.

'Run!' I yelled.

'Wait!' Peter cried, almost simultaneously.

Seconds later, three of us were on one side of the road, and one cranky teenager was on the other, with another thick flood of cars in between. The familiar surge of nausea—that dreadful, primal feeling that accompanies any moment when you think your child is in danger—was already subsiding within me, leaving a curdled mix of bile and the pressing need to blame someone other than myself for this mess.

I yelled at Peter for distracting everyone. I yelled at the cranky son for not paying attention. I yelled at the other son for reasons I can't recall, but possibly because he was yelling when I was yelling. I was not equanimous and I was certainly not silent.

After we finally managed to get everyone on the same side of the road, into the car and halfway home, I apologised to my family for losing my temper. Only then did I fall into silence, but not in any peaceful way. Embarrassed and annoyed with myself, I slid into a familiar pattern of self-recrimination. I was obviously a complete failure at meditation. I was a failure at equanimity. I was a failure at parenting.

I was a failure at life! How could I have become so easily overwhelmed so soon after leaving a Vipassana retreat?

But perhaps, I thought as I reflected further, there was another way of looking at it. Perhaps, had I not learned and practised those Vipassana techniques, I would not have lasted as long as I did, immersed in that hyperstimulated environment, given my longstanding aversion to noise and crowds. In fact, it was possible I would not have even considered an outing to the Big Bash had I not felt so refreshed and recharged by the retreat. Perhaps, too, the added awareness Vipassana had given me—the ability to watch my emotions arise and pass like a violent summer storm—had helped me recover more quickly from this setback, enabling me to make peace with my family rather than stewing or prolonging the recriminations. Everyone else in the car had moved on happily enough—they were busily discussing the highlights of the night and making plans for the following day.

Now I just had to make peace with myself.


Sitting a ten-day meditation retreat in silence was definitely one of the toughest things I have ever done. But after that night at the cricket, I realised this wasn't 'mission accomplished'. The retreat had been a beginning, not an end.

I was reminded of the handful of people I knew who had done detox retreats at health spas like Gwinganna. Returning to work afterwards, they would always insist it had been the hardest week of their lives: they'd given up caffeine, alcohol, meat and sugar, battling their cravings with shots of apple cider vinegar and the occasional raw health ball. Still, as they recounted their experiences of pre-dawn yoga and afternoon colonic irrigations, they would positively *glow*. Pure energy seemed to ooze from their freshly unclogged pores; joy would sparkle in their clearer, whiter eyes.

And then, six months later, I'd spy them in the office canteen ordering a double shot of coffee, or at a friend's birthday party nursing another sav blanc, and they'd look just like everyone else. They'd roll their not-so-clear, not-so-white eyes and confess that they'd stopped getting up early for yoga and had abandoned apple cider vinegar after discovering it could cause tooth decay. They'd often look embarrassed, crestfallen at how the kilos had crept back on and dark shadows were once again stretching beneath their eyes.

I'd reassure them that it's *hard* in the real world, when you wake up in the morning to be greeted not by a personal chef whipping up a delicious tofu scramble or a peppy yoga instructor ready to help you into pigeon pose, but by a sniffling child who has lost his tennis racquet, another who forgot he had an English assignment due today, with no bread left in the pantry for school lunches and a cat that has coughed up a hairball right where your foot just landed.

This time it was me who needed to be reminded: it's *hard* in the real world. It was also a whole lot noisier.

We receive the lessons we are ready for, the ones we most need. I'm sure some guru somewhere said that. Or maybe I read it on an inspirational calendar or on Instagram. Regardless, it was certainly true of our night at the Gabba. The roiling atmosphere of the Big Bash had provided an excellent contrast to the tranquillity of Tasmania. And it was important to recognise that *neither* was typical of real life.

On most days, we don't have to cope with the amplified, sensory jumble of a sold-out sports event. But nor can we expect the perfectly calibrated peace of a secluded meditation retreat. We have to find a balance. And to do that, it helps to identify first where all the noise is coming from—and, importantly, which are the most acute or damaging sources. Then we must find the most effective and restorative sources of silence in our lives, and work out how to access them regularly. Simple, right?

Fortunately, unlike the Desert Fathers and Eastern monks of centuries gone by, who had to rely on instinct, faith and shared personal experiences to guide them, we also have plenty of science.

According to the Australian Academy of Science, 'noise can be identified as any unwanted or offensive sounds that unreasonably intrude into and disturb our daily lives'.[1] The word itself derives from a Latin root meaning 'queasiness' or 'nausea'. In other words, the sounds in your life don't become 'noise' until they irritate you or make you sick.

The problem is, one man's highly enjoyable sporting event can be another woman's splitting headache, as I had discovered. Similarly, you can be exposed to identical decibel levels at a sell-out rock concert as you will encounter standing on an aircraft runway as a jumbo jet takes off, but you're only likely to whip out your credit card to pay for one of those experiences.

What we identify as 'noise' is highly subjective. That's important, because our personal definitions of noise will, in turn, influence what we then identify and seek as 'silence'. There is no absolute silence, as in a complete absence of sound, in the living world within earth's atmosphere. There are only states where the irritating stimuli we think of as noise are reduced dramatically. Both noise and silence, then, are rhetorical shapeshifters, bending and flexing depending on the context and one's personal proclivities.

History demonstrates as much too. The first noise ordinance is believed to have been passed in the sixth century BC, when the good folk of the Greek colony of Sybaris took such umbrage at the clamour made by tinsmiths, potters and other tradespeople that the council eventually banned them from living in the city. They were forced to move beyond the city's walls, along with all roosters, after the poor birds were also found guilty of disturbing the peace. In 44 BC, Julius Caesar was so irritated by the traffic noise of ancient Rome that he intervened, restricting when wagons would be allowed on the city's streets. And in 1595, Rule 30 of London's 'Lawes of the Market' targeted men making 'any such suddaine outcry . . . in the still of night', explicitly banning them from singing, or 'beating hys Wife, or servant' after 9 p.m.

But when the Industrial Revolution swept across Europe and then America in the late 1700s and early 1800s, all of those previous noise complaints suddenly seemed trivial. Roosters, wagons and busy tradespeople were no match for the thundering roar of factories and steam engines. (Shamefully, it would take almost another two centuries for domestic violence to be recognised as more than just a disturbance to the peace in many Western nations.)

Scientists were beginning to take an interest in how soundwaves worked, and particularly in the impact of industrial noise. In 1886, Scottish surgeon Thomas Barr issued the first warning about noise exposure in the workplace, after documenting the considerable damage done to the hearing of a group of 100 boilermakers. However, for the most part it was left to concerned citizens and community organisations to protest what they considered to be the most bothersome sources of noise. Two of the most clamorous cities on the planet at that time—London and New York—were host to some of the most concerted campaigns, with luminaries such as Charles Dickens supporting efforts in London and Mark Twain joining the New York movement.

Things changed dramatically in the twentieth century, and not just because of the arrival of cars and planes, as well as an array of tweeting, trilling personal devices and appliances, all of which contributed to growing noise levels wherever humans were found. The invention of the decibel as a unit of measurement in the 1920s, along with the development of portable recording equipment throughout the century, made it much easier for scientists to draw links between certain types and levels of noise and physiological impacts on the human body.

By 2011, the World Health Organization had reviewed the amassed body of research to estimate the impact of environmental noise on Europeans, expressed as disability-adjusted life years (DALYs): that is, the number of years lost due to disability, ill health or premature death. Its report, *Burden of Disease from Environmental Noise*, quite deliberately sought to focus on the harm caused by exposure to incidental noise, such as road traffic, passing aircraft and trains, construction and neighbourhood activity, separate from workers' exposure to industrial noise. The issue of occupational hearing loss, one of the most common workplace illnesses, was not considered, in part because this problem could be addressed separately, through industrial laws and regulation.

Reviewing data from a variety of large-scale epidemiological studies, the WHO's working group of experts declared that 'there is overwhelming evidence that exposure to environmental noise has adverse effects on the health of the population'.[2] Specifically, they found exposure to excessive environmental noise contributes to ischemic heart disease, tinnitus, sleep disturbances and cognitive impairment (learning difficulties) in children. Many other studies suggesting possible links between noise pollution and an array of other conditions, including ulcers, colitis and other gastrointestinal upsets, headaches and hypertension, were ruled out as inconclusive or lacking statistical rigour.

Using noise-mapping techniques and data, the authors were able to estimate the number of Europeans living in areas where potentially dangerous levels of noise were routinely recorded. From there, they used a complex array of formulae to calculate how many of those people were likely to develop serious health problems, based on the reviewed research. A lack of comparable noise maps from eastern European cities forced them to limit those projections to the west of the continent. Even so, their conclusions were stark: '[T]he total burden of health effects from environmental noise would be greater than one million years in western Europe, even with the most conservative assumptions that avoid any possible duplication.'[3] Three years later, the EU's first noise assessment report offered a similarly dire prognosis, concluding that noise pollution was responsible for 43,000 hospital admissions in Europe annually, and at least 10,000 premature deaths.[4]

Oddly, Australia lags behind in this research area. To be fair, this may be partly due to the luxury of space still enjoyed by most Australians, with relatively few people dwelling in the cramped and close urban environments of many of their counterparts in London, Paris or New York. Indeed, it's worth noting that Australians enjoy an odd #firstworldproblem. In most comparable countries, the most common source of noise complaints is traffic. In Australia, according to at least one review of local council records, it is barking dogs.[5]

Of course, that cannot be expected to last forever.

Assigned to conduct a review of the problem in 2014, a panel of health, environmental and acoustics experts acknowledged that they were hamstrung by 'a lack of systematic data for the Australian context [which] makes understanding and quantifying our noise environment difficult'.[6] Without noise maps and other data that had been available to the European researchers, the Australians were unable to model accurately the impact of noise pollution on local cities and towns. They were also more cautious than the Europeans about accepting as conclusive some of the more alarming research findings, calling for further work in a number of areas.

However, the Australian report did concur that 'there is sufficient evidence of a causal relationship between environmental noise and both sleep disturbance and cardiovascular disease to warrant health-based limits for residential land uses'. Specifically, it recommended that environmental noise around Australian homes be limited to no more than 55 decibels for eight hours at night, and 60 decibels for a sixteen-hour daytime period.[7] In other words, if the noise in and around your home is louder than a normal conversation for prolonged periods during the day, or above the sound of moderate rainfall at night, your health is at risk.

Relatively new techniques such as functional magnetic resonance imaging (fMRI), electroencephalography (EEG) and electrocardiography (ECG), for example, have revolutionised the study of sleep, allowing scientists to observe and document what is actually going on in the brain, rather than relying on their subjects to self-report on the quality or otherwise of their sleep. And so far, the discoveries in this field have shone new light on how insidious noise can be.

The bad news, particularly for those who believe they can snooze through anything, is that noise can erode the quality of sleep at a deep physiological level, even if the subject believes they have not been disturbed. In one 2012 study, for example, Harvard sleep researcher Orfeu Buxton played ten-second clips of different types of sounds—such as doors closing, phones ringing, city traffic and machinery—to healthy volunteers as they slept. With each noise, he noted, various parts of the body roused—measured by spikes in heart rate and neural activity—even when the subjects did not awaken.[8]

Buxton's observations make sense from an evolutionary perspective. There's a good reason why our ears don't have 'lids' like our eyes do. For most of human history, people have not slept securely behind locked doors in alarmed premises on civilised, well-policed streets (much of the world's population still don't have that luxury). At night, while their other senses rested in slumber, our ancestors relied on hearing—the sole sentinel left in the watchtower—to alert them to possible danger.

We remain hardwired to tune in to noise at night, to discern whether it is a threat and prepare to respond to it. Even if we don't remember it, noise can trigger a stress response in the amygdala, the brain's centre for emotion and memory. The amygdala sends a distress signal to the control centre of the brain, the hypothalamus, which then issues a call-out to the rest of the body to prepare for fight or flight.

Only relatively recently in our evolution have our bodies been subjected to so many man-made noises, in such a sustained way, at night and during the day. So it is hardly surprising that our brains are yet to catch up. As a result, many of us exist in a sustained state of 'fight or flight' or hyper-arousal, with associated physiological changes such as increased pulse and quickened breathing, which were only ever intended for emergencies. You don't need a medical degree to intuit that this can be exhausting. At night, however, when the body needs sleep to engage in a range of vital restorative functions, such a state can be downright debilitating, if not ultimately life-threatening.

'I find our current environment and atmosphere highly toxic,' Buxton told *Scientific American*'s Dorian Rolston in 2013. 'We are constantly being pattered by sounds, many of them alerting-alarms or attention-getting in an obnoxious way that activate your response to stressors . . . I greatly appreciate silence and natural noises.'[9]

But while researchers like Buxton may have enjoyed silence as a welcome oasis from toxic levels of noise, it had generally been ignored as a subject for specific research. In the lab, if it was recognised at all, it was merely as a useful control, a blank slate on which more interesting variables could be imposed and scrutinised. When silence finally captured the attention of the scientific community, it was entirely by accident.

In 2006, Italian physician Luciano Bernardi set out to test whether music had the potential to help manage stress, by playing six different tracks to a group of 24 subjects and measuring their physiological changes. He found that almost all the tracks triggered cardiovascular and respiratory shifts that indicated focused attention. But then he noticed even more dramatic changes—in the pauses *between* the tracks. While the musical pieces had relaxed his subjects to differing degrees, it was the intervening periods of silence that had the greatest impact on them physiologically. Bernardi surmised that the silences, contrasted with the musical pieces, were somehow triggering a 'release' in the brain that led to an even greater state of relaxation.[10]

Music as a stimulus also featured in research by biologist Imke Kirste. In 2013, Kirste was researching what types of stimuli might trigger neurogenesis, or the growth of new brain cells, in adult mice. Neurogenesis is arguably one of the most exciting fields of neuroscience, given that until the end of the twentieth century it had been widely accepted that the brain ceases to create cells beyond the initial stages of human development.[11] Hypothesising that the calls of baby mice (pups) might activate new cell growth in adults, Kirste decided to test those sounds in comparison to an array of other auditory conditions, including white noise, silence and the 'baseline ambient noise' of her lab at Duke University.

Looking for additional stimuli that would be unfamiliar to the pups, Kirste added two Mozart sonatas to the experiment. Later, she acknowledged that choosing Mozart was partly a 'tongue-in-cheek' dig at an infamous set of studies done a few years earlier, which had credited the music with improving cognitive performance in human listeners. An international craze for 'Baby Mozart' CDs had followed, with thousands of unwitting infants (including one of mine) subjected to Mozart on high rotation, before the studies were widely discredited.

Initially, Kirste observed that all the stimuli, apart from white noise, prompted some neurological changes in the mice, noting with some surprise that both silence and Mozart had a greater effect than the natural calls of mice pups. But the real shock came a week later. At that point, only the mice exposed to silence showed sustained signs of new cell development, specifically in the hippocampus, which is the brain's centre for learning and memory. Kirste surmised that silence, far from representing an absence of anything interesting, 'might be the most arousing [stimulus], as it is highly atypical'. Indeed, the mice were so stimulated by silence that they had begun generating new brain cells, in preparation for 'future cognitive challenges'.[12]

The findings of scientists like Bernardi and Kirste throw down an incontrovertible challenge to the assumption that silence is benignly peaceful at best, and oppressively boring at worst. At a neural level, at least, silence is an event in itself, and one which may trigger changes and growth we are only beginning to understand. Meanwhile, as a natural prophylactic to the established negative side effects of excessive noise—heart disease, high blood pressure, insomnia and learning difficulties—surely it makes sense for us to seek out and protect the quiet places in our modern world.

# 8

# OVERLOAD

If only we could end the story there, with a recognition that cutting decibels is good for our health, just as we're reminded frequently about cutting calories or kilojoules. It would be so deliciously simple: don a pair of top-notch noise-cancelling headphones and find instant serenity. But not all of the noise that plagues us in the twenty-first century can be measured in decibels. Controlling the external clamour is only part of the equation.

Imagine putting those noise-cancelling headphones on a young professional as she begins her regular peak-hour commute to her city office. We can even give her optimal conditions for this trip: her train offers a 'quiet carriage', and there's a vacant seat waiting for her. Now imagine what our commuter does with her fifteen or twenty minutes of aural peace. Does she meditate? Or immerse herself in some gentle classical music? (Those Mozart sonatas aren't too bad, even if you can't rely on them to boost your cognition.) Or does she scroll through social media, succumbing to Insta-angst about the various lycra-clad influencers whose showcased lives appear so much more #blessed and #blissful than her own? Or scan her newsfeed for the latest crisis in current affairs? Or check her email, fretting that her colleagues or boss will think she's lazy if she hasn't replied already to all those work messages that have flooded in overnight?

No prizes for guessing which three of these five activities are most likely to raise our subject's heart rate and blood pressure, and send her cortisol levels surging, in similar ways to someone who has been exposed to sustained levels of external noise.

My experience at the Big Bash illustrated the same phenomenon. Had external noise been the only issue that night at the Gabba, my stress would have melted away as soon as we left the venue. Instead, the jumble of thoughts rattling around in my head continued to skyrocket, until I was overwhelmed by my anxiety and irritation. I'd had multiple tools on my mobile phone to help me solve the problem of getting back to our car. But somewhere between finding the website with the bus timetables . . . and scrolling Twitter for updates about the game . . . and managing one son's ongoing obsession with Instagram posts . . . and checking Google Maps for the best route to the car . . . and juggling texts from family and friends who wanted to know what was going on . . . I quickly began to feel like I was drowning in information.

In 2015, internationally renowned conservative commentator Andrew Sullivan cited similar feelings when he announced his retirement from blogging, after fifteen years in which he built an avid fanbase for his political writing on *The Daily Dish*. In a compelling essay titled 'I Used to Be a Human Being', published the following year, Sullivan documented how he had ultimately been 'broken' by the endless stream of information, entertainment and interaction available online.

'Over time in this pervasive virtual world, the online clamour grew louder and louder,' Sullivan recounted. 'Although I spent hours each day, alone and silent, attached to a laptop, it felt as if I were in a constant cacophonous crowd of words and images, sounds and ideas, emotions and tirades—a wind tunnel of deafening, deadening noise.'[1]

Noise without sound. A clamouring crowd devoid of any real human interaction. With his eloquent prose, Sullivan had captured the abject awfulness of this thoroughly modern malady: interior noise pollution.

The debut of *The Daily Dish* roughly coincided with my return from New York to Australia, and my entry into the Canberra Press Gallery. John Updike once wrote that 'the true New Yorker secretly believes that people living anywhere else have to be, in some sense, kidding', and, as I tried to settle in a town that had been built arbitrarily on a barren sheep plain (to placate the rival claims of Melbourne and Sydney to being the nation's capital), I began to suspect the joke was on me. The isolation and disorientation, the awkward experience of being the office 'newbie' once again—it all felt like prolonged and acute emotional whiplash. On days when I missed my New York friends and the life I'd built in Manhattan so much it burned, I'd dip into Sullivan's blog, among others, for a little connection back to my former life, and particularly to US politics.

Meanwhile, I was coming to grips with the rhythms of life covering Australian politics, which meant I was on a personal and professional trajectory very similar to that which Sullivan would later describe. Little did we journalists know it, but we were already hurtling towards a time when the refined one-way street of news delivery would be bulldozed, to be replaced by the social media superhighway.

Back in the early 2000s, there were certainly periods that were frenzied: September 11, the Bali bombings and the Canberra bushfires are all etched in my memory. But generally, most of us worked to a few concrete daily deadlines, which endowed the days with a predictable framework around which to research, interview and even reflect on what we were covering. The greatest source of 'noise' was probably Question Time. Given its propensity for generating grabs for the nightly news on sitting days, that period of about 90 minutes in which government ministers field questions without notice is probably what many Australians think of, if they ever think much at all about what their federal government does.

But for all the theatrics and grandstanding of Question Time, most of the Press Gallery's reporting focused on policy problems and the solutions under consideration, with the occasional profile about ministers who had distinguished themselves or other rising stars. Only a few correspondents were given the freedom to express their opinions in columns, where they might also hint at backroom manoeuvring or gossip from behind the scenes.

Big breaking stories aside, the rhythm of the day generally allowed us to check the facts and quotes in our stories, as well as do a lot of routine information gathering through scheduled meetings with contacts, phoning around and ad hoc conversations, not to mention getting coffee and conducting what one former colleague called 'hall trawls'.

A great deal of journalism today is all but unrecognisable from this. Journalists and commentators have become both contributors to the noise but also victims of it, an integral part of Sullivan's 'constant cacophonous crowd'.

So what happened? Looking back, that's easy to answer. A technological revolution happened—and it's still happening.

It's worth pausing here to acknowledge that human beings have always had multiple stressors with which to cope. And for much of human history—and, still, in many less developed countries today—those problems have posed significantly greater threats, in an existential sense, than chronic overstimulation caused by multiple digital devices. But a #firstworldproblem is still a problem—and a significant one too, if soaring rates of anxiety and depression, particularly among our young people, and reports of endemic levels of loneliness and other forms of social dysfunction, such as heightened political polarisation, are any indication.

What is going on? Who—or what—turned up the volume?

In all likelihood, a big part of the answer is sitting close to your elbow, or on your bedside table, or in your handbag or pocket as you read these words. In fact, you may even be reading them *on* it. Although it's hard to quantify, smartphones may well be the fastest-spreading technology in human history. And I have already discussed how our bodies—and, specifically in this case, our brains—cannot and do not adapt as quickly or as efficiently to change as we might like to think.

Instead, when confronted with an influx of stimuli that are new or unfamiliar (in an evolutionary sense), our brains can react with a 'flight or fight' response, and a range of other primal behaviours.

Now, consider the possibility that these reactions are not just random side effects of the new technologies most of us have embraced—but are actually being deliberately provoked and exploited by some of the smartest people on the planet, on the payrolls of some of the most powerful companies on earth. Who turned up the noise? Ladies and gentlemen of the jury, I give you some familiar names: Apple, Facebook and Google.

Before I start sounding like a hysterical conspiracy theorist, or even just a panicky mum fretting over the explosion of mobile devices in her home (alright, there are days when I'm definitely the latter), let's take a step back. First, it's worth taking a moment to fully appreciate the speed, the breadth and the truly revolutionary nature of the changes we have just lived through. Here are two snapshots that help capture just how far we've come.

In 2007, Steve Jobs unveiled the very first iPhone. Glowingly reviewed by *The Wall Street Journal* as a 'beautiful and breakthrough handheld computer', the device combined touchscreen internet connectivity with the convenience of phone portability for the mass market. Today, not much more than a decade later, there are estimated to be more than a billion iPhones in the world, as well as hundreds of millions of similar devices from other manufacturers.

Three years before Jobs made his big announcement, a young geek named Mark Zuckerberg launched his own innovation. Then somewhat clunkily named thefacebook.com, Zuckerberg's baby was not the first social media platform, but it soon became the biggest. Today, Facebook boasts a population larger than any country on earth, with roughly 2.3 billion users, about half of whom are active on a daily basis.

Of course, the massive market success of Apple products and Facebook's social network cannot be held as evidence of a sinister plot to harm human beings. The word 'revolutionary' can describe positive changes as well as negative ones, and I would argue that these innovations have delivered many good outcomes, including connecting friends and families, and enabling exciting new forms of creativity and community building. And yet . . .

In 2010, a behavioural scientist named B.J. Fogg looked back on the changes he had seen over two decades at Stanford University, where he had been a pioneer in the use of computers as persuasive technologies: what he dubbed 'captology'. As you read Fogg's words, it's important to note that he's a self-described optimist and advocate for the use of persuasive design (for instance, he believes that 'the mobile phone is the next step in human evolution, literally'). 'If twenty years ago, I had announced that we would soon be creating machines that control humans, there would have been an uproar,' he noted. 'But today, the uproars around Facebook, around Google's domination, around Apple's seductive products, are small compared to the actual impact this is having in our lives.'[2]

Fogg's research centre at Stanford, now known as the Behaviour Design Lab, became famous as a veritable nursery for Silicon Valley money makers. The students he trained excelled at designing websites and apps that consumers found irresistible; his graduates either were snapped up by the Big Tech firms or launched their own successful startups—or sometimes both. Mike Krieger, for example, left the Stanford lab and started Instagram, which boasted roughly 30 million users when it was bought by Facebook in 2012.[3] Another, Nir Eyal, took what he learned from Fogg and, after starting two tech companies of his own, translated the sum of his knowledge into a bestselling book, titled *Hooked: How to build habit-forming products.*

But not all Fogg's graduates remain as optimistic as their teacher, nor as evangelistic as Eyal about the profits to be made from creating addictive products or apps. Another alumnus, Tristan Harris, ended up working for Google as a product designer after his own startup was bought by the behemoth in 2011. Harris was assigned to work with a team on the development of Google Inbox. But increasingly, as his colleagues focused on the look of the product and how to alert people to new mail, Harris found himself questioning the impact of these intrusions on people's lives.

In February 2013, Harris had what seems, in retrospect, a 'Jerry Maguire moment'. A trip to the Burning Man festival prompted the young techie to reflect on his life and how often he 'felt completely hopeless [and] depressed' about his work at Google.[4] Back in San Francisco, he couldn't shake the feelings, and so began to hunt for ways he could better live his own values. Eventually, Harris sat down and created an ambitious presentation of more than 140 slides, titled 'A Call to Minimize Distraction & Respect Users' Attention'.[5]

'Never before in history, have the decisions of a handful of designers (mostly men, white, living in SF [San Francisco], aged 25–35) working for three companies [Google, Apple and Facebook] had so much impact on how millions of people around the world spend their attention,' he wrote in the slide deck, originally intended for fewer than a dozen colleagues at Google. 'We should feel an enormous responsibility to get this right.'

And perhaps Google, and the other Big Tech companies, did feel that responsibility. Certainly, they acknowledged Harris's thought leadership by inviting him to create a new role for himself in-house. He chose 'design ethicist', and also established an advocacy group outside Google called Time Well Spent, ostensibly to encourage designers to develop products to enhance people's lives, rather than simply capture their attention. But it became increasingly clear that what Google thought were the most important measures of 'getting it right'—market capitalisation, perhaps, and profits, as well as the number of users and the amount of time they spent engaged with the products—were vastly different from the views of Harris, who finally left Google in 2015.

Meanwhile, his 'Call to Minimize Distraction' presentation had gone viral, at least among tech-savvy designers, engineers, investors and commentators. Harris earned the moniker 'the conscience of Silicon Valley', and the support of other insiders who shared his concerns about the direction of the tech giants. As the chorus grew, Time Well Spent evolved into the Center for Humane Technology, which states its mission as nothing less than 'to reverse human downgrading by inspiring a new race to the top and realigning technology with humanity'. Its homepage neatly sums up why so many of us are feeling overwhelmed by the constant noise of alerts, notifications, outrage and other reactions deliberately stoked by social media: 'Today's tech platforms are caught in a race to the bottom of the brain stem to extract human attention. It's a race we're all losing. The result: addiction, social isolation, outrage, misinformation, and political polarization—all part of one interconnected system . . . that poses an existential threat to humanity.'[6]

It sounds frightening. And, frankly, it is. Even the captology evangelist B.J. Fogg has admitted to being surprised there hadn't been a public uproar about how computers were now controlling humans—and that was back in 2010. And the race has only picked up pace since then.

Harris's 'race to the bottom of the brain stem' refers to the mounting scientific evidence that reveals how Big Tech is deliberately targeting and triggering the most primal parts of our brains, particularly to activate 'dopamine loops'. Dopamine is the feel-good chemical involved in motivating or rewarding behaviours, and these loops also light up when an addict is feeding their craving. When Harris describes our mobile phones as 'a slot machine in your pocket', he isn't kidding. The dopamine loops that light up in our brains when we receive likes on Facebook or retweets on Twitter are the same as those in a gambling addict as they feed the family grocery money into a gaudy machine in a dark but noisy corner of the local pub.

But don't take my word for it—or even Harris's. Here's how Chamath Palihapitiya, former Vice President of User Growth at

Facebook, responded when asked in 2017 about his previous efforts to manipulate the behaviour of Facebook users: 'I feel tremendous guilt,' he admitted. 'The short-term, dopamine-driven feedback loops that we have created are destroying how society works.'[7]

Of course, the tech companies aren't pokie machines competing for coins. They are competing for our attention. Harris calls it the 'extractive attention economy'—and our collective failure to understand it probably goes some way to explaining why most of us are also underestimating the amount of digital noise that assails us every day.

If you were constantly reaching for your credit card simply to access Facebook, or if your children were pestering you regularly for more change so they could post on Instagram, you would quickly realise there was a problem in the house. That's because most of us are familiar with a world where companies want us to spend money to buy their products and services; we are therefore used to balancing a budget (or at least trying to), as well as hunting out bargains and spotting false advertising.

In the digital world there are other forms of currency. Tech companies and platforms know that our attention (once called 'eyeballs') is worth something to advertisers, as is the data they can collect on us, based on our behaviour while using their sites. In the attention economy, it is not our money but our focus and engagement that tech companies want most of all.

But while many things have changed in the last decade or so, one thing remains as old as time itself—because it *is* time itself. We still only have 24 hours to spend each day. We can't beg, borrow or steal more time for ourselves. The Big Tech companies must compete savagely for every available minute and second. And if you think 'savage' is too brutal or hyperbolic a word, consider this response from Netflix chief executive Reed Hastings, when asked in 2017 about how he viewed his company's competition. 'Think about it; when you watch a show from Netflix and you get addicted to it, you stay up late at night,' Hastings replied. 'We're competing with sleep, on the margin.'[8] In similar

comments the previous year, Hastings had acknowledged more traditional competitors like YouTube and SnapChat, while also elaborating:
'We compete . . . against everything you do to relax.'[9]

These tech distractors also have another powerful force working in
their favour. Studies have revealed that most human beings find it hard
to tolerate being alone with their thoughts, even for relatively short
periods of a few minutes. Indeed, a series of related studies, conducted
jointly by the University of Virginia and Harvard, found that a substantial proportion of people in this situation would go to the extent of
hurting themselves, just to create a distraction. 'Simply being alone with
their own thoughts for 15 minutes was apparently so aversive that it
drove many participants to self-administer an electric shock that they
had earlier said they would pay to avoid,' investigators reported in a
summary of the studies, published in *Science* in 2014.[10]

In the electric shock study, twelve out of eighteen men and six
out of 24 women who were left for a fifteen-minute period of solitary
'thinking time' chose to shock themselves at least once. Whenever
I read this statistic, I am reminded of a popular quote: 'All men's
miseries derive from not being able to sit in a quiet room alone.' More
than three centuries after French mathematician and theologian Blaise
Pascal wrote those words, science proved him correct!

I'm also struck by an irony: we live in the era of the individual,
of narcissism and self-centredness, and yet many of us are apparently
deeply terrified of the idea of spending time alone with ourselves.
And if some of us will even choose an electric shock to avoid our own
thoughts, then that sets a very low bar for techs and influencers whose
aim is to create content that goes viral, whether it's Candy Crush or
a kitten video.

Regardless of how they win it, once Big Tech has our attention,
the next step is to hold our neural pathways captive, preventing us
from focusing on something else, whether it's Facebook, Twitter or
another social media rival, or sleep, or helping our children with their

homework, or even having sex with a partner (somewhere between 10 per cent and 62 per cent of mobile phone users admit to having checked their phones during intercourse, depending on which survey you believe).[11] The increasing sophistication of artificial intelligence means the tech companies are getting better at that task, particularly when they have big data sets to draw on, which they use to create profiles, or 'avatars', of who we are and what triggers we are most likely to respond to.

YouTube's algorithm has become so good, for example, that under 30 per cent of the videos watched on its site are deliberately sought out by users. The remainder—a massive 70 million hours of video *a day*—is now watched only because YouTube knows exactly what to recommend to a user to keep them engaged after their selected video ends. This is not a conspiracy theory, nor is it even a secret. These figures were cited in 2018 by YouTube chief product officer Neal Mohan, who no doubt appreciates that this sort of expertise is exactly what prospective advertisers want to hear.[12]

'The competition for attention is fierce,' Emily Bell, director of the Tow Center for Digital Journalism at Columbia University, said in a widely quoted speech in 2016. 'The "four horsemen of the apocalypse"—Google, Facebook, Apple and Amazon (five if you add in Microsoft)—are engaged in a prolonged and torrid war over whose technologies, platforms and even ideologies will win. It is as fierce as newspaper rivalries in the 60s and network television in the 70s, but with much more at stake.'[13]

Bell's reference to the newspaper wars was deliberate, for her speech was specifically about how Big Tech, and particularly social media, has changed the way news is produced, distributed and consumed. It explained a lot about why many journalists are now in different careers, and why those who remain in the game feel like they are now working in a deafening wind tunnel, as Andrew Sullivan put it.

Entire books have been written about the havoc wrought on traditional media models by the digital revolution. Suffice it to say that if you've been wondering why the news has become louder—more emotional, more polarised and opinionated—you need look no further than the attention wars.

Today, if you want to compete, you must play by the rules set by Bell's 'four horsemen of the Apocalypse'. For anyone creating content—whether it's a daily news report from Canberra, an influencer's Instagram post about what she's wearing today or a TikTok send-up of the Taylor Swift–Kanye West wars—the aim is to make their work compelling enough to stop a user scrolling through an endless newsfeed and watch or read the entire piece. Then, there's the Holy Grail: getting that user to share the content with their friends and followers.

Of course, many of the ploys the media uses to attract attention are older than social media. Every newspaper editor I've ever worked for has known instinctively that emotions, particularly fear and anger, tend to engage audiences more than rational arguments. Humans are particularly drawn to stories of conflict, perhaps because they intensify those negative emotions further, by projecting them through a tribal prism of 'us versus them'. Similarly, we all carry around an understandable interest in human survival. In the newsrooms of old, the rather tasteless saying that 'if it bleeds, it leads' acknowledged as much—and, depending on the cause of the injury itself, such a story might tap into our fascination with conflict as well.

Novelty is another trigger that is just as likely to capture our attention today as it did when the very first cave painting was unveiled to the other, less artistic members of the tribe. In newspapers, it's long been understood that the headline 'Dog Bites Man' is a bit of a snooze, but if the story is 'Man Bites Dog', you have a winner. That is novelty at work.

But while many of the triggers are perennial, what social media has changed is the speed and brevity with which they must be activated, the context in which that process occurs, and the amplification that is possible when it is successful.

Welcome to the era of 'and what happened next will make you cry!'. In 2017, BuzzSumo analysed 100 million Facebook and Twitter headlines to identify which three-word phrases prompted the most engagement from users. Headlines with the phrase 'will make you' in them triggered twice as many interactions as the next most popular trigram, which was 'this is why'. 'Can we guess' came in third.[14]

Of course, if more engagement means more dollars, and you have analytics tools that can tell you which stories attract more engagement, the next obvious step is to encourage journalists to write more of those stories. And therein lies the crossroads for journalism in the digital era.

In 2019, Melbourne tabloid the *Herald Sun* announced it was trialling an incentives program in which news and sport journalists could earn bonuses of up to $50 for writing stories that increased website traffic and induced would-be readers to buy subscriptions.[15]

The pitfalls were—and remain—obvious. In Melbourne, if you were a reporter covering AFL, the football code which is almost a religion there, your money-making prospects would be far more promising than the reporter covering rugby union, unless some other form of handicap was applied to the system. And pity the poor hack who covers the council rounds—despite the fact that, theoretically at least, we should all care more about whether our rates are being spent efficiently than who's on top of the ladder.

Even without cash bonuses, social media metrics encourage hyperbolic headlines and stories that feature high-profile people, conflict and other polarising emotions. Meanwhile, serious reportage requires research and interviewing and fact-checking, all of which are time-consuming and put a strain on limited budgets.

Enter the professional 'opinionator'. Filling your pages and TV and radio panels full of people prepared to shout their opinions, regardless of whether they have any expertise on a particular subject, while deriding those who disagree with them, costs very little. As the saying goes, 'talk is cheap' (although whoever came up with that adage probably hadn't seen the salary packages of some of Sydney's leading commentators). Without the restraints of balance or fact-checking, opinionators are free to weaponise all the triggers that work in the attention wars, stoking fear, anger and anxiety about difference or the unknown.

The standard response to criticism of such junk media tends to be the same as it is for junk food: nobody is forcing us to consume it, are they? Further, the optimistic argument has even been made—particularly by Big Tech—that the arrival of digital has been an empowering force for democratic good. The fallout from the 2016 US presidential election—the revelations of data mined, bought and manipulated by Cambridge Analytica, the Russian interference, the explosion of 'fake news'—probably struck a fatal blow to that line of defence. But even so, I think most of us know, simply by exposure to the noise and anger around us, that there's a problem here.

Certainly, it is still possible to access quality news and analysis. But much of it now exists behind paywalls, making it unaffordable for some. Plus, as Tristan Harris and others argue regularly, we are now all competing against algorithms drawing on so much data, they effectively know us better than we know ourselves; they are designed to target each of us with content that is most likely to capture our attention, while fake content is becoming increasingly sophisticated.

Even if some individuals can negotiate this minefield and remain relatively well-informed, it's reasonable to assume that large numbers won't be as willing or as able to be so discerning. And the difference between an overconsumption of junk food and a glut of junk media is that the negative impacts of a poor diet are largely limited to the individual (and perhaps their children), while the latter can set the standards of behaviour for entire communities. Just ask anyone who has tried to prosecute a reasoned argument on a controversial topic on Twitter.

Have we reached that point yet? Has the intolerance and personal derision that is modelled by many opinionators, and mimicked and amplified on social media (particularly when users are allowed to remain anonymous), leaked more widely across our culture? We have certainly become less trusting, according to reputable measures such as the Edelman Trust Barometer, and more anxious.[16] Placed under acute pressure, such as during the catastrophic Australian bushfires of 2019–20 and the early stages of the COVID-19 pandemic, Australians have revealed themselves to be capable of appalling antisocial behaviour, such as looting burnt-out properties and hoarding toilet paper. But perhaps human beings have been ever thus. And for every looter and panic buyer, there have also been Australians prepared to step up as heroes in an emergency or to give generously to support their communities.

It would be a stretch, then, to claim that social and traditional media are solely responsible for declining standards of behaviour. Nonetheless, history has repeatedly taught us that it pays to be vigilant against intolerance and incivility.

Free speech is only truly 'free' if it can occur without fear of reprisal, threats and intimidation. And our democratic system can only operate well when our leaders encourage respect for it, which includes a due respect for all of those elected through it. What happens when that begins to break down?

'Rage.'

That was the powerfully succinct answer when I put a similar question to former prime minister Kevin Rudd, seeking his opinion on how digital disruption had impacted the media and Australian politics.

'Rage [was] pioneered by the Murdoch media, in particular the Murdoch tabloids, [initially] in Britain, then Australia, and taken to a whole new plain at Fox News,' the former PM argued. 'By the time social media arrived, that currency of rage had been legitimised by them. And now it is available to hundreds of millions of people. The fear I have is that the politics of rage, pioneered by News, has infected this country and others more broadly.'

Still, unlike this former prime minister—and, for the record, I approached more than one to comment for this chapter—I think it might be naive to hope that the problem we now face is as simple as one media magnate. As powerful as Rupert Murdoch's media empire may be—and it certainly dominates the media landscape in Australia—I suspect that if it closed tomorrow, other media outlets of similar temperament would rise in its place.

In other words, I believe the genie—or demon—is out of the bottle. And it will play havoc unless we get smarter and less complacent. We urgently need to educate ourselves and our children about how our basest instincts are being tweaked and exploited to benefit others more powerful than us.

The first step is to review the evidence that shows that digital noise is bad for our health.

History abounds with moral panics piqued by the latest popular innovation. From the 'penny dreadful' novels that flourished in Victorian England at the time of mass industrialisation to 'video killing the radio star' in the 1980s, the success of a new diversion often prompts fears about what it's replacing or how it will change our culture. But there are some fundamental differences about the way smartphones and other digital devices operate that make them far more deserving of caution than those earlier distractions.

The penny dreadful, the radio, the television, the video recorder and even television-based video games: all were capable of capturing and holding the attention of users. Some still are! But none had the compelling, 24/7 interactivity of smartphones, combined with a portability and power that meant they could track us via GPS, and store our movements, behaviours, keystrokes and even voice commands, for future use and even sale by companies and other third parties. Data mining and the erosion of personal privacy, as well as the way this data can be used to create 'fake news' to manipulate elections, are big problems that are likely to require system-wide responses from governments and other regulators.

While we may not have much power as individuals to counter those issues, we can certainly tackle the amount of digital noise we allow into our lives—and those of our children. How much evidence is enough to demonstrate that this sort of noise pollution—a veritable barrage of cognitive and emotional stimuli designed to keep us engaged—is as toxic as the type measured in decibels, if not more so? Ironically, as I discovered, it's extremely easy to become overwhelmed while reviewing the scientific literature that explains why we are feeling so overwhelmed. But here's a snapshot of some of the more rigorous studies.

Firstly, there is substantial evidence to show that digital noise generated by our devices is eroding our cognitive abilities, such as the ability to focus and pay attention. In 2017, a peer-reviewed study by a group of psychologists and behavioural scientists found that the mere presence of a smartphone, even one that is switched off, generates a 'brain drain' in its owner. Put simply, the urge to pay attention to our phones—a habit ingrained by all those dopamine-inducing likes, email chimes and other rewards—demands energy, and we only have a finite amount to go around, meaning that 'performance on [other] tasks will suffer'. The authors continued: 'Ironically, the more consumers depend on their smartphones, the more they seem to suffer from their presence—or, more optimistically, the more they may stand to benefit from their absence.'[17]

There are multiple implications of this widespread 'brain drain': some muted but invidious, others more obvious and potentially tragic. For example, a study conducted for the US Department of Transportation in 2009 found that commercial vehicle drivers who texted while driving were 23 times more likely to be involved in a 'safety-critical event'.[18]

The addictive lure of our mobile devices has also been shown to have multiple negative effects on our mental health and relationships. According to a study published in the *Journal of Social and Personal Relationships* in 2013, when two people meet, the proximity of a smartphone will degrade the quality of the connection they share, with both conversation and feelings of closeness degraded.[19]

A study of 723 Finnish Facebook users aged between fifteen and eighteen found that 67 per cent of them had been exposed to hate material online, with that exposure associated with poor family attachment, lower happiness levels, physical victimisation in the 'real' world and, perhaps counterintuitively, even higher online activity.[20]

And in 2016, a meta-analysis and review of twenty studies for the American Medical Association's *JAMA Paediatrics* concluded that there was strong and compelling evidence that using or even having access to a screen at bedtime reduced both sleep quality and quantity, as well as increasing drowsiness during the day.[21] As discussed earlier, whether it is caused by external noise pollution or the digital kind, disrupted sleep has many debilitating, even potentially life-threatening impacts on physiological health.

The impact on children and young people is particularly alarming. In 2014, a meta-analysis of multiple studies of bullying involving children and adolescents, published in *JAMA Paediatrics*, found that 'cyberbullying was more strongly related to suicidal ideation compared with traditional bullying'.[22] While bullying was never a positive experience, children bullied online were three times more likely to consider suicide than those who weren't, while children who encountered traditional forms of bullying were twice as likely.

San Diego State University psychology professor Jean Twenge has made a career studying generational differences, even coining the now popular tag 'iGen' to describe the first cohort who spent their entire adolescence in the era of smartphones. In a study she co-authored for the *Journal of Abnormal Psychology* in 2019, Twenge reviewed data from the National Survey on Drug Use and Health, which included survey responses from more than 200,000 adolescents from 2005 to 2017.[23]

Twenge and her co-authors noted a significant spike in mental health disorders among adolescents after 2011, with this group reporting serious psychological distress, major depression or suicidal thoughts, and more attempted suicides. Further investigation revealed a weak correlation between electronic device use and teen depression and suicide, while social media use was also weakly correlated with depressive symptoms, particularly in girls. While the correlation was weak, Twenge was convinced. In a cover story for *The Atlantic* titled 'Have Smartphones Destroyed a Generation?', she stated her case: 'If you were going to give advice for a happy adolescence based on this survey, it would be straightforward: Put down the phone, turn off the laptop, and do something—anything—that does not involve a screen.'[24]

Of course, there are plenty of other experts who say it is too early to make such sweeping statements about the dangers of these relatively new technologies. They argue we must do more research, and particularly more studies that use randomised controlled trials (the gold standard in science), before we can make decisive claims. But even the critics acknowledge that one of the largest impediments to conducting that sort of research is that much of the best data about device use and user behaviour is collected—and very jealously guarded—by the Big Tech companies themselves. They have little interest in releasing it to researchers who want to explore the possible negative impacts of the devices and programs that have made them some of the most profitable companies on earth.

What we do know is that Tristan Harris is not the only conscientious objector in Silicon Valley. In fact, when it comes to voicing concerns about device use, he is in very good company. Microsoft founder Bill Gates would not allow his children to have mobile phones until they were teenagers. In 2017, his wife, Melinda, wrote a column for *The Washington Post* in which she conceded that, in hindsight, even that age was too young. 'Phones and apps aren't good or bad by them-selves,' she acknowledged, 'but for adolescents who don't yet have the emotional tools to navigate life's complications and confusions, they can exacerbate the difficulties of growing up: learning how to be kind, coping with feelings of exclusion, taking advantage of freedom while exercising self-control.'[25]

The late Steve Jobs, co-founder of Apple, also famously limited his own children's screentime, revealing in a *New York Times* interview in 2010 that he was yet to allow them to use the newly released iPad.[26]

In 2018, Tony Fadell, a former executive with Apple and Google parent company Alphabet, called on those companies to 'do the right thing' about digital addiction and overuse, by designing tools to help users monitor and cut down if necessary. 'I strongly believe this is not just a "Facebook problem" or just a "kids' issue",' Fadell wrote. 'All of us, adults and children, have had our lives transformed in the decade since the iPhone was unveiled.'[27]

While it may not be just a Facebook problem, some of Mark Zuck-erberg's former employees have emerged as the most vocal critics of digital noise and intrusion. For example, former Facebook engineer Justin Rosenstein has repeatedly warned of the addictive nature of 'likes' on that social media platform, calling them 'bright dings of pseudo-pleasure'.[28] And he should know: Rosenstein invented the 'like' button during a Facebook hackathon in 2008.

Facebook founding president Sean Parker has also described how its engineers and designers deliberately created feedback loops that 'exploit[ed] a vulnerability in human psychology', recognising that he may not have understood 'the unintended consequences of a network when it grows to a billion or 2 billion people . . . It probably interferes with productivity in weird ways. God only knows what it's doing to our children's brains.'[29]

A few weeks after Parker's comments, another former Facebook executive, Chamath Palihapitiya, urged an audience at the Stanford

Graduate School of Business to take a 'hard break' from their devices, telling them that 'if you feed the beast, that beast will destroy you . . . We have created tools that are ripping apart the social fabric of how society works. That is truly where we are,' Palihapitiya said.[30]

Information, as they say, is power. And it's true that we don't have all the information about the noisy digital tools that have become ubiquitous in our lives. But we have enough. As I watched Palihapitiya's interview, and took in his revelation that he no longer used the social media tools he had helped devise, I felt there was only one question left: 'What will *my* solution be?'

The easy answer would be to turn off all the digital noise. After all, we each have control over our devices. It would certainly be easier to unplug our iPads and PCs, shut down our social media accounts and delete the apps that have flourished like weeds on our phones than to try to control the aural noise in the modern world around us. None of us can turn down the hum of commuter traffic, or the rumble of a jet taking off, or the multitude of other sounds of the city. We can mitigate it to some degree with our choices, but unless we move far away from human development—and that may be an option for some, but won't be for everybody—most of us are still going to be exposed daily to an orchestra of man-made noise over which we have no control.

At home, my study looks directly into the thick canopy of a remnant dry rainforest; our backyard is part of a suburban fauna reserve and even includes a little creek. But my workdays are still punctuated by the sounds from a local school, which carry across a gully from more than a kilometre away, as well as the constant growl of traffic from a distant arterial road, and the occasional shriek and whine of power tools from renovation sites around the neighbourhood.

Still, I think I've achieved a balance that suits my work and family life right now. Nestled in the embrace of bushland on the shoulder of a hill, there is enough quietude and space for me to think, reflect and create. But there is also a bus at the end of the street for my sons to catch to school, and our house—which is just three doors up from my childhood home—is a short drive away from where my parents settled in retirement.

I contemplate this happy auditory balance as my head reels from the avalanche of negative research findings about digital noise. Could it be possible to establish a similar equilibrium in the digital world—the Goldilocks point of not too much exposure and not too little, but just the right amount?

My initial instinct is to go cold turkey: turn off all the devices and return to an analogue world of printed pages and human conversation. But as a journalist, I've experienced firsthand how digitisation has revolutionised research, broadening the information available to us and vastly accelerating the ways in which we can share it. It still seems remarkable that, in my lifetime, we have gone from being limited to material and sources in our immediate vicinity to being able to locate and communicate quickly and easily with experts around the world.

Then there's the enormous personal power of connection that social media has enabled. For every grim story of extremists connecting through the dark web, there are positive accounts of those who may once have felt isolated—gay teenagers, mothers and fathers of children with disabilities, veterans battling PTSD, those struggling with mental health issues—connecting and 'finding their tribe' online.

And I have to acknowledge that, for all that digital noise drove me to seek silence and then to write this book, there were also digital tools that helped me research it. If it wasn't for the internet, I would have struggled to find out about the invaluable work Tristan Harris is doing through the Center for Humane Technology, for example, or discovered the beautiful words of Pico Iyer and been motivated to visit

New Camaldoli. YouTube gave me the chance to watch the lectures and interviews of Sean Parker, Tony Fadell, Justin Rosenstein and so many others. There were podcasts that offered deep dives into some of the subject matter, and Facebook groups that continued the discussions.

While so much of what is pumped into our heads through digital channels is dross, there is undoubtedly gold as well. Our challenge is to hone our skills of discernment and attention in order to detect the good and make use of it, while resisting the distractions designed to capture our attention. That way, we might achieve a balance whereby we make the most of what the digital world has to offer, without being overwhelmed by the noise.

But how? Can we train our brains in the same way that we train our bodies?

For most of human history, that has been an impossible question to answer with any degree of scientific certainty or rigour. But since the advent of MRIs and other imaging technology, our understanding of the human brain has grown exponentially. Along the way, assumptions that had previously dominated conventional medical and scientific thinking, sometimes for generations, have been smashed. One of the most influential was the idea that the adult brain did not have the capacity to change. Only in the past few decades have scientists had the tools to demonstrate neuroplasticity in humans: that is, that the brain can sprout new neurons and forge pathways between them depending on what it experiences throughout life. And if the brain can change, then the odds are that we can train it.

Somewhat ironically, given I was researching ways to calm the mind that had become inflamed by digital noise, it was a Google search that led me to the story of a man who is a master of doing just that.

Yongey Mingyur Rinpoche was born into a noble lineage in Nepal in 1975. His mother was the descendant of two Tibetan kings, and his father one of the few living masters who had studied in old, or independent, Tibet. While still a child, Mingyur Rinpoche was recognised as a *tulku,* or reincarnated lama, and as a result his already privileged status within a respected family was elevated further. In his memoir, *In Love with the World*, Mingyur Rinpoche described his childhood as 'pampered and indulged, and . . . as protected as a hot-house orchid'.[31] Despite these comforts, the young Mingyur Rinpoche suffered severe panic attacks, which could be triggered by everything from storms to strangers. Rather than playing with other children, the nervous young boy would often seek solitude in the caves that surrounded his village in the Himalayas.

When he was nine years old, Mingyur Rinpoche's father began tutoring him formally in meditation practice and philosophy, and at an age when most children in the West are about to start high school, he entered a monastery in northern India to continue his studies. At thirteen, he begged to be allowed to begin a three-year meditation retreat, a highly unusual challenge for one so young, even within a community committed to such practices. (As the mother of two rowdy teenage boys, I must confess I find some appeal in this approach to managing adolescence!)

By the time Mingyur Rinpoche graduated from this retreat, he had completely overcome his panic attacks, and was recognised by his teachers as a prodigy. When his own meditation teacher died, Mingyur Rinpoche was named the monastery's new retreat master at the age of seventeen, and he was fully ordained as a monk six years later. He would go on to supervise three separate monasteries, and oversaw the construction of a new community at Bodhgaya, the place where the Buddha was said to have achieved enlightenment. In other words, here was a young monk utterly comfortable testing the limits, not just of his own capacity but of social convention.

But the West was yet to come, if you'll pardon the pun.

In 2002, Mingyur Rinpoche left his monastery to travel to the American Midwest, at the invitation of a group of neuroscientists who believed the relatively new tools of EEG and fMRI might reveal what goes on inside a person's brain while meditating. Until this point, it had been difficult to test the value of meditation practices beyond subjective reporting by the meditators themselves, who might say that it made them feel calmer or happier, or helped them sleep better—or that it had no effect at all. Scientists had tried some physical monitoring, like measuring heart rates or levels of the stress hormone cortisol, but this had generated few reliable or conclusive results.

Waiting for Mingyur Rinpoche was Dr Richie Davidson, who had founded the Laboratory for Affective Neuroscience at the University of Wisconsin–Madison in the mid-1980s. While the lab was dedicated to studying the interaction between emotions and the brain generally, Davidson was also a long-time meditator: he had sat his first ten-day Vipassana retreat in India almost three decades earlier, taught by S.N. Goenka himself. That experience had left Davidson with a belief in the power of meditation, combined with a scientist's respect for evidence-based investigation. He had been researching its impacts and effects long before it was taken seriously by most of his colleagues, and had been publishing articles about meditation in scientific journals since the mid-1970s.

All of which led to the moment when a bald and smiling 27-year-old from the hills of Kathmandu walked into an EEG lab in Wisconsin and, gathering his crimson and orange robes around him, allowed 256 wires to be attached to his scalp. Davidson, in collaboration with Matthieu Ricard (a French-born molecular geneticist who left that career to become a Tibetan Buddhist monk), had mapped out a detailed running sheet for the experiment. Over three carefully timed cycles, Mingyur Rinpoche would be prompted to alternate between a one-minute compassion meditation and a 30-second resting, or neutral, state.

The researchers had no idea what to expect. Later, Davidson would admit he had misgivings about the script he and Ricard had devised, fearing it would not allow Mingyur Rinpoche enough time to achieve a deeply meditative state. But as the first cycle began, something extraordinary occurred. The computers monitoring the feedback from Mingyur Rinpoche's wired skullcap lit up with a huge surge of electrical activity. The spikes of colour and light were so great that the scientists assumed the young monk must have shifted in his seat, accidentally triggering the highly sensitive electrodes. But Mingyur Rinpoche sat serene and still before them, and the dramatic brainwaves on the monitors continued. They subsided when he stopped meditating and entered the rest phase, but never faded completely.

Then, as Mingyur Rinpoche began the next meditation phase, another series of pixelated spikes rolled across the computer screens, as jagged and dramatic as the Himalayas themselves. 'The lab team knew at that moment they were witnessing something profound, something that had never before been observed in the laboratory,' Davidson wrote later in *The Science of Meditation*, published in 2017 with Daniel Goleman. 'None could predict what this would lead to, but everyone sensed this was a critical inflection point in neuroscience history.'[32]

After the EEG, Mingyur Rinpoche was invited to submit to fMRI testing. This second machine would give scientists a 3D image of the monk's neural activity, allowing them to locate more precisely the part of the brain that had been generating those enormous electrical surges. This time, the surprise wasn't so much the source of the neural intensity—as Mingyur Rinpoche meditated on compassion, the neural circuitry associated with empathy lit up—but its intensity. During his meditation, the activity level in this part of his brain increased by 700 to 800 per cent.

'Such an extreme increase befuddles science,' Davidson and Goleman wrote. 'The intensity with which those states were activated in Mingyur's brain exceeds any we have seen in studies of "normal" people. The closest resemblance is in epileptic seizures, but those episodes last brief seconds not a full minute. And besides, brains are *seized* by seizures, in contrast to Mingyur's display of intentional control of his brain activity.'

Later, after conducting similar tests on a number of other yogis, Davidson sat down to review the data with a colleague, Antoine Lutz. They detected another remarkable pattern, or 'neural signature', among the long-term meditators: all had sustained periods of high gamma oscillations, the fastest and most intense brainwaves.

Most human beings generate only a second or two of gamma at a time, in those rare but delicious 'aha!' moments of synchronicity when a number of brain regions fire together; for example, to solve a puzzle or generate a particularly evocative memory. But Davidson's research found that expert meditators such as Mingyur Rinpoche were able not only to sustain that activity, but to switch it on and off at will. Considering this phenomenon in *The Science of Meditation*, Davidson and Goleman speculated that a heightened gamma state might explain why the Buddha himself earned that title. Returning from his quest for enlightenment, the former prince Siddhartha Gautama was asked by a group of yogis whether he was a god. According to legend, he responded, 'No. I am awake.' The Sanskrit word for 'awake' is *bodhi*— thus Siddhartha became known as the Buddha. Davidson and Goleman continued: '[Gamma] seems to lend a sense of vast spaciousness, senses wide-open, enriching everyday experiences—even deep sleep, suggesting an around the clock quality of awakening.'

Put like that, who wouldn't want to learn how to meditate? After all, it's free to practise, it can be done anywhere, without special clothing or equipment, and the risks of negative side effects are exceptionally low (except in those who have serious pre-existing mental health issues, particularly related to trauma or extreme anxiety disorders, who should discuss the option first with their supervising doctor or therapist). But then again, at the time of testing, Mingyur Rinpoche was estimated to have spent more than 62,000 hours of his life meditating. That's equivalent to more than seven years of nonstop practice, without sleep.

The other yogis studied by Davidson as part of those initial studies averaged about 34,000 meditation hours each: not quite in Mingyur's league, but still a formidable amount of time.

Relatively few people have the possibility of devoting their lives so completely to a contemplative practice. And there are other variables that might have influenced the monks' unusual brain patterns. You don't have to be a scientist to recognise that their diet, exercise, sleep patterns and general lifestyles, as well as their genetics, are likely to be quite different from those of the average Westerner. So setting out to surf our gamma waves like a super-yogi may be the wrong goal to begin with. But is it possible that quietening our minds through meditation (sometimes referred to as mindfulness, although that term has broader applications) could help counter the toxic effects of digital noise and overload?

There's little doubt that meditation is the Next Big Thing in wellbeing. According to the leading US public health agency, the Centers for Disease Control and Prevention, it is the fastest-growing health trend in that country, with the number of adult Americans practising meditation set to eclipse those practising yoga in 2020 if growth continues at the rate measured in 2017.[33] (And if you've seen the number of yoga studios in New York and Los Angeles particularly, you know that's saying something.) In 2018, Apple named mental wellness and mindfulness apps the number one app trend of the year.[34] And in its 2019 Wellness Trends Report, the Global Wellness Summit predicted that meditation was about to 'go plural', with a proliferation of methods and practices, having acknowledged that it was already 'installed—along with a healthy diet and exercise—as one of the three pillars of wellbeing'.[35]

You would think this would make long-term meditation practitioners and advocates like Richie Davidson and Dan Goleman very happy. But instead, the bestselling authors have been highly vocal, warning that much of what we are reading and hearing about the benefits of meditation is unsubstantiated hype. Indeed, their book quoted above (and published elsewhere as *Altered Traits*) was prompted by what they saw as an increasing need to separate the science from the snake oil. They had two goals in mind: to ensure that people taking up meditation were not driven by false expectations, and to help guide future research into the practice, by identifying gaps in understanding or evidence.

Davidson and Goleman spent more than two years reviewing the published research into meditation, ultimately sifting through more than 6000 academic studies. They discarded many, even some published by otherwise respectable peer-reviewed journals, for being not rigorous enough in their definitions, or not specific enough in what was being tested, or too small in sample size, or simply for having results that were yet to be replicated in other studies. Reviewing the remaining 'gold standard' research, Davidson and Goleman found compelling evidence that meditation can alter four main neural pathways: those used for reacting to, and recovering from, stress; those governing attention and focus; those linked to compassion and empathy; and, finally, the pathways related to our sense of self.

The first two of these are particularly pertinent if our goal is to help manage and mitigate the impact on us of digital noise each day. Recall that, earlier in this chapter, I cited research that suggests digital devices, particularly iPhones, create a significant cognitive 'brain drain' in their distracted users. There were also plenty of references to heightened levels of emotional stress, including anxiety, loneliness, disconnection and bullying experienced by those living their lives online. If we cannot disentangle ourselves completely from digital devices in the modern world, then perhaps we need to work proactively to strengthen and protect the neural pathways most impacted by them.

Regarding stress, the 'gold standard' studies cited by Davidson and Goleman showed a strong dose-related impact; that is, the more subjects meditated, the more subdued their stress reactivity became.

Much of the research in this area involved experiments in which subjects were put in a range of difficult or challenging situations, while scientists monitored activity in the amygdala, the part of the brain that is responsible both for directing our attention and for intense emotional reactions. For example, in one study subjects were asked to look at a range of photos, including some of patients with extreme burns; in another, participants were required to solve complex mental maths problems in front of an unsympathetic panel of 'judges'. Scientists in a third study strapped metal plates to their subjects' wrists, before gradually heating them. (Speaking of digital distraction, at this point in my research I stopped and typed a query into Google: 'Do participants in scientific research get paid?' The answer is often yes, but whatever the amount, it's surely not enough.)

Summing up the conclusions from these and other stress studies, Goleman and Davidson noted that 'more daily practice seems associated with lessened stress reactivity'; that is, meditators were less upset by negative situations, and those with more experience tended to be the calmest in unpleasant circumstances. Perhaps most dramatically, in the case of the hot wrist plates experiments, published in 2009 and 2011, the brains of experienced Zen meditators were not only markedly less reactive when processing the increasing heat, but also had a pain threshold that was 2 degrees Celsius higher than that of non-meditators.[36]

As for encouraging better focus and attention, it didn't surprise me at all to learn that several 'gold standard' studies have shown that a meditation practice strengthens a person's 'selective attention'—their ability to focus—and increases the time they can sustain attention. After all, on the first three days of my Vipassana retreat, all I had to do was sit perfectly still and train my attention on the small area of skin beneath my nose, and by 9 p.m. I was exhausted! Now I know why. I was building up my neural pathways for attention at an intensity I'd never attempted before.

One way scientists have of measuring attention is by monitoring what is known as the 'attentional blink': the moment when the mind relaxes or 'celebrates' after it has recognised or spotted something it has been looking for. Until relatively recently, it was assumed that this blink was a fixed part of neural processing and could not be trained. But then Richie Davidson decided to measure the attentional blink in a group of meditators before and after they had been on a three-month Vipassana retreat.[37] Using a common test, he showed each of them a long series of letters, each flashed up at about 1/20th of a second. The meditators were told that mixed in randomly with the letters were one or two numbers they needed to look out for.

After watching the series, they were asked what numbers, if any, they saw. Typically, if the two numbers are shown in close succession, most people will miss the second one as their attention 'blinks'. And so it was with the meditators before their retreat. But after three months, Davidson's subjects showed an average 20 per cent reduction in their attentional blink compared to the control group who had not attended the retreat, shattering the conventional scientific wisdom that held it was hardwired. A seasoned meditator himself, Davidson surmised that the meditators' brains, trained in maintaining a state of calm non-reactivity, had not 'celebrated' with an attentional blink after spotting the first number, and had therefore remained alert enough to spot the second one.

Two years after that study was published, a 2009 German study compared results between age groups and found that meditation training could also help offset the increasing frequency of the attentional blink that commonly happens as we age, degrading our ability to remain alert; older meditators in this study did better than those in a younger group.[38]

Again, not everyone has the ability to withdraw from the world on long meditation retreats. But this is just a taste of what is possible. Other studies noted as 'gold standard' by Goleman and Davidson found reductions in the attentional blink after just seventeen minutes of mindfulness practice by a group of beginners, although the authors caution that this improvement is unlikely to last without more practice.[39]

Similarly, University of California researchers found that even a short mindfulness session, in which participants counted their breaths for eight minutes, improved their concentration and lessened mind wandering.[40] The same researchers then ran a two-week course in which volunteers did a total of six hours of mindfulness training (exploring mindfulness in daily activities like eating, in addition to the breathing practice), plus daily ten-minute sessions at home on their own. Again, the volunteers practising mindfulness showed improvements in attention, as well as in working memory, compared to a control group who had studied nutrition instead. And perhaps the biggest selling point: the mindfulness group achieved a 30 per cent improvement in marks on their entrance exams for graduate school.[41]

As mentioned above, meditation alters other neural pathways that are not directly related to mitigating the effects of digital overload, but are nevertheless worth considering when we feel overwhelmed by negativity in a noisy world. Currently, for example, there is a surge of research interest in loving-kindness (*metta*) meditation, which aims to cultivate compassion for all beings. Studies have already found this form of meditation is the fastest at delivering a positive sense of well-being—in as little as seven minutes—although again this is likely to be transitory without further practice. But according to one study published in 2018, a two-week training period was enough to alter the neural circuitry related to altruism and responses to suffering.[42]

Of course, feeling good is very different from doing good. But there is a growing body of scientific literature that suggests teaching loving-kindness meditation, particularly to people working in caring occupations such as teaching or health, and to those who have to serve the public in high-pressure environments, may have a broader social impact. The prestigious Stanford Medical School is just one institution taking the research seriously: it now incorporates the Center for Compassion and Altruism Research and Education, which has educated more than 100 Compassion Cultivation Training (CCT) teachers to lead courses around the world.

And it would be remiss of me not to note just one more potential benefit of meditation, if only because this one has been highlighted by an Australian—and not just any Australian, but the first and only Australian woman to win a Nobel Prize. Born in Hobart, Tasmania, biochemist Elizabeth Blackburn jointly won the 2009 Nobel Prize in Medicine or Physiology for the discovery of how chromosomes are protected by telomeres and the enzyme telomerase.

Blackburn often characterises telomeres as similar to the plastic tips on the ends of shoelaces that prevent them from fraying. In this analogy, the shoelaces are our chromosomes, which must be protected and copied in full when our cells divide in order for us to remain healthy. In the early 1980s, Blackburn discovered that our chromosomes had 'tips'—the telomeres—with a particular DNA, which protected them from being broken down. However, she also observed that with each cell division, the telomeres usually became shorter. As they did so, the cells aged, with the associated risk of diseases like diabetes, heart disease and cancer increasing.

This made her next breakthrough particularly exciting. In 1984, with her then PhD student Carol Greider, Blackburn co-discovered telomerase, an enzyme that regulates the length of the telomere, controlling the ageing of cells. In some cases, telomerase even replenishes and rebuilds the telomere, potentially reversing the ageing process. When awarding the Nobel Prize to Blackburn, Greider and their colleague Jack Szostak in 2009, the committee said their work had 'added a new dimension to our understanding of the cell, shed light on disease mechanisms and stimulated the development of potential new therapies.'[43]

But what has this weird biological shoelace tip got to do with meditation? For one thing, Blackburn's discovery inspired studies on how to boost telomerase production or deliver more of it to the body—through creams or pills, for example. But in 2000, Blackburn received an email from a psychologist, Elissa Epel, who had been studying the impact of stress on mothers caring for chronically ill children. Epel wanted Blackburn's opinion on whether that sort of sustained pressure might show up at a biological level, in a carer's telomeres.

'I suddenly saw telomeres from a whole new viewpoint, from a completely different mountain,' Blackburn told Cameron Stewart, *The Australian*'s Washington correspondent, in 2019. 'She [Epel] was interested in ageing, in how people famously get haggard when they are under long stressful situations. It was a great question—it was so simple but no one had asked it.'[44]

As a working mother herself, Blackburn was particularly interested in the challenge. The research that followed confirmed that stressed people did indeed have unusually shortened telomeres. That was the bad news. The good news: people can slow their own ageing process at a cellular level by making good lifestyle choices. In 2017, Blackburn and Epel published *The Telomere Effect: A revolutionary approach to living younger, healthier, longer*. The book recommends many familiar lifestyle changes: exercise more, eat more nutritious foods, get more sleep. But it also notes that a wandering, unfocused mind, or a ruminating, negative one, can increase the sorts of stress that decrease telomerase activity and shorten telomeres.

Since winning the Nobel, a major focus of Blackburn's research has been on how meditation techniques can calm the mind, disrupt negative thought patterns and, ultimately, increase anti-ageing telomerase activity. Blackburn is the first to admit that this research is still very new—but she is also now a dedicated meditator.

In other words, meditation can no longer be dismissed as 'woo-woo', the province of 'trippy hippies' or just 'some voodoo nonsense'. As I type those dismissive comments, all of which I've heard myself over the years, I can't help but wonder about how much money is spent every year on more 'mainstream' products and services that promise to help the consumer lose weight, or slow their ageing, or boost their sexual prowess, with little or no scientific research to back the claims, and potentially more dangerous side effects.

Of course, it's richly ironic that the proliferation of digital devices within our lives has made access to meditation training and advice so much easier. Apps like Headspace, Calm, Insight Timer, 10 Percent Happier and Waking Up all offer great tools for establishing a meditation practice, as well as courses by highly regarded teachers, many of them for free. Rather than be a purist and refuse on principle to engage with digital devices, I'd prefer to take the good with the bad, especially if the good can actually mitigate the bad.

These days, I try to meditate for at least half an hour each day. If I can, I try for two sessions: one in the morning and one before bed. It's less than Goenka recommends for graduates of his ten-day Vipassana retreats—he prescribes a two-hour minimum—but the science outlined above suggests that even the amount I'm doing will have positive impacts that are likely to build if I maintain the practice.

I'd love to say that it has made me superhuman, and that I am now completely impervious to the temptations of social media or the digital rabbit hole that is news and analysis online. But I'm not. What I have noticed is that I am much more alert to those moments when my mind wanders, so much so that I have removed social media apps from my phone, and work with a productivity tool that blocks internet access on my computer at certain times of the day.

More compellingly, although it's sometimes confronting too, I find myself more aware of the stories I reflexively tell myself when the going gets tough, and more inclined to take a step back and watch them with a degree of dispassionate interest, rather than get swept up in the drama of it all. A confession: I am an anxious person, prone to chronic insomnia. Deadlines—including the one that looms as I type these words about the calming effects of silence—often trigger my anxiety and sleeplessness. (And yes, I can see the irony in piquing my anxiety by writing about peace and quiet!)

Meditating hasn't completely cured these conditions. But it has certainly given me the ability to recognise how my Monkey Mind starts chattering—*You're crazy! Who will read this? Why do you even bother? You should get a real job! You're being financially irresponsible and will die in poverty! Why don't you do the laundry since you've got nothing better to do than write? Or what about some Netflix? Twitter?*—when faced with a challenge like writing. Once you begin to see it like that, it's easier to be amused by your little monkey's attempts to distract you from something it thinks might be boring or hard or threatening. 'Nice try, monkey, but I've got this. Now, go and sit over there and we can binge-watch old episodes of *Suits* later.'

I still yell at my kids. But I think I do it less often. I explain it this way: by resetting my brain regularly to a quieter level, with less mess from multiple sources, it makes it easier to spot when there is a new noise or input that demands my attention. Too often I think we lose it with our kids because our brains are already overloaded with the noise of the day, and it only takes one more thing—'But he poked me first!'—to push us over the edge.

External, man-made noise still tests me. I think it tests all of us in the modern world, more than we know. Which is why I have become passionate about the spaces that are naturally—as in, 'of nature'—quiet.

# 9

# NATURE

Every December, my family—my parents, siblings and now our children—turn our faces to the north and travel to the sea. We have been doing it for more than 40 years, this journey to the coast, but I hadn't recognised it as an intergenerational ritual until one day a few years ago, when my elder son paused while eating breakfast.

A Moreton Bay breeze had drifted in from the back deck, nudging a hint of tangy salt ahead of it. Outside, the sun was gaining power, reminding us that in a few months' time it would not just be shining. It would be hurling beams that would land on the skin with a sizzling thump.

'Soon,' my son decreed, not quite pausing between mouthfuls of cereal, 'we'll be going to Noosa.'

He didn't need a calendar. The scent in the air, the quality of the light told him everything he needed to know. It was almost summer—and that, for our family, meant travelling to the beach.

The town of Noosa Heads has changed dramatically since I first holidayed there as a six-year-old. Back then, it was little more than a fishing village tucked in beside a national park. Long before that—for tens of thousands of years, in fact—it had been a sacred area for the Kabi Kabi people, but it took a bunch of surfers to 'discover' its delights on behalf of white tourists in the late 1960s.

We stayed in a tiny unit in a dilapidated weatherboard shack. I don't remember much about it, apart from it always being dark regardless of the weather outside, with a pervasive smell of mildew and an orange vinyl couch that clung aggressively to the backs of sweaty legs. None of that mattered, though, because the turquoise Pacific glimmered just across the back lawn, and over the side fence was a tangle of rainforest where we could play hide-and-seek for hours.

A few doors up Hastings Street, there was a hamburger shop run by a diminutive, gravelly voiced woman named Betty. She had an Australian accent as broad as the Nullarbor, and she often cooked barefoot, having stepped out of her thongs, but Betty was a very savvy businesswoman. She'd worked out that if you installed a grill behind a basic counter in a sandswept concrete arcade leading to the beach, you could forget the niceties of decor or table service. Just keep frying up meat patties and onions and that smell would drift across the sand and out to the surfers and the swimmers, who would come in their hordes, salt-crusted and starving.

Apart from Betty and the lure of her famous $1 burgers, our favourite haunt on Hastings Street was the souvenir shop. To my child's eyes it was a treasure trove: coral painted in garish colours, jewellery boxes encrusted in shells, and an array of 'naughty' items like a pen with a cartoon swimmer etched on its barrel; when you picked the pen up to write, the swimmer lost her bikini. For those on a budget, there were always postcards with an array of lewd cartoons and messages, often inspired by a nearby beach that had become popular with nudists: 'I went to Noosa and got crabs!' 'Bum-tiddy-bum! Hi from Noosa!'

That Hastings Street is barely recognisable today. After twenty years behind her grill, Betty was forced out by a property developer with big plans for that unpretentious arcade. Opulent apartments now cram the shoreline, while their tenants' luxury cars cram the road. Along the street, designer boutiques and chain stores vie for space with swanky cafes and gelaterias. Nobody has embraced Betty's philosophy of keeping prices so low they become legend.

But one thing about Noosa Heads hasn't changed much. The Noosa National Park remains the highlight, for me, of our annual holiday. So many memories were made here: first topless sunbathe, first naked swim, first X-rated canoodle in the surf . . . you get the idea. There's something primal about this place, something so fresh and vivid that it has the power to override the executive function of the brain— the part where we make to-do lists and work out what time we need to leave to beat the traffic home, not to mention where we remind ourselves to put on sunscreen and debate the legalities or otherwise of topless sunbathing—and demand the full attention of the senses.

Perhaps that's why I have never felt comfortable visiting the national park with earphones in my ears. Over the years, I have walked, jogged and run its coastal track many times. But I've never lasted long with music or podcasts—and for the longest time I couldn't work out why. Believe me, I'm not someone who likes running, and when the temperature climbs into the high twenties by early morning, and the humidity soars even further, I usually welcome anything to distract me from the pain. But pumping artificial noise into my head while visiting this little piece of heaven feels sacrilegious.

So I walk, stripped bare of noise, and remember. I remember the spot just past Tea Tree Bay where I once used urgent hand gestures to explain to some excited German backpackers that the brown snake coiled on the path was *really* best left alone. And the place where you'd smell a pungent blend of musk and eucalypt, alerting you that koalas are somewhere overhead. And the headland where, years ago, I glanced down and spotted an enormous turtle lazily stroking its way into an inlet between the cliffs, unperturbed by the enormous waves exploding onto rocks nearby.

It isn't silent. Far from it. For much of the track, you're accompanied by the sound of breakers: their hiss and hum as they collapse onto sand, the rattle and clackety-clack when they snatch and grab at volcanic stones and small boulders. There's one particular spot where the acoustics can take you by surprise. Rounding a bend high above another bay, you sometimes hear conversations from below as clearly as if you were walking with the speakers. Usually the voices belong to young men, joking, carousing, sometimes insulting. It can be unnerving if you're on your own—until you realise that a shift of the wind has carried these sounds up from the surfers on the point below, across a natural amphitheatre formed by the curve of the coast.

But my favourite part comes towards the end of the trail. Fewer people make it here, because the path is still unsealed and rocky, and there are fewer trees to provide relief from the heat. Out on this headland, battered by wind and scorched by the sun, only the toughest survive: kangaroo grass and wallum banksia, hardy casuarina and the occasional smattering of rice flowers and golden everlasting daisies.

As you turn onto this section, something else changes as well. At first, you may think you hear thunder, and scan the horizon for massing clouds. But even when the sky is clear, the booming bass is present. Then you might notice what's missing: the endless crashing of breakers. That gives you a hint. The low, sonorous rumble is the sea itself. Here, away from the gentle slope of beaches and coves, the cliffs of Noosa National Park plunge into deep ocean. That resonant booming is the sound the sea makes as it shifts and shudders against the land. If our planet breathes, this is the sound I think it must make.

Up here, alone on this rocky outcrop, I feel my breath steady into a rhythm set by something much larger than me. Up here, I feel spacious, clean. Sometimes, I feel almost timeless. It is healing. But is it silence?

'Silence isn't the absence of sound. It is the presence of everything.'

I don't recall where I was when I first read those words. But I do remember when I first heard the person who wrote them, because his voice stopped me in my tracks.

Back when I was still commuting to and from work in Sydney, I had started listening to podcasts. Guiltily, at first, because I felt certain there were more important things for me to read—economics briefs, policy analysis—as well as breaking news to listen out for on the radio. But for reasons I didn't understand then (they're glaringly evident now), I started listening to Krista Tippett's *On Being* podcast and was quickly hooked. If you haven't heard of it, *On Being* began on American public radio, albeit under another name for a while, as a small corner where Tippett, a softly spoken journalist turned diplomat turned Yale divinity scholar, could interview guests about religion, faith and spirituality. Very often, when exposed to the subtle heat of Tippett's intellect and boundless curiosity, those topics would melt and expand, and conversations about the meaning of life itself would begin to flow.

Usually the guests are theologians, philosophers, poets or scholars, with the occasional scientist, social activist or psychologist thrown in. But one day I tuned in and heard a voice that sounded . . . well, had I known what the voice sounded like, I probably wouldn't have stopped in my tracks on a side street in Neutral Bay, as joggers dodged me with exaggerated huffs of irritation and parents tugged fractious toddlers out of the gate of a nearby day care centre. There was something about Gordon Hempton's voice that I couldn't place. I found it compelling, with a tone and a turn of phrase that lodged in my brain like an earworm.

It's hard to capture the unique cadence of a voice in words on a page (or on screen). But if you had to choose someone—anyone in the world—to tell your child a bedtime story, a story they had to make up on the spot, filled with greater meanings and told in tones both mystical but also calming, a tale that would send your cherished little one off to sleep with a serene smile on their face, a few good options would quickly come to mind. I'd let you have J.K. Rowling. You could also have A.A. Milne or C.S. Lewis. (Is there a rule that the best children's authors can't reveal their first names?)

I would choose Gordon Hempton. Perhaps he'd tell his story about how the earth is really a solar-powered jukebox. Or how, in autumn, enormous Roosevelt elk bellow guttural mating calls across the Pacific Northwest of the United States, but if you're listening from a few kilometres away, in a very quiet forest with the acoustics of a cathedral, those bold declarations of virility are somehow transformed into 'a magic flute' by the time they reach your ears. Or about an isolated beach in a corner of America where there are logs so large you can crawl inside them and hear music, because the quality of their wood makes them hum with the ocean like nature's largest violins.

Hempton isn't a children's author. He is an acoustic ecologist and sound recordist—or, as he prefers to describe himself, a 'sound tracker'. It's a vocation that found him, rather than one he sought out. When he was 27 years old, Hempton was on his way to university to study plant pathology when he pulled off an interstate highway between Seattle, in Washington state, and Madison, in Wisconsin, to rest in a cornfield. While he was lying there, a large thunderstorm rolled across the landscape. 'It was on that day that I really discovered what it means to be alive as another animal in a natural place,' Hempton told Tippett in an interview for *On Being* in 2012. 'That changed my life. I had one question and that was: how could I be 27 years old and never truly listened before?'[1]

Hempton decided to ditch university and devote his life to collecting the sounds of the world. Almost four decades later, he has circled the globe three times and recorded more than 60 albums of soundscapes, which are used in films, TV shows and video games, and by fans simply seeking listening pleasure. In 1992, his television documentary *The Vanishing Dawn Chorus* won him an Emmy.

It might seem odd that Hempton is also a passionate activist for silence. But his definition is specific—he describes silence as a natural acoustic state, free of intrusions from modern, man-made noise—and it's a quality he has seen steadily eroded, disappearing over the years from many of the formerly pristine natural environments he knows so well.

As a benchmark, Hempton aims to identify places with a 'noise-free interval' of fifteen minutes or more. That may not sound particularly remarkable, but Hempton estimates there are only twelve locations left in the continental United States where he can be confident of recording nature unblemished by man-made noise for that amount of time. He keeps them on a personal register he calls 'The List of the Last Great Quiet Places'; he won't reveal most of them, as there are no laws protecting them from intrusion or noise pollution.

His favourite wilderness spot on the planet is the Hoh River Valley, a temperate rainforest in Olympic National Park, which is close to Hempton's home in Washington state. In the Hoh, with its centuries-old Douglas firs, Sitka spruces and western hemlocks soaring up to 100 metres high, and its annual average of 480 centimetres of rainfall that deters noisy tourists but encourages thick, noise-absorbing moss, Hempton had previously been able to record hours of pristine natural sounds. But with the explosion of air travel across the United States, that interval was slowly eroded; the rumble of commercial flights— and, more recently, training runs by the US Navy's fleet of Growler fighter jets stationed on a nearby island—can now disrupt the Hoh's tranquillity several times a day.

Troubled by the steady encroachment of noise back in 2005, Hempton walked 6 kilometres into this ancient forest and placed a small red pebble on a moss-covered log. There, he declared—silently, and with no audience at all—that this was 'One Square Inch of Silence'.

For a quiet act, it resonated around the world. It led to Hempton's voice being heard on Capitol Hill in Washington, DC, where he lobbied politicians and bureaucrats to protect One Square Inch by banning flights over Olympic National Park. It led to a book, *One Square Inch of Silence*, co-authored with John Grossman, and then to Hempton's views being aired in countless media interviews. More recently, it led to a guest podcast, *Sound Escapes*, in which Hempton showcased some of his favourite soundscapes from around the world, in the hope that listeners would be seduced by nature's myriad symphonies and join his campaign to protect them.

Eventually, Hempton's voice would be heard as far afield as India, in the very noisy city of Mumbai, where highly successful tech entrepreneur Vikram Chauhan would decide not just to join the campaign, but to kick it up a notch. Together, Chauhan and Hempton would found Quiet Parks International in 2018, which is dedicated to identifying and protecting quiet spaces around the world.

Hempton's campaign also led to that conversation with Krista Tippett. And then his voice bounced around the world several thousand more times to podcast listeners, before it was eventually heard by a burnt-out communications professional in early 2017 as she stood bewitched on a busy Sydney street at twilight.

Funny how things work like that.

Remember, back then I was yet to go to Gwinganna, or to New Camaldoli, or to Tarrawarra Abbey. I was yet to have conversations with monks, or to meditate silently in the Tasmanian bush for ten days. All that lay ahead of me. Back then, I was still fervently hoping that someone would simply give me a prescription that would erase the noise from my head so I could get on with my noisy job in the noisy city, and continue my noisy life. I'd tried sleeping pills. I'd tried exercise. I'd tried the occasional spa break. Now, as I held my own against the joggers snootily making it clear that Sydney footpaths are for *hustling*, not for epiphanies triggered by tales of libidinous bugling elk on the other side of the world, I decided that the Sound Tracker would know what to do.

I'll confess that when I finally made contact with him via email, I may have been hoping Hempton would simply hand over his List of the Last Great Quiet Places, or at least the Australian section of it, so I could book a trip and get my head clear. But you don't spend

40-plus years listening as Mother Nature reveals herself and not learn a thing or two about human nature as well. Like Father Michael Casey, I suspect, Hempton had encountered a few noisy people—or people with noisy heads—seeking a quick fix. It became clear he was not going to surrender his list just because I asked nicely. Indeed, he neatly dodged my requests for him to name the best places in Australia to listen to silence. He was always charming, and often highly entertaining. But as our emails flitted across time zones over weeks and months, I began to feel a bit like the slow but well-meaning kid in the class. I was asking lots of questions, but I wasn't really getting it.

Meanwhile, Hempton told me he was busy planning a trip to the Zabalo River, in Ecuador, a part of the Amazon he considers the most pristine soundscape he has ever heard. Given that the western Amazon is arguably the most densely biodiverse spot on the planet, it is also one of the noisiest. But the din of howler monkeys and scarlet macaws, not to mention the thrumming of fat drops of rain falling from plate-sized leaves, is an all-natural one. It therefore triggers very different sensory reactions in humans—who are, after all, animals too—than the din of construction sites and food court muzak and iPhone notifications. Hempton's vision was to accompany small groups on listening tours of the Zabalo, with the cooperation and input of indigenous owners, who were keen to find viable economic opportunities that would help them resist pressure from oil and mining interests.

'The Cofán's tribal land is as close to a world undisturbed as I've ever seen,' Hempton said. 'Nature's symphony has been evolving undisturbed there for millions of years and it is absolutely remarkable. For people who live amid noise pollution, which science has made abundantly clear is bad for your health, coming to a place like the Zabalo River is an opportunity to discover new ways of listening and hearing.'

Maybe an Ecuadorean adventure would fix my head. But I couldn't stomach the thought of my family's faces, if I announced over dinner that I was draining the holiday savings account to go on a camping trip to the Amazon without them.

I was, however, intrigued by how an often cacophonous jungle orchestra could rejuvenate someone who had been overwhelmed by urban noise. Hempton's descriptions brought to my mind the tumult of sounds around Noosa National Park: the variety of bird calls and wind playing with different types of leaves, the crashing surf on sand and the constant, low-throated thrumming of the ocean. On a decibel meter it, too, could be a very noisy place. But like the Zabalo, could it also be a place to commune with silence?

Hempton answered by painting a word picture—or, more precisely, a soundscape. 'To my ears the most musical beach in the world is Rialto Beach, on the Olympic Peninsula,' he began. 'It is there on a windless day that the Pacific delivers one of the most peaceful and relaxing concerts. At low tide, the sand is exposed so the swells break with a resounding thud, but briefly, and all is quiet and I can hear my footsteps, seabirds feeding, and the echo of the surf faintly returning from the forest nearby.

'As the tide level rises, the swells reach the pea gravel, where bright highlights then tip the thuds with a delicious accent. When the tide rises further, we enter the pebbles and cobblestones and this increase in substrate size scales downward the tone. If the wave is large enough, it is possible to hear the whole beach at once, as if fingers sweeping across the keys on a piano.

'But every place has its music, when we listen closely. If it is quiet enough, you might be able to discern the faint meaningful uniqueness of each place. And the quiet between the notes is key.'

So yes, it seemed I could experience the power of silence on a beach.

Hempton added that his ocean soundtracks were always bestsellers, and he had a theory as to why. 'The first place we hear nature's music is inside the womb,' he said. 'There, in that safety, we hear the beating of our mothers' hearts. When we emerge, our breath becomes our own spiritual metronome. And when we hear waves pounding on a shore, we're reminded again of that primal essence, and we will unconsciously synchronise our behaviour.'

Hempton offered to send me a copy of his book, *Earth Is a Solar Powered Jukebox*, in which he expands on such thoughts. It is a delightful mix of highly specific technical advice for sound recordists—how to factor in topography when recording thunderstorms, how to build a wind shield for your microphone and so on—embroidered with the observations of a philosopher-poet: 'Silence is the think-tank of the soul—not the absence of something, but the presence of everything . . . In quiet, we hear who we were, who we are, and who we need to be . . . The art of listening is the art of self-quieting. The art of self-quieting is the art of being. Simply be still and observe.'[2]

Reading this reminded me of a quote I had once stumbled across in a compilation of lectures given by the Tibetan lama Thubten Yeshe when he'd visited Australia in the 1970s. '"Silent" does not mean closed,' Lama Yeshe had told an audience keen to learn more about Buddhist meditation. 'The silent mind is an alert, awakened mind; a mind seeking the nature of reality.'[3]

Hempton does not profess to be religious; he told Krista Tippett he was raised Episcopalian but doesn't go to 'church that's inside of buildings'. Nonetheless, he certainly seemed to share the core Buddhist belief that the calm awareness that can be found in silence will lead us to enlightenment. His highly regarded commercial library of natural sound effects includes an entire section titled *Quietudes*, or recordings made in environments where most sounds occur at the very threshold of human hearing. 'Perhaps the noblest application of *Quietudes* will be the raising of your audience's awareness of the eloquence of silence,' the Sound Tracker advises his aspiring sound recordists, 'which opens the door to spiritual transformations and perhaps ultimately, to legions of more committed citizens of Earth.'[4]

As a newcomer to the idea that spiritual peace or awakening could be found in nature, the mysticism filtering through Hempton's writings fascinated me. But it turns out Hempton was a newcomer too, relatively speaking. Indeed, even the Desert Fathers and Mothers, who sought enlightenment amid the rocks and sand of Egypt in the third century AD, and the bhikkhus of Buddhism, who took retreat in mountain caves, were predated by a far more ancient tradition that ties wisdom to the natural world.

White Australians are still so used to looking to foreign shores for greater knowledge and higher authorities, and it hadn't occurred to me to look in my own backyard. But one day, while researching Christian contemplative traditions online, I stumbled across a video discussion that utterly humbled me.

On the left side of the screen sat a familiar character: Father Laurence Freeman, a Benedictine monk who is the head of the World Community for Christian Meditation. When not hosting retreats in the WCCM's centre in Bonnevaux, south-west of Paris, Freeman travels the world promoting the use of meditation in education, as well as in business and politics; he famously introduced Singapore's founding prime minister, Lee Kuan Yew, to meditation, and he counts the billionaire hedge fund tycoon Ray Dalio and the International Monetary Fund general counsel Sean Hagan among his greatest allies. In his flowing white robes, with wire-rimmed spectacles framing an intent gaze, Freeman looked as serene at this meditation conference, hosted by the Australian Catholic University, as he was when engaging in interfaith dialogue with the Dalai Lama.

Beside him sat a small, grey-haired woman in a pink cardigan, her name tag slightly askew and her handbag tucked next to her chair. You don't often see women like Miriam-Rose Ungunmerr wired up with a headpiece to address a conference audience. There are at least two reasons for this. One is that Ungunmerr is a Malak Malak elder from the Northern Territory, and Aboriginal leaders are rarely invited to contribute to public discussions in modern Australia, beyond the remit of 'Indigenous affairs'. The other is that Ungunmerr prefers to teach at home in Nauiyu, a remote Aboriginal community on the banks of the Daly River, about 250 kilometres south of Darwin. By her own admission, she's never in a hurry to get to the city.

That is doubtless our loss, because Ungunmerr knows a great deal about how to educate and inspire. After graduating as the NT's first fully qualified Aboriginal teacher in 1975, she went on to become a long-serving primary school principal and the driving force behind getting the visual arts incorporated in the Territory's primary school curriculum. She received an Order of Australia in 1998, in recognition of her work in education, and was appointed to the National Indigenous Council in 2004.

Ungunmerr knows that not all learning—perhaps not even *most* learning—should take place behind a desk in a classroom, and it certainly should not stop after a person reaches adulthood. In 2017, she released a video online, in which she spoke at length about the concept of *dadirri*, a state of being as much as a spiritual practice that involves 'inner, deep listening and quiet, still awareness'.[5] It captured the attention of contemplatives around the world, even inspiring Irish folk singer Luka Bloom to write a song about it.

'This is our most unique gift,' Ungunmerr said of the value of *dadirri* to Indigenous people. 'It is perhaps the greatest gift we can give to our fellow Australians ... It is something like what you call "contemplation".' Ungunmerr is a practising Catholic, and sees her two forms of spirituality as complementary, not contradictory. But, like Hempton, she has no need of man-made churches or chapels to practise the deep listening she espouses. 'I can sit on the riverbank or walk through trees; even if someone has passed away, I can find my peace in this silent awareness. There is no need of words. A big part of *dadirri* is listening.'[6] That, it seems, is the big hurdle for non-Indigenous folks, particularly those from big cities, to overcome as they grapple with the concept.

After posting her video, Ungunmerr was inundated with requests to teach others how to practise *dadirri*, and to travel nationally and internationally to lecture on the topic. She joked with Freeman that there were often so many cars parked outside her house in Nauiyu that she had considered installing a parking meter there to raise funds for her not-for-profit foundation, which is committed to creating opportunities for Indigenous youth. (It's not hard for visitors to cause a stir in Nauiyu: its population is just 304 people, according to the 2016 census.)

Ungunmerr speaks to school groups and cultural immersion tours when they make the effort to get to the remote community, but she told Freeman that, once there, visitors often struggle to slow down and let go of the distraction of their devices or the comfort of tightly controlled schedules.

'I can't [just teach *dadirri*],' she said. 'It's not a one day thing, or a few minutes thing. You actually have to live it . . . If you're trying to find yourself and find your spirit, we've got layers and layers and layers of things on top of us that we've got to keep tearing off to find [ourselves].'[7]

According to Ungunmerr, it's natural for Aboriginal people to spend time in the natural world, to release the pressures imposed on them, particularly by white people in faraway cities who framed constantly changing policies. 'I just disappear into the bush . . . I've got the sun and the birds to tell me what time it is,' she said. When asked by Freeman whether she took books or anything else with her to help her practice, Ungunmerr did a double take. 'What for? I'm reading the bush, not a book!' Both laughed heartily. I suspect Freeman appreciates better than most the absurdity of trying to assign words to describe what is silence.

It angers and embarrasses me that white Australians have been denied knowledge of 60,000 years of Indigenous history in this country. Our forefathers and civic leaders may have decided that it was more comfortable to simply deny the brutal impacts of colonialism. Not only has this left great injustices unanswered and festering, tainting all of us, but the refusal to recognise the humanity of those living here before the arrival of Europeans denies all of us the chance to share and learn from wisdom such as this.

'To be still brings peace—and it brings understanding,' Ungunmerr wrote in a longer, text version of her *dadirri* contemplation. 'When we are really still in the bush, we concentrate. We are aware of the anthills and the turtles and the water lilies. Our culture is different. We are asking our fellow Australians to know us; to be still and to listen to us.'[8]

And so I turned to nature to still my soul and quieten my mind. I was yet to experience Vipassana, and was still a novice at any form of meditation. I was guided by instinct, looking for anything that would help the clench of my mind and heart unfurl. It took me a while to be comfortable being physically still, so instead I walked. Not as exercise, for the cardio benefits or to burn calories, or because a knee or hip needed to be rested after too much running. And not for the usual practical reasons—that it's cheaper than a cab, or faster than a bus.

It surprised me at first how unfamiliar this simple activity felt. Walking without any particular time frame or goal, without company, without distraction—simply putting one foot in front of the other and looking, listening, smelling, feeling—seemed self-indulgent. Or just plain nuts.

With no podcasts or music or news and current affairs analysis to amuse it, my brain rebelled: *This is boring. This is a waste of time. You look weird. You look like a loser. You're vulnerable here on your own.* But I kept going—slowly, deliberately—and eventually I started noticing more of what was going on around me. Like a teenager deprived of her favourite mobile device, who tantrums because she is so bored she's 'going to die', my brain eventually calmed down and found other things with which to occupy itself: how the light played on the eucalyptus leaves, how those leaves sounded different from those of the Moreton

Bay figs when a southerly breeze swept through, how the leaf litter and soil smelt after an afternoon shower.

I was embarrassed by how little I knew. When I ran my hand over the trunk of a tree, I wanted to be able to name it: the one that was hard and smooth as marble, the delightful sponginess of the one whose bark peeled away under my fingertips, and the one whose trunk seemed to carry a topographical map of the land around us in shades of mauve and grey. Bird calls that had once blended into an amorphous background chorus now introduced themselves individually, in delicious aural curlicues. I wanted to identify them, too, as if assigning a name or a label would somehow mean I knew them better. And I wanted to know what was responsible for the smell by the creek that sat greasily at the back of my nose and throat, and for the lemony tang that billowed as the track headed upwards into the sunshine.

I knew I could just whip out and turn on the phone that I still kept in my pocket as my security blanket, but I was determined to resist the urge to enjoy the instant gratification of googling for pre-packaged information. Or, my mind told me, I could take photos and make recordings and post them on social media, and they would attract not just the answers I sought, but also the warm glow of 'likes' and other endorsements. But the very intensity of my urge to do those things alerted me that they were probably exactly what I needed to deny; how else to discover what existed on the other side of this quiet *unknowing*?

In those moments, Miriam-Rose Ungunmerr's words would float in my head: 'This was the normal way for us to learn—not by asking questions. We learnt by watching and listening, waiting and then acting. Our people have passed on this way of listening for over 40,000 years. There is no need to reflect too much and to do a lot of thinking. It is just being aware.'[9]

For someone who had excelled at school and then at work by researching, thinking and asking as many questions as possible, this seemed awkward and unreliable. I thought that, as a journalist, I'd become adept at asking the right questions and listening well to the answers, but Ungunmerr seemed to be saying that this was not 'deep' listening—that it excluded more than it invited or accepted.

Similarly, Gordon Hempton often described listening, as it is taught to us in most modern schools, as 'controlled impairment'. Now that was beginning to make sense. 'When we're taught to focus our attention,' he told me, 'what we're doing is learning to listen for a particular sound while screening out everything else as unimportant. But when you go into nature, just listen to the place. Listen to it, just as it is. Ask yourself: can I be here, just as it is? Can I be here, exactly as I am?'

There, with only the trees for company, I grappled with this very new, very old form of learning. What I learned first was not primarily about the natural world, but about myself. Specifically, I learned how this frantic rush back to the intellectual, rational world was actually just my way of maintaining control—or, more correctly, of maintaining the comforting sense that I could be in control. After all, if everything could be classified and ordered and explained, then the world could be expected to behave in predictable, logical ways.

How often had I made that mistake? How often had I been confronted by a decision in my own life and driven myself crazy ruminating on it, telling myself that if I just thought about it hard enough and long enough, one simple, fail-safe solution would emerge? How often had I been frustrated or irritated by the behaviour of others, wondering why on earth they would behave in ways that seemed completely illogical?

Some things just *are*.

Briefly, I allowed myself a flicker of irritation. How often did I have to learn this lesson? Everywhere I looked—in nature, in monasteries and meditation cells—the answer was to stop thinking and controlling, start listening and experiencing. Still, somewhere in that lesson was also the message that I had to be forgiving of myself. Some things just *are*.

I had learned something else, too, by the time we made the decision in early 2018 to move to Brisbane. Having ready access to the natural world—to be able to write while looking at trees; to walk and feel earth underfoot, not concrete—was no longer a 'nice to have' for our next home. It was an essential.

We decided to rent a house until we got our bearings again. It was lovely: a raucous gang of kookaburras would gather every afternoon in the surrounding gum trees, like a gaggle of old mates having a beer after work at the local, while a glamorous pair of king parrots made eyes at one another on the sprawling back deck. But it wasn't ours.

One day, almost a year after we moved, I took a deliberate detour to drive up the street where I'd grown up. Our family had moved from that house when I was about eleven, but my most vivid childhood memories were posited there.

While living in New York in my twenties, I'd begun having a recurring dream about the view from my bedroom in that house, which backed onto the bushland of a fauna reserve. In my dream, I saw the uneven stone steps that led down to our backyard, and even the thick moss that grew in the crevices. I saw our old iron swing, painted maroon and veiled in spiderwebs; we'd rarely used it because the thick wooden seat was slowly disintegrating, and would plunge splintered daggers into the backsides of those who wriggled too much. Beyond the swing, I saw the track, choked with lantana, that led into the bush. I could smell the pawpaws that grew overhead, although few survived the screeching hordes of fruit bats that visited at night. I also saw the creek that flowed through the bottom of the reserve. Sometimes, when I was small, I'd dreamed that the water was rising and there were crocodiles living in it. But I never felt scared. Twenty years after overlooking that view as a child, I would wake on the Upper West Side; the only screeching would be from sirens and brakes, the only trees the tenacious Callery pears that could survive the sidewalk assault of snow, salt and dogs.

Another twenty years on, I was looking at that view again—and at a 'For Sale' sign three doors up from our old house. Was it meant to be? As I write, many of the trees that imprinted themselves on my childhood imagination are part of the canopy outside my study window. I walk among them as often as I can. The lantana has been cleared—and I haven't seen any crocodiles yet.

Being back in Brisbane means that I can more easily get in my car and head north to the sea. Not just in summertime, with my family, but sometimes on my own, when I am feeling frazzled or overwhelmed. I drive for about 90 minutes, and then Noosa National Park greets me like a prodigal child. These days, I care less about what I look like; I let my fingers trail over the silky textures of the paperbarks, stop and place my palms flat on the cool, mottled surface of a towering eucalypt. Periodically, I try to learn their names and classifications. But when I am there, I focus simply on being present.

I find one of my favourite bays, one that is often unoccupied, or just about. I lie on the sand until the sun's heat has penetrated skin, flesh, muscles and finally bones. Then I walk slowly into the breakers. I don't swim; not at first. Often, I just stand under the vast dome of the great southern sky and let the sea do its work, the waves pummelling me, the salt scouring me clean.

Sometimes I hear Miriam-Rose Ungunmerr's voice, describing her own connection with water: 'There is nothing more important than what we are attending to ... We are River people. We cannot hurry the river. We need to move with its current and understand its ways.'[10] And other times it is Gordon Hempton: 'Ask Silence the questions you have. Just ask—and take note of the answers.'

Science, too, offers plenty of reasons for why human beings might benefit from more time in nature. Our first human ancestors appeared somewhere between 5 million and 7 million years ago, probably in Africa. But it has only been about 250 years or so since, during the Industrial Revolution, we began moving en masse from the fields and the forests into factories, shops and offices. In other words, for most of human history—well over 99.99 per cent of our time on earth—men and women have been intimately connected to, and dependent on, the natural world.

When you think about it that way, it shouldn't be at all surprising that we often feel better and healthier when we have spent time in the outdoors. If anything, the real mystery is why we would expect anyone to spend 40 hours a week or more in an environment of artificial light and recycled air, for 48 weeks a year, and continue to perform at peak productivity.

This is a point made often by Chiba University's Professor Miyazaki Yoshifumi, one of the world's leading researchers on the physiological effects and benefits of *shinrin-yoku*, which translates to 'forest bathing'. In 1990, Miyazaki conducted the first experiments to measure the levels of the stress hormone cortisol in people visiting a cedar forest on the Japanese island of Yakushima. The results were promising: visitors' cortisol levels dropped significantly after 40 minutes spent walking among the cedars, some of which were centuries old. But Miyazaki faced the same challenges that confronted Richie Davidson and others when they attempted to explore the impact of meditation in the last decades of the twentieth century. Their instincts were good, but the tools available to test them were still unreliable.

By 2004, the technology had evolved, and Miyazaki and his colleagues had accumulated enough data about the positive impacts of spending time in nature that they were able to convince the Japanese government to commit significant funds (about 270 million yen, or A$4 million) within the country's health budget to drive further research into *shinrin-yoku* and other forms of what's known as 'nature therapy'. Since then, more than 60 forests across Japan have been endorsed as

'Forest Therapy Bases', after scientific evaluation of their natural assets, with each offering at least two forest therapy trails.[11] Hundreds of thousands of Japanese visitors walk the trails each year, either casually or in groups led by guides trained in *shinrin-yoku*. The government funding has ensured that what otherwise might simply be outdoor activity or leisure continues to contribute to science, with visitors often asked to call in at on-site clinics to have their blood pressure and other vitals measured, with the results added to a general database.

For a scientist like Miyazaki, these are dream conditions. Since 2004, he has been able to measure the impact of forest bathing on hundreds of participants, using different physiological and psychological metrics, and in differing conditions. In one extensive experiment, Miyazaki and another Chiba University scientist, Juyoung Lee, studied 756 Japanese university students around the country. Groups of twelve students were each assigned to a different forest across 63 locations. Once on site, the groups were again split in half, then directed to walk either in the forest or in an urban area on the first day. On the second day, they swapped locations. Researchers at each location took a variety of physical measurements from the students after each walk. Cortisol levels were almost 16 per cent lower in those who had been walking the forest trails than in those who had walked the city streets. Those in the forest also returned with a lower blood pressure and heart rate than the urban walkers, but with dramatically higher activity in the parasympathetic nervous system, which is responsible for rest and recovery. Some students were also asked to spend time just sitting in the forest; even those periods produced more positive physiological results than those in the city', although not as strongly as walking.[12]

Health benefits continue even after walkers have left the forest. In 2017, Miyazaki studied office workers, some of whom had high blood pressure, to test the sustained effects of a forest bathing session. He found the average blood pressure of the workers dropped significantly while in the forest, and remained lower for five days.

Meanwhile, immunologist Qing Li, of the Nippon Medical School in Tokyo, focused on how exposure to nature might boost the immune system, particularly by impacting a particular group of white bloods cells known as NK cells, or natural killer immune cells. These form the body's front line against aggressors such as infections or cancers, but stress is known to suppress their activity, making us more vulnerable to a range of serious illnesses when we're stressed. Over three studies, Li found that NK cell activity increased in office workers with weakened immune function after just two hours of forest bathing.[13] The effects continued, increasing by 53 per cent on the base rate after a second day of forest exposure, and lasting for at least a week. Male participants in Li's studies fared particularly well, continuing to enjoy a boost in NK cell activity for up to a month after their forest visit. These findings prompted Li to urge city dwellers to spend at least two hours in nature every two to three weeks, in order to reduce their stress levels; to boost immunity, his 'prescription' was a two-night stay in a forest environment.[14]

The studies spurred Li to try to identify the specific element of the forest that was responsible for the glowing health impacts. He focused on the natural oils, or phytoncides, released by trees. These chemicals protect trees from marauding insects, but they also endow them with their signature smells. Li decided to use hinoki oil, drawn from a cypress native to Japan, for an experiment. Rather than exposing his volunteers to a forest, Li assigned them to city hotel rooms for three nights, with some sleeping in rooms with hinoki oil diffused through vaporisers, and others in unscented rooms. At the end of their stay, Li took blood samples and found that those sleeping in hinoki-infused rooms had enjoyed a 20 per cent increase in their NK cells, while the levels in the control group remained the same.[15]

Such research has burgeoned in the past ten years or so, and now incorporates and tests all manner of potential 'nature therapies', not all of which require time spent outdoors. For example, in one study published in 2014, Miyazaki took 85 high school students, and asked half of the group to concentrate for three minutes on a view that included three common ornamental house plants, while the other group focused on the same view without the plants. The first group reported feeling more comfortable and relaxed after their session, and their physiological measurements reflected as much: they recorded an average 13.5 per cent increase in parasympathetic nervous activity and a 5.6 per cent decrease in sympathetic nervous activity (the fight-or-flight instinct) after looking at the plants.[16]

It's not clear why scientists focused so intently on the benefits of green spaces when they began exploring the physiological and psychological effects of exposure to nature. Perhaps it was just convenience, and a reflection of the average proximity of trees to the average university or research facility. But there are plenty of blue spaces out there too—oceans, beaches, rivers and lakes—and evidence is beginning to mount that their health effects on humans may be just as powerful, if not more, than the green variety.

Ironically, it was a thoroughly modern invention, and one associated with much of our stress, that helped shift researchers' focus onto the benefits of exposure to water. In 2010, researchers at the London School of Economics designed an experiment to map how the environment and other factors impacted on people's mood. They devised an app which would send subscribers a 'ping' at random times throughout the day, prompting them to record their mood, where they were and who they were with. If they were outside, respondents were invited to take a photo of their location and submit that as well. The so-called Mappiness Project was intended to gather data from 3000 users over two months. But the app proved so popular that the researchers extended the study, ultimately capturing more than a million responses from 20,000 people.[17] Mappiness 2.0, which will take the study global, is currently in development.[18]

Some of the findings were pretty predictable. 'Intimacy [and] making love' was rated as the most effective activity at raising one's happiness levels, followed by attending a theatre, dance or concert. Taking care of children was rated a long way down the list, behind drinking alcohol, religious activities, hunting, fishing, sports, hobbies, gardening . . . I could go on. Conversely, the only activity that made people worse than when they were 'working/studying' was being sick in bed. Data from the timing of people's moods also only confirmed what most people already know: the weekend is when most of us feel happiest, while Monday is when we feel most depressed.

But when the researchers turned to location—where respondents were when they recorded their mood—they were surprised. Being closer to water had a marked impact on mood, with those respondents rating their happiness (regardless of activity) as six points higher than those in urban environments. In one interview, the researchers likened this margin as similar to the difference in mood or happiness between someone going to a concert or exhibition and someone doing the housework.[19]

Recognition of the potential value of blue spaces, and research into that possibility, has increased dramatically since Mappiness 1.0. In 2017, the Barcelona Institute for Global Health conducted an analysis of 35 blue space studies, and found that 22 were of 'good quality' and demonstrated 'a positive association between greater exposure to outdoor blue spaces and both benefits to mental health and well-being'. However, they also called for more systematic work to be done.[20] Meanwhile, across the European Union, experts and researchers from various disciplines have been united by the BlueHealth program, which focuses on harnessing the benefits of coastal margins and urban waterways 'to promote health and wellbeing across Europe's cities'. It is due to make recommendations in 2020.[21]

Why does the brain respond so positively to stimuli from the natural world? Different hypotheses exist, but one of the most enduring and widely quoted is Attention Restoration Theory, developed by psychology professors Rachel and Stephen Kaplan, who specialised in environmental psychology at the University of Michigan, in the 1980s and '90s. The Kaplans proposed that the modern world of emails, phone calls, reading and writing demanded sustained 'direct attention', of the type that fatigues our brain's frontal lobes. It is then that we feel 'fuzzy' or mentally exhausted, and find it difficult to continue focusing. While human beings have always faced situations that require such intense attention, the Kaplans theorised that the brains of our ancestors got more chance to rest and recover. That often occurred in natural environments that encouraged 'soft fascination': a state where the brain has stimuli that is interesting, while not needing to be focused on one particular thing. The presence of stimuli is important—a bored brain is not a happy brain (just ask a device-deprived teenager)—as long as they are not too demanding or confronting.

Nature, the Kaplans found, was particularly good at creating conditions that are 'softly fascinating'—ripples on a pond, the changing colours on clouds as the sun sets, the sound of rain on leaves—and their studies confirmed the neural benefits: the brains of those who had viewed images of nature recovered faster, on measures such as executive attention and cognitive performance, compared to those who had looked at urban imagery.[22]

Of course, as Richie Davidson and Daniel Goleman compellingly argued in their own book, one scientific study (or a couple of them) does not make for concrete evidence. Many nature therapy studies have involved relatively small samples, or conditions that have not been replicated, or their results may have alternative explanations. For example, would a person sitting in a cedar forest checking their work emails on an iPhone have a better or worse physiological response than a person sitting in an office meditating with the scent of a pine tree wafting from a diffuser? In a real-world situation, a large range of variables must be factored in.

Meanwhile, I have a confession to make. My deep dive into the science of nature therapy did not immediately prompt me to go out on a bushwalk. What it triggered was an internet search to buy hinoki essential oil. It's bubbling away beside me in a diffuser as I type, a gorgeous fresh smell that is a little like a Christmas tree and a little like a day spa. And what's not to love about those two things?

For Christmas in 2017, just before we moved back to Brisbane, Peter gave me a remarkable gift. He had travelled a lot, both domestically and overseas, in the years since we met. Sharing domestic life with a foreign correspondent—or someone who carries the correspondent's itchy-footed gene in their DNA—means accepting that plans will change often, and sometimes at the last minute.

It helped that I had been on the road as a journalist myself, and shared Peter's insatiable curiosity for new places and experiences. But it didn't help that I was now usually the one left at home in Sydney, with a demanding job and two boys to juggle, yawning through Skype calls about fascinating people in exotic locations while wondering whether there was enough bread for tomorrow's school lunches.

There were so many good things about our life together that it usually didn't bother me too much. But then there was the time Peter convinced me to submit to my younger's sons entreaties for a puppy, insisting that, as the former owner of several dogs himself, he would take care of the house-training and other challenges of adopting a fur-baby. A breeder was found, and we all predictably fell in love with a bundle of black fur with eyes like melting chocolate.

Then, on the day we were due to pick up our new family member, the plans changed—or, as Peter would put it, they were updated. We would not only be welcoming a new puppy into our home that night; we would be welcoming an entire film crew, who needed to shoot some footage for his latest documentary film! Oh, and the next day he and the crew would be heading off for a three-week shoot in France, which had been rescheduled.

I didn't think it was possible, but my noisy life was about to get noisier. The yelping of a lonely pup at 4 a.m. will do that. So too will the bellowing of a son who has just found the TV's remote control in the puppy's mouth, and the yowling of a cat who does not appreciate being asked to share her space, and my own shrieks after stepping in something unspeakable before I've had my first coffee for the day.

Suffice it to say, when Peter arrived back, I was ready for a break. Which is why his Christmas gift to me that year was so wonderfully perfect: the proceeds of his travels—his frequent flyer points—bestowed to me. I think he already knew what I would do with them, as I'd been talking about the Hoh Rainforest for months, in the breathy, reverent tones other people use when they gush about Paris in the springtime, or Aspen in the ski season, or 'Vegas, baby!' at any time. The point of travelling to One Square Inch of Silence was, of course, to explore silence, which was why Peter also offered to stay at home and care for the boys for the two weeks I would be away.

Two weeks! It had been more than a decade since I'd spent that amount of time alone, responsible for nobody else's bedtime or meals or miscellaneous clothes. Perhaps only parents (particularly those who have raised children alone for a number of years, as I had) will truly grasp how outrageous, even seditious, it felt to be booking a trip that included a writers' retreat at a Zen farm outside of San Francisco, followed by several days of hiking in various parts of Washington state.

I deliberately made the Hoh the last stop on my itinerary, as I wanted to factor in plenty of time to wind down before visiting. But even so, when I finally arrived at Olympic National Park, I was overcome by an insistent urge to rush. Sprawling over almost 400,000 hectares, Olympic boasts glacier-capped mountains, ancient temperate rainforests, stunning lakes and several beaches along more than 100 kilometres of wild Pacific coastline. It has been declared a World Heritage Site and International Biosphere Reserve by UNESCO in recognition of this diverse array of pristine ecosystems. In other words, I had arrived in a sensory Eden—and I didn't want to miss a thing.

Long ago, as a university student, I used to marvel at how restaurants like Sizzler, with its all-you-can-eat buffet, would bring out the worst behaviour in people, including my own cash-strapped friends and me. Rather than savour a meal, we were compelled to try a bit of everything, piling our plates high and repeatedly, lest we somehow miss the one *really* good dish that was on offer. The result: we'd waddle out like geese fattened up for Christmas (and we always agreed that the potato skins were the best). I dubbed this urge to overdo it 'the buffet reflex'—and, surveying the maps and tourist leaflets for Olympic, I realised it wasn't just an array of food choices that could trigger the urge to gorge. Confronted by such an array of spectacular destinations, I wanted to see everything in a few days. I had started rushing, rather than savouring my trip and focusing on the reason I was there in the first place. Fortunately, nature intervened.

Late on my first day in the region, I decided to do a short walk to Sol Duc Falls. It was an hour or so closer than the Hoh to the B&B where I was staying, so I thought it would be an easy first trail before I tackled the 10-kilometre return hike to visit One Square Inch. The falls didn't disappoint. Although it was already April, the northern mid-spring, generous drifts of snow were piled high amid emerald-green moss and ferns, creating a vivid patchwork as I followed the trail. Overhead, the red cedars stretched so high that I had to curl backwards, hands on butt to keep my balance, to try to spot their crowns. More snow was clearly feeding the Sol Duc River, which was icy-cold and clear as it roared towards a gorge, falling several metres in a spectacular waterfall before settling in a brilliant blue pool far below.

If this was a sample of what I could see in this part of the world, I was determined to cram in as much as possible. As I walked back to my car, I was already calculating the time left before nightfall and the distances I could cover on the road and on foot. I grabbed the map as I sat in the front seat with the engine off, studying it for several minutes. But when I looked up again, I was no longer alone. Four black-tailed deer had emerged from the woods and were surveying the car keenly. One even leaned into the passenger-side window, nose twitching, tossing its head imperiously when it decided there was no food on offer. Eventually, it moved away and I began to reverse—only to discover another deer behind the car. It peered inquisitively, almost directly, into the reversing camera, all dark-rimmed, come-hither eyes, and for the first time in my life I fully appreciated the power of the description 'doe-eyed'.

I didn't want to scare or hurt these beautiful animals—nor did I want to risk the rental car being damaged if they panicked and ran into it. I could do nothing but sit and wait, and admire the graceful creatures that were paying me an unexpected visit. That's when I realised I really had no reason to hurry anyway—and that if I did rush, I risked missing moments like these. Weren't they part of the reason I'd come to the other side of the world in the first place, to experience what it was like to be more present and aware?

The next morning, I rose before dawn to drive two hours to the Hoh. Throwing back the curtains in my hotel room, the only lights I could see were in another country, across the Strait of Juan de Fuca, in Canada. Dawn's mists were beginning to roll away by the time I stopped for a breakfast snack by the breathtakingly beautiful Lake Crescent. The low levels of nitrogen in its water restrict algae growth, creating startling clarity and colours spanning from brilliant cobalt to turquoise and teal. It began to rain in earnest after I hit the road again. I had never hiked in a downpour before. At least it meant less chance of other visitors—and therefore noise—on my way to One Square Inch of Silence. The low cloud also reduced the possibility of aircraft noise; perhaps I would experience the rainforest the way it had been when Gordon Hempton first fell in love with it.

The last leg of the drive, along the Upper Hoh Road, was like melting slowly into a fairytale. Giant trees crowded the road, their massive branches laced with crystal frills of snow and ice. The car and I were dwarfed within this still, green corridor, which felt simultaneously mystical and familiar, a fragment torn from a dozen children's stories: Narnia, Red Riding Hood, Snow White and the Seven Dwarfs.

There were few cars when I pulled into the Hoh visitors' centre parking lot. As I crunched across the gravel, I spied a gaggle of people ahead of me, but most seemed to be branching off to a shorter trail through the Hall of Mosses. I paused for a moment, uncertain. I'd read about the Hall of Mosses, a green cathedral full of ancient trees, gnarled and bearded with hanging ferns and moss, like the Ents of Middle-earth. Perhaps, I told myself, I should do this trail first, in case I was too tired when I returned from One Square Inch? I was procrastinating—because to take the first step on the longer trail, knowing I would be alone in this soft quiet for several hours, felt like a very big thing. And I suddenly felt very small and exposed.

However, the idea of going home without visiting One Square Inch was too embarrassing to bear. My 'grown-up brain' took over, pushing me on and insisting I pay careful attention to *everything*: my breathing, my pace, the detail of the leaves, the smell of the air. After about a kilometre, the rest of me was thoroughly sick of my brain acting like an earnest science teacher on a field trip, demanding we show avid interest in the pond slime growing in a suburban lagoon, or the dusty collection of rocks we'd collected at a bush reserve.

For a while I sang to myself, and occasionally I became lost in thought, usually pondering the same theme: *What's a nice place like this doing with a president like him?* How odd it seemed that my mission to immerse myself in silence had brought me to a country whose leader governed mostly via shouty abuse on Twitter and hyperbolic grabs for television attention.

The sheer size of the trees never lost its novelty for me. Once, pausing by the Hoh River for a snack and some water, I tried to measure the trunk of a fallen giant that had been washed up on the bank. Leaning against the crosscut section, against the hundreds of rings that documented its life span, I stretched my arms above my head. Still, my fingers couldn't reach to the outside rim of bark. Even in death, this tree towered over me.

After about two hours of walking, the doubts I had faced at the beginning of the trail flocked back—and they'd been practising their lines. Did I really know where I was going? What if I mucked up the directions Gordon Hempton had given me? With no official signs marking Hempton's spot, was I sure I'd know when to turn off the track and onto an elk trail that would take me through boggy grass and ferns to One Square Inch? Hempton had told me that silence was the presence of everything; what he hadn't mentioned was that, in your head, 'everything' can include every piece of criticism and self-sabotage you have absorbed through your life.

Pretty soon I was not just berating myself for thinking I could do a hike like this on my own, with my poor sense of direction. Having claimed some territory in my attention, my inner critic now acted quickly to consolidate. I was self-indulgent to be here. I was delusional to think I might discover something here, on the other side of the planet, that I couldn't have attained at home in Australia, where there were plenty of pristine spaces available. I was embarrassing myself. The Sound Tracker himself was probably laughing at me behind my back, scornful of my pathetic attempts to understand something that was beyond my ken.

The steady drizzle hadn't dampened my spirits, but this excoriating stream of consciousness quickly penetrated where the rain had not. By the time I spied the enormous Sitka spruce with its trunk split so high and wide you could shelter there during a storm, I was trudging forward on pure will alone. I had already travelled more than 12,500 kilometres;

according to Hempton's notes, I now had less than 100 metres to go to make it to One Square Inch. Even so, I managed to convince myself again that I was lost, when in fact I was only a few metres away from the little red pebble. It seemed so easy for me to assume that I would do the wrong thing, rather than give myself credit for getting things right.

Finally, I spied the pebble and settled down next to the large, moss-covered log that served as its pedestal. After walking more than 5 kilometres, stilling my body was easy. Stilling my raucous mind, awash with ripples of irritation, was tougher. Two mosquitoes buzzed hungrily around my head. Raindrops fell with solid *thoks* on my hooded jacket. If I pulled back the hood to hear better, the rain trickled off my nose and chin and formed rivulets that disappeared down my neck. The mat I had brought with me to sit on, in what I thought was a stroke of genius, crackled every time I moved or even drew breath.

But slowly, through all of this, I noticed something else. Towering above me, the Sitka spruces and red cedars, the western hemlocks and Douglas firs, and clustered around me, the huckleberry bushes and deer ferns and wood sorrel—all were simply present. The noise of my mind had affected nothing here. Everything was still and calm, and quiet in a way that I swear I could have touched in the air.

I had felt this kind of presence—a quality of the atmosphere that is as evident as a scent—in other places, particularly around parts of Uluru and Kata Tjuta. So much of what was present had been here long before I was born. Some of it before white men set foot in my country, or on this land. And life would go on here after I left, regardless of how I spent this time. Slowly, my thoughts rolled away like clouds. Perhaps I was delirious, or possibly simply exhausted, but I felt the silence settle on me like an embrace. The trees themselves seemed to lean in slightly, to greet this small, clueless child at their feet.

Before I returned to the trail, I spent some time sitting in the trunk of the split spruce that marked the threshold to One Square Inch. Something about the enormity of this tree, the fact that I could sit right inside it—its great weight stretching above me, the density of its living tissue wrapped around me—was almost incomprehensible. Here, in this hidden spot in the quietest forest I had ever known, I felt safe in a way I couldn't remember, at least not since I entered the adult world.

By the time I hiked back to the car, the only part of me that wasn't wet were my feet. Good hiking boots and socks are a modern marvel. I drove for two hours, stopping only at a restaurant in Port Angeles to buy a pasta meal for dinner. Later, I realised the venue had been made famous by the *Twilight* film about a teenage girl falling in love with a vampire. I wonder what the staff made of the drenched, muddy, crazy-haired woman stumbling in from the rain that night to order Bella's mushroom ravioli.

I rarely write poetry. But later that night, by the fireplace in my room, I jotted some notes to mark my visit:

HOH RAINFOREST
*In a forest*
*In a secret grove*
*There is a Sitka spruce*
*Who can teach you all you*
*Need to know about love.*

*She is waiting for you.*
*I can take you partway there.*
*But it is best for you to arrive*
*On your own*

*With raindrops across your cheeks and nose*
*Like freckles*
*And fingers blue with cold*
*And wondering:*

*'Why am I here?'*
*And*
*'How much further?'*
*And*
*'Am I too old and tired*
*To be doing this anyway?'*

*And you can crawl*
*Beneath her,*
*Right inside her,*
*Where it is dry and almost warm.*
*And near this tree's big heart,*
*Her roots embrace you like a mother.*

*She will not ask you*
*Why it took so long*
*Or remind you that she has been here*
*Two hundred years*
*Or more.*
*She will not ask you*
*What your plans are*
*Or where you are going*
*Or what you wish to be.*

*Because you are enough.*
*Right here*
*Right now*
*In this secret forest.*
*And you can stay with her*
*As long as you wish*
*Or not long at all.*

*Sometimes I wonder*
*If we lined up all the world's leaders*
*(You know the ones)*
*And took them*
*One by one*
*Into this wet, waiting forest*
*To sit in the heart of a tree:*
*Would the world be a more peaceful place*
*Afterwards?*
*I think so.*

*But for now*
*It is enough*
*To tell you of the Sitka spruce*
*Who can teach you all you need to know*
*About love*
*And to know that she is waiting*
*For you*
*For me*
*For all of us.*

# 10

# WORK

Gordon Hempton has dedicated much of his working life to finding and protecting places where natural silence can stretch for more than fifteen minutes. In contrast, my professional career includes a stint in an office where silent periods of a mere five to ten seconds once prompted consternation among my colleagues.

In Sydney in 2017 I had been charged with building a new communications team, which meant interviewing candidates for a variety of positions, some of whom would be required to support the CEO of our organisation with daily media advice. Recruiting can be difficult at the best of times. With senior communications roles, one of the greatest challenges is finding people who have the capacity to convert complex information into simple, compelling messages, the emotional maturity to deal with an array of personality types—including business execs, political leaders and tough-talking journalists—and the energy to master new tools in a rapidly changing media landscape.

As is often the case in the modern workplace, I was tackling the recruitment task while juggling my normal duties. It seemed ironic that in order to lighten my workload, I first had to increase it substantially for weeks, and then months, as the job search continued. As the teetering stacks of résumés spread across my desk, there were times when I wondered whether the effort was worthwhile.

I had divided the applications into three categories: bright young things who knew social media inside out, but who I suspected would be either overwhelmed or bored by complex policy detail; old-school communications professionals who were still managing media via press release and over long lunches with favoured contacts; and the notorious slush pile of applicants who seemed to be applying for another job altogether. None really fit the bill.

So I was thrilled when I heard a rumour that a former colleague, whose professional skills and personal integrity I had always admired, might be on the market. A few phone calls and an informal coffee confirmed as much. He agreed to come in for a preliminary interview, in which he would be assessed by two senior colleagues from outside the communications division, as well as me, before potentially meeting the CEO and other senior execs. I was convinced I had found the 'unicorn': a candidate who blended the wisdom of Solomon with the digital smarts of a Kardashian.

By my reckoning, his performance in the preliminary meeting only confirmed that view. My colleagues, both highly accomplished specialists in their own fields, posed a series of challenging questions directly and sought his opinions more obliquely on a number of fraught scenarios. He gave answers that not only demonstrated both knowledge and insight, they frequently 'added value', incorporating information that none of us had considered. At the end of the meeting, I walked him to the elevator, trying hard not to grin too much when I double-checked his availability for a final interview.

My colleagues had already done a quick debrief when I returned to the meeting room. 'He's great,' said one. The other nodded in agreement. 'There's just one problem.' More vigorous nodding from the other. 'What's with the pauses before he answers questions?' she asked.

'He can't wait that long to talk!' the other declared. 'The boss won't put up with it! It'll drive everyone crazy.'

I was so surprised that I had to take a long pause of my own before answering. I intended no irony; I was simply lost for words. I too had noticed how our interviewee had taken a few moments before answering some of the trickier questions. I'd even counted: he would pause up to eight seconds before offering his thoughts. But those answers, when they came, were so good that I was hardly concerned about a pause that might simply have been a sign of nerves.

This is a book about silence, not office politics, so I'll cut to the chase and say I made darn sure that candidate came back for another interview. He got the job—and he excelled. Not only was his advice impeccable and his work rate remarkable, but in an organisation that had its fair share of prickly personalities and turf wars, he was universally adored for his lovely manner. As I said, he was a unicorn. A unicorn that occasionally liked to stop and think before he spoke.

We remain good friends, although we have both since moved on from that organisation. But my memory of that post-interview discussion with the other panel members lingers, because it says an awful lot about the culture of the modern workplace, in particular which skills and traits are prized, and which are undervalued.

In the scenario I've outlined, the 'cost' of receiving good counsel was several seconds of quiet thought. Over the course of an hour or so of intense discussion, this may have added up to about 30 to 40 seconds of silence. Certainly, there are some environments where such hesitation before proposing a course of action would be a legitimate deal-breaker. But we weren't interviewing for a position in a hospital emergency department, or for a bodyguard to provide close personal protection to a controversial political leader, or for an air-traffic controller. Split-second responses would not be required in this job; nuanced, astute advice would be.

Why, then, the discomfort over the few seconds of quiet reflection it might take to provide it? I believe it springs from a widespread epidemic of 'performative busyness' in our workplaces, where contributions that are quick, disruptive and often loud are valued over those that are slower, considered and detailed.

Before we explore that idea, let's take a step back and consider the broader context in which we're all performing. Most business, political and community leaders would agree they are operating in environments that are more complex than ever before. But we also live in a world where we are more impatient than ever, where we want problems solved immediately, and we are highly intolerant of uncertainty. It is human nature to try to impose certainty, even control, even if it's illusory; neuroscientists have shown that the brain will reach for an available narrative, or construct one itself, rather than try to function in an ambiguous situation.[1]

This tendency has only been exacerbated by the lightning-fast feedback loops of social media, as well as by traditional media's moves to protect and consolidate niche markets by playing to the biases of their audiences, and by the governing ethos of the Silicon Valley firms that increasingly dominate global culture: 'move fast and break things'. It has become the norm to jump swiftly, even reflexively, to a hardline stance on even the most ambiguous questions, and to assume that any problem can be solved if you are confident enough, sometimes to the point of outright aggression.

In this environment, many leaders in politics, business and the media feel they must be the ones to move first and speak loudest—and that has had a ripple effect on their staff and workplaces.

But what if there are problems that aren't solved so quickly? For example, economic growth has slowed or even stalled in mature economies in recent years, and as this book reached the final stages of editing, the COVID-19 pandemic threatened to throw several countries into recession. Even before this most recent crisis, wages growth had flatlined in many parts of the world. Already, many employees have survived waves of redundancies, 'efficiency drives' and other workplace overhauls, and now feel they are working harder than ever before, and yet earning less, relatively speaking. In many cases, they would be right.

There are many different workplaces in this modern world. Some of us, like me, work behind computers, while others work behind counters; some on factory floors and others at front of house. But I'd hazard a guess that almost all of us, regardless of our workplace, have heard that the only way we can improve our lot as a nation is to be more *productive*. That, we are told, is what will drive economic growth, and therefore push up wages. The problem is that nobody—not the economists nor the Treasury advisers nor the business whiz-kids—appears to have come up with a foolproof way of doing this.

This is echoed at the micro level—on the shop floor or in the office, for example—by managers, section heads and bosses who have very little idea how to improve productivity within their own remit. In some cases, a fundamental problem is that productivity has never been rigorously defined, in terms of key goals and outputs, in the first place.

Stuck on this hamster wheel, working harder for longer with no clear metrics for success, how do employees react? According to Safe Work Australia, about 91 per cent of workers compensation claims involving a mental health condition are linked to work-related stress. Perhaps surprisingly, 'work pressure' is cited as the most common cause of this stress, ahead of the more highly publicised (and certainly more serious) problems of bullying and harassment. And while mental health claims represent only a tiny fraction (about 6 per cent) of all workers compensation claims each year, when they occur they are serious: the typical compensation payment is 2.5 times more than the average for all payouts, and those affected spend almost three times as long off work.[2]

Fortunately, most Australians will never suffer this level of workplace stress. But many of us will have experienced or witnessed the warning signs. Safe Work Australia lists unplanned absences and high staff turnover among the more obvious ones. But I was fascinated by another term: 'presenteeism'. In many workplaces where stress is rife, staff work long hours—but not at optimal or healthy levels. In layman's terms, they are 'going through the motions'. Often, they may also contribute to a more widespread phenomenon I refer to as 'performative busyness'.

Performative busyness is the workplace equivalent of 'virtue signalling': those glib acts by which people in the public eye—celebrities, CEOs, political leaders—demonstrate their ideological bona fides by embracing certain social causes, without committing to anything truly significant. Consider, for example, the politician who dons a white ribbon on a certain day each year to signal a concern about men's violence against women, but fails to push a serious policy agenda to tackle the issue.

At work, one of the easiest ways for an employee to signal their virtue is to elaborately showcase their own busy-busy-busyness. They're the folks who circulate reading material via group email on issues that are of peripheral interest at best, always seeking feedback. Or the superior who floats from desk to desk, 'checking in', making a show of collaboration. Or the colleague who asks plenty of questions in routine meetings, not because they're affected by a particular issue or have any responsibility for it, but simply to demonstrate how 'engaged' they are. And the person who schedules all those 'routine' meetings to begin with (more about that later).

Back in my McDonald's days, I quickly learned that anyone who wasn't cooking food or serving a customer was likely to be targeted by a manager reciting the popular company mantra: 'Time to lean, time to clean!' One day, I decided to conduct an experiment. After taking a storeroom inventory, I spent an additional twenty minutes or so wandering the floor of the restaurant with my clipboard and pen. Provided I had those accessories, I discovered, and a look of concentration in my eyes, I was left alone. Everyone assumed I had been assigned another task. I shared this secret with a mate, who confessed he'd observed a similar effect when he strode around purposefully wielding a screwdriver. 'I walk around for a bit and then eventually I just duck outside for a smoke,' he grinned.

Being busy for its own sake has little to do with productivity, of course; nothing got marked off on my clipboard or tightened by that screwdriver. But to the untrained eye, or the eye of a superior who has no clue what else to do, or who has not developed their own metrics for evaluating performance, it *looks* impressive. Nobody could ever accuse this busy bee of not working hard enough!

If performative busyness just wasted the time of the performer, it wouldn't be such a big deal. I certainly didn't mind mooching around that dining room with my clipboard back in the day. But back then, that job was just a money-earner for me: I wasn't building a career, so had limited investment in the overall success of McDonald's. Once we enter the adult world of work and start building our actual careers, though, most of us have more complex tasks to perform, and many more nuanced and important interactions with our colleagues each day. We are likely to place greater expectations on ourselves and our work, especially once it's a full-time commitment, rather than a part-time gig for pocket money—and we are almost certainly going to have greater expectations placed upon us. And yet it is almost impossible to conduct quiet, thoughtful work for any sustained length of time in a workplace dominated by a busy performer. They actively require an audience to witness their efforts—that's the whole point.

Performative busyness erodes silence and generates 'noise' in a number of ways. In some case, the noise is literally auditory, but in many others it is digital noise that intrudes on our attention, heralded by the *ping* of an incoming email or the *blip* of another meeting invitation. Over time, a workplace's culture can be defined by these behaviours. In such an atmosphere, work requiring sustained concentration—the sort that I believe is necessary to foster strategic insight, creativity or problem-solving—becomes so rare that, should it occur, it is sometimes even viewed as suspect. The person who seeks time alone at their desk (or elsewhere) to work uninterrupted for a couple of hours may be labelled lazy, incompetent or, perhaps worst of all, 'not a team player'.[3]

As a journalist, and then as a consultant and also as an in-house employee, I've had the opportunity to observe many workplaces and the leaders who drive them. I've learned that the three most pervasive manifestations of performative busyness are the open office plan, ritual meetings and email overload—and they are often top-down behaviours, endorsed or modelled by the leaders of the organisation. Each one of them generates intrusive noise that detracts from the productivity they are supposed to enhance.

Open offices date back to the 1940s, but in the Anglosphere for most of the twentieth century they were really only intended for the vast banks of secretarial and administrative staff who supported the men who did the 'real work' behind closed doors. (If you've watched *Mad Men*, you'll understand that an awful lot of that behind-closed-doors toil involved whisky, with clothing optional.) But in post-war Germany, more dramatic changes were afoot. Business leaders were keen to signal a shift to a more democratic approach to running things, and thus *Bürolandschaft*, or the open-plan office, was born. It may sound like a sneeze you've tried to suppress while ordering bedroom furniture from IKEA—*Büroland . . . schaft!*—but it translates roughly to 'office landscape', and in this case that working landscape was intended to be more organic and natural.

It was during the 1990s that the open office became genuinely fashionable in English-speaking countries, as the first wave of the tech boom was born out of converted warehouses, lofts and even garages that were available to young entrepreneurial geeks. However, it took Google to make the concept of the open-plan office *really* hip. Of course it did. Back in 2005, the world was still in awe of Silicon Valley—and who was going to criticise a company that built its workers in-house climbing gyms and gave them three free meals a day, plus snacks? Tasked with designing what would become known as the Googleplex—the company's headquarters in Mountain View, California—architect Clive Wilkinson eschewed cubicles and corridors in favour of bright open spaces with lots of colour and glass. 'The attitude was: We're inventing a new world, why do we need the old world?' Wilkinson told *Fast Company* years later.[4]

In 2012, Twitter founder Jack Dorsey took *Forbes* on a tour of the headquarters for Square, his new mobile payments company, drawing attention to how his developers and marketing staff sat at long tables in communal spaces. 'We encourage people to stay out in the open because we believe in serendipity—and people walking by each other teaching new things,' Dorsey explained.[5]

Not to be outdone, Mark Zuckerberg commissioned legendary architect Frank Gehry to design Facebook's new headquarters in Palo Alto, California. Posting a picture of the newly completed building on his own Facebook page in March 2015, Zuckerberg highlighted that 'we designed the largest open floor plan in the world—a single room that fits thousands of people'.[6]

The tech titans had spoken: open plan was the new black.

The assumption was that people at single desks or in contained offices created silos of information, while shared spaces would encourage impromptu information sharing and collaboration. When one designer ran into another on the way to his next free massage, who knows what idea might be born when the two tech bros decided to play foosball in the games room instead—perhaps the right new type of *ping* to alert you that another email has arrived in your Gmail account.

If I'm sounding a little cynical here, it's partly because I've spent much of my adult life in newspaper newsrooms, which were open plan long before that design was cool. And in my own experience, if you allow a bunch of creative folks to roam freely around the workplace, the outcome is often an impromptu game of cricket, ending with someone being hit in the back of the head with a rolled-up newspaper and everyone arguing vehemently about whether that's six and out. (Or perhaps that only happens in the Parliament House Press Gallery in Canberra.) Certainly I've witnessed those freewheeling environments encourage innovation, usually by grumpy colleagues trying to ensure their chairs aren't stolen by their co-workers and replaced by the one with the dodgy height adjustment mechanism. People can be very creative in their use of padlocks, chains, signage and, in one memorable incident, sticky tape and razor blades.

More seriously, you don't have to be a closet Marxist to recognise that the open-plan office design, lauded as a glorious innovation for worker creativity, also happens to be a glorious innovation for the bean-counters in charge of corporate cost-cutting. You can fit a lot more people into a space when you remove walls, doors and corridors. It has also been observed that the hip new open-plan office is a better way to 'monitor staff'—in a casual, not-at-all-Big-Brothery way, of course.

Regardless of initial intent, it seems pretty obvious that an open-plan office is also going to be a noisier workplace, especially when it incorporates lots of polished concrete and glass in a bid to be 'on trend'. It is also very likely to encourage performative busyness. Why? Because its design signals to employees what sort of work is valued here: collaborative and interactive, rather than quiet and focused. That's fine in some industries, but many workers in the 'knowledge economy' actually still need time to think, plan, create and write. 'Collaboration' in this environment often ends up as 'a constant stream of interruptions'.

Journalists are expected to work anywhere, in any conditions. I've filed copy from scorched bushland near a devastating fire front, from the grandstand during a U2 stadium concert, and from raucous street protests and political rallies. Others far braver than me have done so under fire on the front lines of wars and coups. But I've also observed that many of my co-workers chose to work from home if they needed to focus on a big project. Or they would come in early or work late, to avoid the daily hubbub of the office. I often did the same.

More than a decade after the birth of the Googleplex, a plethora of research on how employees behave in open-plan offices has confirmed that we are not alone. In 2013, researchers from the University of Sydney reviewed the workplace satisfaction of one of the largest

data sets of office workers available, drawing on a survey of more
than 42,000 employees in the United States, Canada, Finland and
Australia. They found that exposure to uncontrollable noise, as well as
a lack of privacy, in open offices undermined staff morale. 'Open plan
office layouts have been touted as a way to boost workplace satisfaction
and team effectiveness in recent years,' author Jungsoo Kim explained
when the study, based on his PhD research, was released. '[But] our
research . . . clearly indicates the disadvantages of open plan offices
clearly outweigh the benefits.'[7]

More recently, Harvard Business School researchers used sophisticated tracking technology in an experiment that shattered the
conventional wisdom about open-plan collaboration and productivity.
Professor Ethan Bernstein asked employees at two Fortune 500
companies to wear tracking devices and microphones, designed by his
collaborator Dr Ben Waber, so he could assess their interactions with
colleagues for several weeks before and after they transitioned to open-
plan offices. The staff also granted Bernstein and his co-author, Stephen
Turban, access to their electronic communications during that time. Their
study, published in 2018, found that face-to-face interactions actually
dropped by roughly 70 per cent when the workers moved to open plan.
Meanwhile, staff use of email and instant messenger spiked dramatically,
by 67 per cent and 75 per cent, respectively, in one workplace.

The authors also observed that many employees adopted overt
cues, such as wearing large headphones, to buffer the noise around
them and signal they did not wish to be disturbed. Privacy, Bernstein
later observed, was a 'fundamental human desire', and had also been
shown in other studies to actually increase productivity. The workers
who tried to ward off interruptions, even in ostensibly antisocial ways,
were actually behaving in entirely natural ways that were also likely to
enable more focused work.

'My hope is that this research throws a bucket of ice water on the
idea that there's no trade-off—that you will naturally both save in

real estate costs and get more collaboration from this kind of design,' Bernstein told the Harvard Business School's digital newsroom. 'In general, I do think the open office space "revolution" has gone too far.'[8]

It's important to note that Bernstein also stressed that open plan offices themselves weren't the problem. Rather, he pointed the finger at the failure of management to be clear about what they were trying to achieve. For example, if an organisation required a combination of focused work and collaborative teamwork, it might be better to design an office with a mix of private spaces—cubicles or offices, for example—and 'breakout' rooms for meetings and group interaction. Companies that were under budget pressure to fit more staff into smaller spaces might also consider giving their employees greater leeway to work remotely or with flexible hours, Bernstein suggested.[9]

You might think that all the extra collaboration we're supposedly enjoying in these open-plan offices would reduce the need for what I call 'ritual meetings', those recurring events on the calendar that muster staff regardless of any specific development or event. Unfortunately, the reverse is often true. Certainly, in workplaces where performative busyness is endemic—that is, where even the leaders confuse activity with productivity—meetings proliferate.

One of the greatest culture shocks I experienced when moving from the media, where deadlines are often incredibly tight, to communications consultancy and then in-house work was the vast swathes of time spent in ritual meetings. They went by an array of different titles—staff meetings, status meetings, campaign updates, progress reports, policy round-ups, conference calls—but all shared a few common features. They usually involved far more people than those directly involved in any decision-making, and concerned routine information that could be more quickly and efficiently disseminated via a written report.

For those individuals who relish performative busyness, ritual meetings provide the perfect stage and a captive audience. For office psychopaths, they can be a target-rich environment. For professional rivals, they represent turf to be battled over and won. And for consultants—some of them, at least—they're an easy way to make money by prolonging a discussion and exacerbating, rather than solving, problems.

In hindsight, I'm reminded of Gordon Hempton's warning that the wrong type of listening is simply 'controlled impairment'. Listening to the noise of agenda items in which you have little stake, and over which you have no control, does not come without a cost. It requires a necessary screening out of other information (controlled impairment), and erodes the time available for taking in the bigger picture.

For a while, however, I was like the boy in 'The Emperor's New Clothes'. If everyone else kept turning up for this pantomime, I figured, it must be me who was missing the point. It turned out I wasn't the only one thinking the Emperor was a little light on the essential details—or at least that their ritual meetings were.

In 2014, a global study of almost 4000 full-time professionals found that meetings were proliferating like weeds in workplaces around the world, and were an almost universal source of discontent.[10] Almost 90 per cent of the respondents from Australia and New Zealand said they were attending more meetings than ever before, the survey by Ovum and LogMeIn found. But two-thirds of the workers said these meetings were of no value to them.[11]

Forcing people to sit through events that they perceive to be worthless is obviously not great for staff morale. But the costs go a long way beyond irritation and boredom (and providing the occasional platter of unappealing pastries). I'm not going to lie: there were occasions when I welcomed a scheduled staff round-up as a chance to kick back and have a coffee. If it was a conference call, even better; thanks to Bluetooth, I've occasionally managed to do yoga, put on a load of laundry, start dinner and walk the dog while having my voice heard on those musters.

But that is entirely the point. Ritual meetings expect little more of most employees than simply showing up and staying awake, which strikes me as a pretty poor measure of productivity, particularly when you consider the trade-offs.

Tech entrepreneur Jason Fried is evangelical about boosting productivity, so much so that he co-founded a highly successful company, Basecamp, that builds web-based productivity and project-management tools. In 2016 he wrote a scathing blog post on the Basecamp website, titled 'Status meetings are the scourge'. 'Eliminate them,' Fried urged, 'and you'll actually know more, save a pile of money, and regain dozens of hours a month.'[12]

He encouraged readers to apply a simple formula to calculate the value of the next ritual meeting they attended. First, count the number of people in attendance and multiply that by the duration of the meeting. That will give you the true 'time cost' of the meeting; for example, a 30-minute meeting attended by ten people actually equates to a meeting of five 'worker hours'. You can also use average salaries or hourly rates to estimate how much it actually costs to have that many people in a room or on a call at one time. 'How would you feel if you had to regularly expense $1200 so you could "tell a few teammates something"', Fried asked. 'Think that would go over well?'

It can be an eye-opener to apply this metric to your own calendar. In my last office job, I found myself routinely taking work home to complete after dinner or on weekends. After hearing Fried in an interview, I applied his maths and realised I was spending an average of almost eight hours in unproductive routine meetings every week—roughly an entire work day! That kick-back coffee didn't taste so good after that (and the pastries never did).

Having been so scathing about the hip open office plans made popular by Big Tech, I should probably acknowledge that it is generally tech execs like Fried who are challenging the stultifying conventional wisdom about routine meetings. In Australia, for example, Atlassian's Dominic Price wrote in 2019 about wiping all meetings from his calendar, after finding he had little time left for meaningful one-on-one engagement like coaching and mentoring, or for the thoughtful work required in his role as 'work futurist'.[13] With every cancellation, he sent a note to the meeting organiser, asking them to clarify whether his attendance was specifically required and, if so, in what capacity; whether someone else could add as much value or more in his place; and whether the meeting itself was still of use, or whether it had morphed into a 'zombie meeting'.

After taking account of the responses, Price cut his total meeting load by one-third. 'Of the meetings that did come back to me, just clarifying my role massively reduced my cognitive load,' he wrote. 'In most of them, I was turning up and performing a very different role than what was intended (mostly because I was on auto-pilot). Now I don't have to guess anymore, and my contributions to those meetings are far more valuable.' Put simply, Price had increased his value by cutting the noise of performative busyness.

Of course, not every employee will have the seniority or the bravado to challenge a workplace culture of ritual busyness and noise. That's where insightful leaders can help. The execs at Dropbox did just that in August 2013 when they sent out a company-wide email with the subject line: 'Armeetingeddon has landed'. The Dropbox IT team had been instructed to erase all meetings, the message announced, apart from those with external stakeholders, between section heads or for recruitment.

'Two years later, Dropbox employs nearly three times as many people at its San Francisco headquarters, yet it has only approximately doubled the number of conference rooms,' Bob Sutton, a professor of organisational behaviour at Stanford, wrote of the initiative in *Inc.* magazine in 2015. Following the change, Sutton noted, 'meetings are shorter and more productive, with less rambling discussion and more focus on making decisions'.[14]

The name Armeetingeddon, by the way, was intended as a permanent warning against this form of performative busyness.

In a world where remote work is becoming more prevalent, some of us may be lucky enough to stay out of noisy office environments and dodge ritual meetings. But the third of what I consider the Unholy Trinity of performative busyness is much more difficult to avoid.

According to modelling by Radicati, a Silicon Valley–based market research firm specialising in technology, almost 246 billion emails were sent each day in 2019, with the majority (roughly 52 per cent) generated by business accounts. Breaking those figures down further, the average worker with a business email dealt with 126 emails each day, receiving 96 (about twenty of which were spam) and sending 30.[15]

Although studies vary, there is no doubt that all this email traffic demands a lot of time and energy. In a 2012 study, McKinsey Global found that knowledge workers—those people employed to 'produce or analyse ideas and information', according to the Collins Dictionary—spent 28 hours a week writing emails and 'collaborating internally' using social technologies.[16] In 2019, the *Harvard Business Review* calculated that the average full-time worker in America spent 2.6 hours a day on emails,[17] while research on the 'digital day' of UK adults in 2016 found that they devoted slightly more than an hour daily to that task (although that figure probably underestimates the time spent on work emails, as it represents the time divided evenly across work days and the weekend).[18]

Meanwhile, an array of other software options has come onto the market, promising to further streamline professional communications and collaboration. Today, on top of that punishing load of emails, the average knowledge worker might also be expected to participate in discussions on group texts, WhatsApp, Slack, Skype, Zoom, Google Hangouts, Microsoft Teams or Facebook Workplace, among others. Theoretically, these tools were meant to reduce the need for email; some, like Slack, promised to replace it altogether. But that hasn't occurred in most businesses—and, without proper thought or guidelines for use, the danger of introducing multiple communication tools is . . . well, multiplying the communication. And that means increasing the noise.

These changes have both short-term and long-term impacts on individuals and the organisations they work for. Firstly, in an 'always on' culture, where technology enables instantaneous communication and leaders prioritise rapid response and busy collaboration over thoughtful research and problem-solving, most workers keep their email open, and Slack or similar apps running, at all times—which means their attention will be disrupted multiple times during the day. Researchers call this phenomenon 'attention fragmentation'—and it takes a severe toll on employees and their productivity.

Professor Gloria Mark, of the University of California, Irvine, is a widely cited leader in the study of this phenomenon at work. One of her most commonly referenced studies found that the average amount of time people spent focusing on a single task at work before being interrupted was about three minutes.[19] This was in 2006—before the advent of the iPhone, and most of the software options for workplace collaboration outlined above.[20] It's hardly a surprise that multiple studies and surveys have shown increasing rates of interruption since then. For example, researchers in another study by Professor Mark recorded participants checking their email about eleven times per hour, while another group of researchers found that 84 per cent of users keep their email up in the background at all times, and that 64 per cent of users used notifications to access email at least some of the time.[21]

Across the Atlantic at Loughborough University in the United Kingdom, Professor Tom Jackson has been researching the cost of email overload since 1998, and has even devised an 'email cost calculator' for employers to calculate how much email management costs, in time and money, across their workforce.[22] In 2013, a team led by Professor Jackson monitored the heart rate, blood pressure and cortisol levels of government workers as they went about their work, including dealing with email. They found that 83 per cent of employees showed physical symptoms of increased stress while sending and receiving email, with that number rising to 92 per cent when the workers also had to multi-task email management with face-to-face meetings and phone calls.[23]

While we may already know we are stressed at work, or particularly stressed by the avalanche of email interruptions, some of Professor Gloria Mark's work has delved further into exactly why that is. 'Interruptions change the physical environment,' Mark explained in an interview with Gallup's *Business Journal*. 'For example, someone has asked you for information and you have opened new windows on your desktop, or people have given you papers that are now arranged on your desk. So often the physical layout of your environment has changed, and it's harder to reconstruct where you were. So there's a cognitive cost to an interruption.'[24]

It's worth noting that Mark also found these disruptions did not necessarily detract from workers' productivity in the short term. In fact, they often compensated by working faster. But over time that extra effort took a toll, with people 'experiencing more stress, higher frustration, time pressure and effort'.

Mark's work threw further doubt on a shibboleth that was already beginning to be challenged by researchers, after dominating the workplace for decades: the idea that the ideal employee was someone who could 'multitask', juggling multiple challenges simultaneously, without breaking a sweat.

In 2009, a group of scientists from Stanford unveiled a series of three multitasking experiments. Not only was juggling multiple high-tech inputs inefficient, their study found, but it could actually *impair* cognitive control. Ironically, the research by Clifford Nass, Eyal Ophir and Anthony Wagner began as an exercise in identifying what high multitaskers were really good at, because they had assumed that the students they saw checking their emails while talking to friends and watching a football game on TV, for example, wouldn't multitask like this if it was difficult for them. The trio had even each laid a bet on what the 'superpower' might be: an exceptional ability to filter out irrelevancy, a talent for switching attention quickly, or perhaps a highly organised memory. The research subjects sat a series of tests, including one in which they had to recognise red rectangles while filtering out blue ones as irrelevant, and one where they had to switch attention between letters and numbers.

'We were absolutely shocked,' Nass said of the results in an interview with PBS program *Frontline*. 'We all lost our bets. It turns out multitaskers are terrible at every aspect of multitasking. They're terrible at ignoring irrelevant information; they're terrible at keeping information in their head nicely and neatly organized; and they're terrible at switching from one task to another.'[25]

Nass, who died after suffering a heart attack in 2013, said he found the results deeply troubling. He warned of the potential damage to the cognitive function of children, who were multitasking on devices from increasingly young ages, as well as the growing pressures on employees. 'Multitasking is one of the most dominant trends in the use of media, so we could be essentially dumbing down the world,' he noted.

That was in 2009. Recently, Anthony Wagner reviewed the body of work that had accumulated since he, Nass and Ophir published their headline-grabbing study. He came to the conclusion that, 'in general, heavier media multitaskers often exhibit poorer performance in a number of cognitive domains'. While some studies did not find that heavy multitaskers performed worse than others, the very best they could expect was a 'null effect': no better or worse than their peers.[26]

So if all this additional noise can stress and potentially damage the health of individuals, and even 'dumb down the world' at large, what is the impact on workplaces? One clear risk is that as the noise of multiple forms of communication grows, the sheer volume will begin to drown out other goals, redefining how an organisation sees itself and its core work. Slowly, over time, rather than being a means to an end, all this communication and collaboration becomes an end in itself.

How does this happen? How do otherwise experienced industry leaders fall into the trap of noise over thought, demanding lots of activity with very little meaningful output?

In his excellent book *Deep Work: Rules for focused success in a distracted world*, computer science professor Cal Newport writes of the danger of 'metric black holes': behaviours that resist easy measurement. According to Newport, in the growing knowledge economy, where many individuals are working in large organisations on complex issues or problems, it can be extremely difficult to measure the value of individual efforts or outputs. Meanwhile, some of the busy behaviours and noisy practices outlined above offer something that generative and thoughtful 'deep work' can't. They're easy. They're obvious. They are the bright, shiny things that offer an instant payoff, when most of the real work has longer and more complicated timelines.

Of course, this is no coincidence. As we saw in Chapter 8, if there's one thing Big Tech is better at than making it easy for you to click on a diversion, it's giving you a big dollop of dopamine to keep you there.

But Cal Newport is a computer scientist too—albeit one who works in the buttoned-down environs of Georgetown University in Washington, DC. And here is where he empties a big bucket of cold water on the brilliance of his bros in their West Coast hipster havens.

Being constantly connected is just not that great, Newport argues, if you want to create something truly valuable. 'No one's ever made a fortune by being really good at sending and receiving emails,' he told Shankar Vedantam, the host of the *Hidden Brain* radio show and podcast. 'Right now, we're [in] the early stages of digital knowledge work [and] we've adopted this workflow that's very convenient and very simple, which is let's just give an email address to every person and let work unfold in this sort of ad hoc, ongoing conversation that happens with ... messages going back and forth and back and forth.

'And it's very easy, and it's very convenient, but it's also drastically reducing the human brains that are the main resource of these organisations. So my way of thinking about this is that we've built up a culture of convenience and simplicity in knowledge work at the cost of effectiveness and true productivity. And this is something that we need to change.'[27]

Of course, rarely, if ever, do most of us have the luxury of full freedom of choice over the work we do. Those of us with children or others who need our support (like ageing parents or family members with a disability) know this truth intimately.

Beyond our individual circumstances, we must participate in an employment market that is currently characterised by two oddly contradictory scourges. At one end, particularly in the professional white-collar world, many complain of chronic overwork. In the space of a generation, technology has made it easy and cheap to be connected 24/7—and suddenly work is as close and constant a companion as the devices we carry in our pockets and handbags. Much of this overtime is barely acknowledged, much less paid, and yet many feel they cannot question what has become the status quo.

At the other end of the spectrum, plenty of Australians can't get enough work to pay the bills. They juggle casual jobs with poor security, and so have limited say over their conditions. From their perspective, sitting at a desk in an open-plan office probably doesn't sound too bad at all, although some of the other experiences outlined above—the time-sucking nature of meetings and check-ins, for example—might be familiar.

My own experience as a single working mother when my boys were young makes me acutely and uncomfortably aware of the privilege bound up in this chapter. At that time in my life, I was simply glad to have a job that gave me financial security and a little flexibility. Only relatively recently have I been lucky enough to step off that treadmill of angst and overwork and take stock of the options, as well as the wider impacts of our current work culture.

I don't think we can change the way organisations operate or do business—at least, not in one fell swoop. But a little clarity can certainly help. Having a clear idea of the values that are important to you—and the reasons *why* you give them pre-eminence—may help you navigate the workplace more effectively or negotiate better with a boss. For example, it may give you more confidence simply to know that there is a strong body of scientific evidence confirming that quiet, deep work is ultimately more productive.

At the very least, this knowledge might liberate you from the destructive assumption that there is something wrong with *you* when you feel overwhelmed. The rate of diagnosed anxiety disorders has surged in recent years (although there is some debate about whether this reflects a greater incidence of anxiety or an increase in reported cases).[28] Yet there is rarely a discussion about the possibility that anxious individuals are actually experiencing a very healthy reaction to unhealthy environments. In other words, it might be the workplace culture that is flawed, not you.

I speak from experience, as someone who spent years berating herself that she just had to work harder and she would eventually feel better—less like an impostor and more like a success. In an ailing work culture, working harder may not only be futile, it can be counterproductive. When goals are unclear, or busyness is confused with productivity, expending even more energy will have limited impact—apart from possibly heightening your own sense of frustration.

Deconstructing the noise and busyness of the modern workplace helped me to understand that there was often nothing personal in the counterproductive assignments or frustrating interactions I experienced professionally. But it also gave me insight into myself. I know now that workplaces that foster or demand high levels of performative busyness, with little acknowledgement of the value of quiet work, are not places I want to be.

Then again, it's equally important to recognise how easy it is to fall into the trap of busyness individually, even—and perhaps especially—when we find work we love, subjects we are passionate about, causes we believe in. When I first began researching what I thought was a thoroughly modern scourge—performative busyness—I expected that it would represent a complete break from many of the topics I've explored in this book's earlier chapters. But I'd forgotten what listening in nature had taught me: that all worlds are interconnected, across time and through shared experiences, thoughts and philosophies.

So I laughed when I discovered that, more than half a century ago, Thomas Merton had formed a strong opinion about busyness too, as he observed the turbulent changes of the 1960s from the silence of Gethsemani Abbey in Kentucky.

'There is a pervasive form of modern violence to which the idealist . . . most easily succumbs: activism and over-work,' Merton wrote in *Conjectures of a Guilty Bystander*, published in 1966. 'The rush and pressure of modern life are a form, perhaps the most common form, of its innate violence. To allow oneself to be carried away by a multitude of conflicting concerns, to surrender to too many demands, to commit oneself to too many projects, to want to help everyone in everything is to succumb to violence.'

Had he lived today, would Merton have tweeted his thoughts instead, in a staccato stream of #monk #deepthought? Would he have been available on email? Or maintained a Facebook page? Or would he have observed us all, rushing and roiling, clamouring and clashing, and simply smiled, before retreating to the hermitage, where he could be at peace with his thoughts?

# 11

# ACTION

Silence doesn't have to mean passivity. It's not the same thing as acceptance. Nor should it be assumed to imply complicity or surrender. Silence can be fierce. Focused. Courageous, ingenious, even revolutionary. But it took me a while to learn all that. Looking back, this may have been the most difficult lesson of all.

You see, there's one problem with discovering how blissful it feels to strip away the noise of the modern world: all the pings and dings of mobile devices, the ranting of ego-driven commentators, the social media feeds that tweak envy, feed fear and fuel anxiety, and the manufactured, often meaningless hustle of the modern workplace.

The problem? The modern world thinks it's just fine, thank you very much. And very few of us have much option whether or not we continue participating in it. Had I wanted to take a vow of silence or enter a contemplative order, either as a Christian or a Buddhist nun, or perhaps pursue a career as a park ranger or lighthouse keeper, I would have to have committed to that a long time ago.

Life just doesn't work that way. You don't get dealt all the cards you need at the start of the game. Sometimes you cop a few lousy ones instead. You learn a little, do your best to get rid of those—jettisoning, trading, bluffing, whatever it takes—and eventually things might improve. I turned up the card that said, *Pssst, silence is a really good thing!* in my late forties. And don't get me wrong: I'm immensely grateful I received it at all. But I can't help but suspect there's a dealer somewhere with a smirk on his or her face. Because by then, the other cards I was holding included two rambunctious boys, a career in the clamorous worlds of journalism and communications, and a yowling mortgage. Tricky to discard any of those without folding.

So here I was, with a new-found love of silence in the same old noisy world. How would I find a balance? Was it even possible?

I'd love to say I applied some wisdom borne of my meditation and quiet practices. But instead I decided—albeit briefly—to turn to the philosophy of the late Kenny Rogers, who once advised all gamblers to know when to hold 'em and when to fold 'em, as well as when to leave the card table altogether.

Of course, that was it. I was going to run away.

Once, a green turtle almost convinced me to flee the noise of the city, in favour of a life more fully dedicated to quietude and silent practices.

We were gliding together through the glorious blue of the Coral Sea, about 50 kilometres off the coast of Far North Queensland. Well, the turtle was gliding. I was snorkelling, and trying to kick powerfully enough to keep pace with him. Or her.

All seven species of marine turtle are endangered. However, the Great Barrier Reef still offers a relative abundance of nesting and feeding sites, and this green turtle seemed pretty contented with its lot. It was somehow able to set an impressive pace while appearing completely unhurried. Its dreamy, slow strokes were hypnotic, and as I paddled along in its thrall, I could almost hear Thich Nhat Hanh leading a meditation: 'Stroking, I pull my flippers back; gliding, I move through the sea . . .' This was a very Buddhist turtle, I thought. Or perhaps Buddhism is a very turtle-ish spirituality.

Not far away was the outermost edge of the reef's eponymous barrier, beyond which the ocean floor plunges more than 2 kilometres, forming a deep-sea playground for all sorts of 'megafauna'. But here I felt none of the normal unease of being out of my depth in a wild expanse of water. Here, I felt nothing but presence and calm.

It was a state I had embraced since arriving in the tropical north a few days earlier. I'd left behind a chilly house and a family made skittish by the westerly winds that roar into Brisbane in late winter, stirring up dust and irritation. Arriving in Port Douglas, I'd shed layers of clothes as naturally as a python, eager to let the unfamiliar honeyed beams of sunlight sink deep into my bones. Everything felt healthier: the lush rainforest that swathed the nearby mountains, the sweeping curves of sand bleached clean by the sun, the slower pace of the locals working to 'tropical time', and the happy Euro-accented chatter of backpackers burnished to caramel hues.

Very soon—and like many visitors before me, no doubt—I was plotting a sea change, a permanent move to a slower, quieter lifestyle, nestled in the embrace of Mother Nature. Our move from Sydney back to Brisbane had opened my eyes to the quality of life we could achieve as a family when we weren't scrambling to cover the cost of living in an overcrowded capital city. Now, as much as I loved our house in Brisbane, I found myself wondering how much further I could take that idea. If our little slice of backyard bushland could bring such joy, perhaps it was worth really immersing ourselves in a life more closely aligned to the rhythms of the natural world? And my encounter with the turtle seemed just the sign I was looking for. Surely we all needed to be more present and steady, just like this creature, content in its quiet corner of paradise?

Sure, I knew it would be hard to get journalism work here, and corporate communications positions would be almost non-existent. But to be honest, that was part of the dream. Having embraced silence and established some quiet, contemplative practices, I'd noticed how hypersensitive I'd become to the mad scramble of the modern media, and particularly the amped-up volume of public debate. I was beginning to wonder whether I still had a place in that world.

But then I tilted my gaze away from my shelled companion. Was this *really* paradise? Here in this coral garden, there were certainly glorious specimens of branching coral and luminescent fish, the types that have gained the Great Barrier Reef international renown as a natural wonder of the world. But there were also tracts of desolation: puckered brown scars of slime, and the occasional eerie forest that appeared to be made entirely of bone, like skeletal hands reaching to the heavens in one final, desperate plea for salvation.

I had travelled north on the commission of a British media outlet that was seeking a feature story on coral bleaching. What future, if any, was there for the world's coral reefs if the climate continued to warm? I was interested in the brief: like most Australians, I knew there had been two recent mass bleaching events reported on the Great Barrier Reef, in 2016 and 2017. But I had been so busy with corporate work at that time that I hadn't made the effort to learn much about them.

Plus—I'll be honest—when a news outlet from a foreign country with a good exchange rate comes knocking, offering an attractive payment rate per word, most experienced freelancers will tell you it's like being offered a free beer at the pub. You take it whether you're thirsty or not, because you never know when the next one might come along.

In Port Douglas, I'd located someone I suspected would be perfect for the story. John Edmondson was a marine biologist by training and a commercial tour operator by profession. As the former, I expected he would be keen to highlight the devastation of mass coral bleaching, and to call for urgent government action to curb climate emissions, as an overwhelming majority of scientists in this field had already done. But as the latter—a businessman dependent on tourist dollars—Edmondson would also have a strong incentive to show his paying customers the best coral available, to generate plenty of Instagrammable moments and positive social media reviews to support his tours. Given this tension— or balance—I figured that accompanying Edmondson on one of his commercial snorkelling tours would provide as close as I would get to a 'real' snapshot of the health of the reef in this area, rather than a curated view intended to support only one side or the other of a polarised debate.

In addition, Edmondson offered to take me separately to some sites where he was working in partnership with scientists from the University of Technology Sydney on a project to repair reefs damaged by bleaching. Led by Associate Professor David Suggett, the Coral Nurture Program was launched in early 2018, when Suggett, Edmondson and their respective teams installed ten artificial 'coral nurseries' around Opal Reef. The nurseries, made of aluminium screens weighted down with concrete blocks, were then stocked with 1500 coral fragments from ten different species. If they grew successfully, the intention was to harvest them and use them to repopulate parts of the natural reef where coral had been damaged or killed by bleaching and extreme storm events.

'I prefer to call it stewardship rather than reef restoration, because we're maintaining coral in a particular area at a particular level,' Edmondson explained. 'There is an ecological value, but . . . you wouldn't want to think we're making a massive ecological difference or fixing the entire reef. If you want to "save the reef", there's all sorts of issues . . . and the big one is that we have to address the amount of carbon dioxide in the atmosphere.'

My first surprise, as I followed Edmondson from reef to reef over several hours, was not the damage or otherwise, but the noise. I had expected it to be quiet underwater. But coral reefs are busy places, and my snorkelling was accompanied by a staccato backing track, like somebody crinkling and popping bubble wrap in a nearby room. He explained that this was the sound of the parrot fish—exuberantly coloured creatures with bird-like beaks—chomping insatiably on tiny nuggets of coral. The sand below, I learned, was predominantly made up of that same coral, chewed and digested and ultimately excreted by parrot fish, as well as by a few other marine species, as part of the food chain.

Sometimes the simplest stories deliver the most profound messages. And so it was with this tale of parrot fish poo. Less coral meant less shelter for little fish, like the clown fish made famous in *Finding Nemo*, as well as less food for medium-sized fish like the parrot fish. Fewer smaller fish like these meant fewer of the big fish that fed on them—and less sand excreted to the sea floor. Less sand meant fewer crustaceans and other organisms that 'bottom-feed', and fewer coral cays. And so it goes. Here was the simple calculus describing the potential death of an entire ecosystem, should one piece of it be endangered or removed.

Another stark piece of maths: if the average global temperature rises to 1.5 degrees Celsius over pre-industrial levels, according to the broad consensus among marine scientists (including those working in agencies advising the Australian government), between 70 and 90 per cent of the world's coral reefs will be lost, including on the Great Barrier Reef. Given the planet has already reached the +1.0 degree mark, and the ocean will continue absorbing carbon dioxide from the atmosphere for decades even if carbon emissions on land are curtailed, it is not at all alarmist to suggest we may be the last generation of Australians who can marvel at the full beauty of the Great Barrier Reef.

It's an awful thing, watching a natural wonder die on your watch. But that is what Edmondson experienced in 2016, when the first of the back-to-back bleaching events swept through the waters off North Queensland. Visiting one of his favourite spots on Opal Reef, which had featured only months earlier in the BBC's documentary *Blue Planet 2*, he noticed that the coral there had begun to fluoresce, a phenomenon in which the distressed organisms erupt in intense pigmentation, possibly in a bid to protect themselves from harsh sunlight. Powerless to intervene, Edmondson could only wait for the next stage, bleaching, in which the dying corals turn skeletally white, before being slowly consumed by algae.

'You just feel overwhelming sadness and hopelessness,' Edmondson recalled. 'But I also felt really angry—because this is a human-caused thing. Why aren't we doing something about this? You want people to know about it.'

Back aboard Edmondson's cruiser, my earlier daydreams of a bliss-fully quiet sea change evaporated faster than salt water on the sunny deck. The tourists were happily trading pictures and tales of what they had seen—a pair of sleek barracuda, the green turtles with their chilled-out vibe, a pod of eight whales that had cavorted around our boat on the way out—while planning where they would catch up for a drink back on land. But I had no one to distract me from my memories of the more desolate vistas I'd surveyed with Edmondson, or from fretting about the dire outlook we'd discussed.

I'm no stranger to grim topics, having written regularly and in depth about the horrors of sexual assault, domestic violence, child abuse and murder in my years as a journalist covering what is sometimes called 'social affairs'. Often, what gives you the energy to keep going is the possibility of changing things for the better. You may not be able to achieve anything single-handedly. But when you have the privilege of working for a major media outlet, there is always the chance that some-thing you write will put pressure on an otherwise dismissive political leader, or attract attention from experts and oversight from the right agencies, and ideally prompt constructive change.

Your article may even help fuel a slow but powerful shift in public opinion. As I began my career, for example, domestic abuse was still considered by many to be a matter best left behind closed doors, report-ing on suicide was completely taboo, and paedophilia was rarely even mentioned. As one editor assured me, these were subjects that 'nobody wanted to read about over their cornflakes'. But over time, with the efforts of diligent journalists and committed editors, that view has been challenged.

Yet something felt different about the impending scourge of climate change. Unlike those other problems, there had already been widespread discussion of this one. There were plenty of good envi-ronment and science journalists reporting on the intensifying threat, and on some of the possible solutions, as well as political journalists covering the responses of various governments. But none of it seemed to matter—or to matter *enough*. The United States had abandoned its commitment to the 2016 Paris Agreement, under which nearly 200 nations had pledged to cut greenhouse-gas emissions in a bid to contain the average global temperature rise to 'well below' 2 degrees Celsius above pre-industrial levels. Apparently, US president Donald Trump thought it was possible to isolate his own country from changes in the climate; perhaps he thought it was as simple as building an enormous wall to keep out the weather? Meanwhile, in Australia, brutal political tribalism and media point-scoring made it impossible to even begin a constructive public conversation about transitioning away from our reliance on fossil fuels.

This silence was not good or nurturing or restorative. It felt oppressive and wilfully ignorant, even cruel.

A few days after I flew home from Far North Queensland, the federal environment minister visited the same region. *The Weekend Australian* reported Sussan Ley's trip in a front-page story, with a large picture of the minister snorkelling just as I had done, accompanied by the headline 'Great Barrier Reef Is Better Than Expected'. The first paragraph read: 'The Great Barrier Reef is not dead, is not dying and is not even on life support, federal Environment Minister Sussan Ley has declared after her first official visit to the World Heritage-listed site.'[1]

This, despite warnings from multiple renowned marine scientists about the devastation wrought by the mass bleaching events of 2016 and 2017, and a formal declaration from the government's own agency, the Great Barrier Reef Marine Park Authority, that the reef's long-term outlook was 'poor'. Two weeks later, when GBRMPA issued its latest five-yearly report, downgrading that assessment to 'very poor', the same newspaper buried the news back inside the paper and low on its website, as if the parlous state of an Australian icon was of little import. (As I edited this chapter in March 2020, the GBRMPA had just released a statement to confirm that mass bleaching was once again occurring on the reef, with a high mortality of corals expected in some sections.[2] But with the pandemic of COVID-19 sweeping the world, the slow death of a natural wonder attracted little attention.)

Reading the effusive newspaper report about Sussan Ley's visit to the reef while sitting in the bleachers at a school basketball game, I had to grind my teeth to prevent the profanities pouring out, as a wave of rage surged up my throat like bile. I may actually have growled out loud. The parents around me smiled nervously, perhaps assuming I was just carried away by the skills of the mighty 7Es. So much for silence. After several weeks reviewing the best research about coral bleaching and global warming, and interviewing a range of local experts, I wanted to call this newspaper's coverage out for what I sincerely believed it to be: selective reporting that deliberately downplayed science in order to favour a particular political position.

Yes, I was writing my own coral bleaching story for a foreign news outlet. But my story would be published online, and was unlikely to attract much attention in Australia. It didn't feel like enough. *Nothing* felt like enough, not when national politics seemed hopelessly grid-locked on an issue of such existential urgency, and the largest media organisation in the country seemed determined to deny the problem.

How could I find joy in silence now, if it meant biting my tongue rather than speaking up when something seemed wrong? How could I walk away from public debate, when we so urgently needed more voices? And what was this new emotional state which had extinguished the warm glow of quietude, leaving my values like cold ashes in my mouth?

'Your silence will not protect you.' A poet named Audre Lorde wrote those words in the late 1970s, not long after I was hauled out of my quiet reverie in that kindergarten cubbyhole. They echoed now across the decades—and somehow, despite all the ways silence had improved my life and outlook, they still rang true. 'My silences had not protected me. Your silence will not protect you.'

Lorde first wrote—and spoke—those words in 1977, in a paper titled 'The Transformation of Silence into Language and Action', presented at a conference of the Modern Languages Association in Chicago and later published in her book *Your Silence Will Not Protect You*. A few months earlier, doctors had warned her that a lump in her breast was 60 to 80 per cent likely to be malignant. Lorde had to wait three weeks before surgery could confirm whether that was the case, all the while knowing that a positive cancer diagnosis would almost certainly be a death sentence. These were early days in breast cancer research—before pink ribbons and charity runs—and the treatment options were limited and generally severe. Ultimately, she received good news: the growth was benign. But by then the trauma had seeped through the poet and onto paper.

'In becoming forcibly and essentially aware of my own mortality,' Lorde wrote, 'and of what I wished and wanted for my life, however short it might be, priorities and omissions became strongly etched in a merciless light and what I regretted most were my silences.'

Her words were profoundly political, just as every act of her daily life had become political. As a black lesbian feminist in the 1970s and '80s, Lorde wrote regularly about the multiplicity of ways in which she experienced being an outsider from the social movements of the day.

She acknowledged that speaking up could feel embarrassing, even terrifying. Indeed, the bloody history of the civil rights movement had demonstrated time and again that speaking up could be lethal for black Americans. But Lorde's own brush with death had left her with 'a harsh and urgent clarity' that staying silent in the face of injustice was not a viable option. We could censor ourselves, she concluded, and 'still be no less afraid'.[3]

As I was working on my story about the future of the Great Barrier Reef, I had shared what I had discovered with my sons, as I usually do. I had shown them the pictures of dying coral, their delicate bodies turning white and then brown with slime, the microscopic animals that inhabit them literally dripping away in tears of sludge.

'Why are adults letting this happen?' one son asked me repeatedly.

'What are *you* going to do?' the other pushed.

It never ceases to amaze me, this superpower children wield: the ability to strip us bare with their gaze. It's as if they have X-ray vision, acute enough to penetrate our most elaborate white lies, hypocrisies and justifications, and powerful enough to demolish all those carefully constructed exercises in self-deception, until our very hearts and souls are exposed in the rubble.

What *was* I going to do? As a mother, hadn't I always encouraged my boys to speak up when they saw something wrong or unjust? And as parents, don't we bear a responsibility to do everything we can to deliver our children a better, cleaner, safer world? Remaining silent no longer felt defensible. And writing another story, while remaining at arm's length from the issue, did not feel like enough either.

And so, one brutally hot day a few weeks after my own story was published, I joined about 30,000 other people in a Climate Strike march that snaked its way from Queens Gardens, once a central part of Brisbane's very first convict settlement, across the river to Musgrave Park, a site with an even deeper history as a longstanding meeting place for local Indigenous people.

This was not a march of extremists or anarchists or eco-terrorists, as some hysterical media commentators and condescending politicians had predicted. There were grandparents pushing strollers, and mothers shepherding small clusters of schoolchildren, their broad-brimmed hats bobbing and waving in the sun like fields of flowers. There were Indigenous elders, and tradies in high-vis representing their unions, and even a smattering of CBD office workers who must have left work early, trading their heels for sneakers beneath pencil skirts or sensible slacks.

All had turned out to support the Global Week for Future, a series of international protests driven largely by high school students, in support of teenage activist Greta Thunberg's appearance at the United Nations Climate Summit in New York.

Later, I would discover that Thunberg had also called out a potentially toxic kind of silence, just as Audre Lorde had decades earlier. In her book, *No One Is Too Small to Make a Difference*, Thunberg wrote: 'To all the political parties that pretend to take the climate question seriously. To all the politicians who ridicule us on social media . . . To all of you, who choose to look the other way every day . . . Your silence is almost worst of all.'[4]

Clearly, I was not the only one uncomfortable with that type of silence. An estimated 300,000 Australians marched in actions around the country that day in September 2019, with a total of 6 million or so believed to have done so across the suffering planet. In Brisbane, some high school kids had brought instruments and formed a marching band, which occasionally broke into a jaunty reggae beat, lifting the spirits of the crowd just as they began wilting in the heat. The appearance of a group of pretend pallbearers, carrying a cardboard coffin to represent the multiple species that were likely to be killed as global temperatures soared, only served to add a colourful 'Day of the Dead' atmosphere to the experience.

But even shoulder-to-shoulder in a crowd of 30,000 people, I felt exposed. Like Audre Lorde, I felt that this experience of speaking up was 'never without fear—of visibility, of the harsh light of scrutiny and perhaps judgement'.[5]

Yes, I wanted to add my voice to this cause, but did I really want to be recognised, laughed at, dismissed? Like politics, the media in Australia is extremely tribal; I knew colleagues who would roll their eyes at my involvement, not to mention important contacts in politics and business. Some would likely disown me: I was not to be trusted, no longer on their 'team'. And potentially that meant dollars: freelance jobs assigned to other writers, communications advisory work given to other consultants. It would have been easier to stay silent—and I had a ready-made excuse to do so: as a journalist, I was supposed to remain impartial, above the fray, right?

But I wasn't just a journalist. I was a trained listener, someone who had heard the resignation, the weariness and the frustration in the voices of scientists who had dedicated their lives to researching climate change and its impact on species and ecosystems. Most would never make the money or win the recognition enjoyed by those dominating the public and political debates. And yet they likely knew more than all of them put together.

Also, I was an unashamed fan of democracy, as geeky as that sounds. Having graduated from university with a double-major in politics—Australian and American—I still believed in the gift and the power of democratic participation, not to mention the right of free speech.

Finally, I was a mother too. And I wanted to know that when my boys were grown, they would still have the opportunity to swim through one of the natural wonders of the world as I had, and to glide through the brilliant blue in the quiet company of a green turtle.

My participation in one street protest was hardly going to change the world. But it had changed me. Adding my voice to this issue did not feel the same as simply jumping on an ideological bandwagon or joining the sound and fury of a confected media debate. For some, I'm sure a street protest can be about those things: the adrenaline-charged tit-for-tat of politics. But for me, and I suspect many others, it came from a different place entirely.

I realised that the time I had spent in silence and stillness had grounded me. By stripping away the noise and pressure of what others were saying and might think, as well as an ever-changing array of trivial distractions, I'd rediscovered my own moral compass: what felt right and necessary to me. In an era of disposable opinions and public posturing, I had discovered I could draw on something more solid and empowering: conviction. Acting with that as a guide feels entirely different from floating along with the zeitgeist or screaming for the sake of a headline.

Perhaps there is something innate in human nature—most likely that something is called 'the ego'—that predisposes us to believing that when we encounter a difficult problem, we must be the first individuals ever to have done so, and that when we solve it, or at least achieve some greater insight about it, this must be because we are somehow wiser than most. Alas, I soon discovered I was no guru. With a bit more research and reading, I soon discovered that I was far from the first person to ask whether it was possible to live a contemplative and 'quiet' life while engaging with the world at large.

Remember Thomas Merton, the Benedictine monk who continues to be a bestselling author, more than half a century after his death? Reading his memoir, *The Seven Storey Mountain*, at New Camaldoli, I had felt estranged by his passionate avowals of commitment to the rituals and traditions of the Roman Catholic Church, pre–Vatican II. Merton had come to Catholicism in the 1940s after a hellraising youth; to me, his new-found religious zeal then smacked of an entitled masculinity, his experiences nothing like those of a child raised in that religion, nor a woman relegated to its fringes.

But Merton's life and writings didn't stop there. By the 1960s, social change was sweeping America, the shockwaves strong enough to penetrate even the walls of Gethsemani Abbey, the Kentucky monastery in which Merton lived. As a student at Columbia University in New York, Merton had become familiar with the Harlem neighbourhood, even volunteering for a while at Friendship House, a local Catholic-run community centre, and eventually considering whether this was his vocation. Decades later, when Dr Martin Luther King Jr wrote his 'Letter from a Birmingham Jail' in 1963, Merton responded with 'Letters to a White Liberal', challenging the complicity of white Christians in maintaining a system that advantaged them. It formed the basis of a book published the following year, *Seeds of Destruction*, which alienated many conservative Catholics.[6]

But as a monk, Merton saw himself as a marginal person, and he continued to align himself with those who felt themselves to be powerless or victims of injustice, while opposing the Vietnam War, and nuclear weaponisation particularly. He also drew the ire of many in the Church hierarchy for adopting a meditation practice, and exploring the similarities between Buddhism and Christianity. (A few months before his premature death in 1968, Merton met with the Dalai Lama, who decades later continued to refer to him as a good friend and 'spiritual brother'.[7])

By the mid-1960s, Merton had convinced his abbot to allow him to live alone in a basic cottage more than a kilometre from the abbey, but his time in even greater silence only seemed to fuel his writings. Clearly, Merton (then known as Father Louis) was not only aware of this apparent contradiction, but grappling with it. In an essay titled 'Is the World a Problem?', published in the Catholic magazine *Commonweal* in 1966, Merton signalled to the reader that both he, and the world as a whole, had changed dramatically in the years since he had converted to Catholicism, and then become a Trappist monk.

'As long as I imagine that the world is something to be "escaped" in a monastery—that wearing a special costume and following a quaint observance takes me "out of this world," I am dedicating my life to an illusion,' he declared.[8]

Instead, Merton mounted an eloquent argument for engaging passionately with the problems of the world at large, even from the silent isolation of his hermitage. If God had created the world and every person in it, he argued, then surely a Christian must be dedicated to caring for the good of all, rather than simply pursuing his own autonomous piety.

'If the deepest ground of my being is love, then in that very love itself and nowhere else will I find myself, and the world, and my brother and Christ,' he wrote. 'It is not a question of either/or but of all-in-one. It is not a matter of exclusivism and "purity" but of wholeness, whole-heartedness [and] unity.'

What an enormous relief to realise that greater minds than mine had recognised the futility, even disingenuity, of insisting that life be an either/or. If you're a perfectionist—as so many anxious people in this hypercompetitive modern world are, having come to believe that only perfection can protect them from life's uncertainties—you may be prone to this kind of absolutism. An exercise routine is only worth-while if we *never* miss a session. A presentation at work either *nails it*, without a single pause or error, or it is *nothing*. Our children must be perfectly behaved and completely happy all the time or we have *failed utterly* as parents.

The truth is that for an awfully long time after my first ten-day Vipassana retreat, I bought into the either/or mindset. I did *not* want to compromise, refusing to accept that, sometimes, simply maintain-ing ten minutes of silence in the real world is enough. Having tasted silence's power, I wanted more of it. I wanted it *all the time*. As a result, I spent a lot more time beating myself up for not being silent than I did actually practising silence. Not a particularly productive approach . . .

Ironically, I'd asked a Buddhist monk about this very challenge years before I found myself plotting a sea change on the Great Barrier Reef. (Call me a slow learner.) After my visit to Gwinganna, I had sought out a three-day silent retreat near Sydney, where the women slept in what felt like a communal aircraft hangar, and the men in what looked like an old train carriage, atop a beautiful but brutally cold mountain. On the final morning, the sun came out and the monastery cat played at the monk's feet as he gave his final lesson.

When he invited questions (at this point we were allowed to speak), I asked whether there were any Buddhist teachings specifically about how women, who were commonly the primary carers of children or other loved ones, might maintain peace amid a hectic daily routine.

The monk nodded slowly, his face folding into a smile. 'Being a mother—that is the hardest job in the world.'

And that was all he said. Which, of course, only made me want to scream.

I don't think we are socialised anymore to accept that some things just *are* bloody hard. Certainly not those of us who live in advanced capitalist societies. When we have a problem, we consult an expert and we want it fixed—*now*! We're happy to pay, provided we don't have to be uncomfortable anymore. The idea of experiencing the problem, simply being aware of it and choosing to live with it and see what happens next, feels ridiculous, and sometimes unbearable.

(This might explain why most monasteries don't charge for their retreats, preferring instead to rely on donations. Imagine the stampede for refunds from customer service, should enlightenment not be acquired after three days of communal sleep!)

The reality—for most of us, anyway—is that the world is a messy, demanding place. Modern work is often messy and demanding, as is the art of leadership, and the process of creativity. Love, in all its forms, can be messy and demanding, as we discover almost every day in our families, our relationships, our friendships, our parenting. If we're going to embrace silence within this environment, we can't be purists about it. It can't be either/or.

'There are many approaches, many ways,' a woman originally known as Diane Perry once responded when asked a similar question to the one I'd posed to the monk on the mountaintop that day. 'What is unrealistic, however, is to become a mother or a businesswoman and at the same time expect to be able to do the same kind of practices designed for hermits. If women have made the choice to have children then they should develop a practice which makes the family the dharma path. Otherwise they'll end up being very frustrated.'[9]

Diane Perry is better known today as Jetsunma Tenzin Palmo. In the late 1960s, when she was barely out of her teens, she became one of the first Westerners ordained as a Buddhist nun. However, after several years of life in monasteries in India, she became frustrated, partly because of sexist traditions that prevented nuns from gaining access to the full Buddhist teachings. She decided it would be better for her spiritual progress to practise alone, in seclusion. Provocatively, she declared that she intended to attain enlightenment in the female form—'no matter how many lifetimes it takes'.

In 1976, Tenzin Palmo hiked up a mountain near her village, to a small cave that sat more than 4000 metres above sea level. With less than two square metres of living space, she slept upright in a small elevated box, which she used during the day for meditation. While some basic supplies could be brought up the mountain in summer, she spent her winters alone, often snowbound.

Ultimately, the diminutive Englishwoman spent twelve years living in that cave, including the final three in complete retreat (without visitors). When she came back down the mountain, Tenzin Palmo discovered a world that had been transformed by the second wave of feminism. Everywhere she went, in her new role as a teacher and ultimately as head of her own nunnery, women were railing against religious traditions that empowered men to pursue their own spiritual advancement, while the burden of care and domestic life was assumed to fall on women.

Often she was asked whether her own example had simply proven that women had to turn their backs on things like family if they wanted to match the spiritual development of men. In her characteristically direct style, Tenzin Palmo defended her choice, arguing that going into retreat certainly could advance a practice more quickly, because the practitioner could focus exclusively on that single goal, away from all other distractions. (Of course, we see this principle already applied in the secular world, to achieve top results in sport, ace their exams or finish a creative project like a book, if they're very lucky.)

'It's ridiculous to become a nun or a hermit because of some ideal when all the time we would be learning more within a close relationship or family situation,' Tenzin Palmo told her biographer in *Cave in the Snow*. 'You can develop all sorts of qualities through motherhood which you could not by leading a monastic life. It's not that by being a mother one is cutting off the path. Far from it! . . .

'Whether one is a monk, a nun, a hermit or a businessman or woman, at one level is irrelevant. The practice of being in the moment, of opening the heart, can be done wherever we are. If one is able to bring one's awareness into everyday life and into one's relationships, workplace, home, then it makes no difference where one is.'[10]

I realised that by approaching silence and noise like an absolutist— *silence = good, noise = bad, therefore I must run away from the city and commune with the turtles*—I was engaging in exactly the type of 'ridiculous' behaviour Tenzin Palmo had described, and that Thomas Merton had ultimately eschewed. I was casting my dilemma in black-and-white terms and insisting that I choose a side for myself, while forgetting that much of the complexity and wonder of life exists in the shades of grey.

Very few of us have the option of dedicating our lives entirely to silent practices, no matter how good they make us feel. But whether we are supporting an ailing parent, tackling a complex work project, cooking the family dinner or playing sport with friends, the quality of almost any activity is improved when we are fully present, focused and fuelled by the sort of calm awareness that silence fosters.

So the challenge becomes clear: we must identify specific practices that can be integrated into our daily routines without becoming an extra chore on an already overcrowded to-do list. I've found that it helps to remind myself that there is no single, perfect silent practice that is more beneficial than others. This is partly because silence itself can shapeshift, manifesting in different ways depending on the situation and the person.

It's also important to acknowledge that silence is not always positive. Sometimes, it can be a political act. When imposed on us by others, it can be hostile and repressive. When self-imposed, it may be driven by fear, serving only to reinforce our feelings of weakness or shame.

For silence to be wholly positive, it must be freely chosen and founded on respect for oneself and others. Even then, it can have an array of qualities. To articulate them best, I find myself deferring not to a Buddhist or Christian contemplative who considered these things from behind the walls of a monastery, but to a Dutch priest, psychologist and theologian named Henri Nouwen.

Nouwen spent extended periods in Trappist monasteries, and his writings often draw comparisons with those of Thomas Merton. He was also a popular public speaker who taught at both Yale and Harvard at different times. But Nouwen was not content to remain in such rarefied institutions when he saw social injustice beyond, and he spent much of his life living with the poor in Central and South America, and ministering to those living with disabilities. His extensive body of written work reflects a lifelong effort to incorporate two apparently contradictory qualities—community and solitude—within a spiritually meaningful life. Considering silence specifically, he acknowledged its multifaceted nature, that it was both a discipline and a mystery, a redemption and a renunciation.

'First, silence makes us pilgrims,' Nouwen wrote in *The Way of the Heart*. 'Secondly, silence guards the fire within. Thirdly, silence teaches us to speak.'[11]

These seventeen words have become a touchstone for me. Within them, I know I can always find a compelling reason to return to silence, even when the world is brandishing so many bright, shiny things to distract me. (In fact, returning to silence can be *particularly* important when bright, shiny things abound.)

Nouwen's conceptualisation of silence was founded in a deeply Christian faith, but I believe his concepts can be applied more universally, just as the search for greater meaning tends to be universal.

First, *silence makes us pilgrims*. That is, after all, exactly what I had been doing when I hiked to the Hoh River Valley and meditated at a retreat in the Tasmanian bush, when I travelled to a hermitage on the cliffs of Big Sur and another tucked into farmland on the banks of the Tarrawarra River. But a pilgrimage does not refer only to physical territory. It is an interior journey as well. In Nouwen's view, when we choose silence, we retrace the footsteps of the Desert Fathers and Mothers, who walked into a barren landscape as an act of rebellion against a world preoccupied with indulgence, gossip and hyperbole. Carving out time to nurture your interior silence involves a pilgrimage that exposes first your thoughts, then your feelings, then your soul itself—if you let it.

If that all sounds uncomfortably airy-fairy, Nouwen's second aspect of silence promises some solid practical benefits as well. *Silence guards the fire within.* It nurtures the embers of our inner humanity: the glow of strength, the spark of creativity, the crackle of passion. In a world where everyone and everything seems to demand more—more effort, more productivity, more action, more connectivity—silence recognises that we are enough as we are. It is the safe respite after too much noise and too much busyness. Silence allows us to simply *be*—and, in so doing, it stokes the flames of our inner resources until we are ready to venture out into our world again.

Finally, *silence teaches us to speak*—from the heart of wisdom, rather than the lizard brain of primal instinct. Time spent in quietude may open us to essential truths, greater meanings and intuitive knowledge. Surely that was what fuelled the passion for social justice that burns in Thomas Merton's later writings? Just as importantly, it trains us in the art of listening with equanimity. We become comfortable with our own silence and stillness, and more discerning about what we say. Our words, when they come, are likely to be more deliberate, more insightful and, perhaps, more magnanimous. They certainly have more potential to be that way than when we speak from a defensive mindset or from reflexive emotion.

My time in silence endows me with an equilibrium, and a stronger and clearer sense of myself and my values. That is why I recognised eventually that I needed to do more about the challenge of climate change, by taking part in protests and speaking up as someone who wants action, rather than continuing to fly safely under the radar. Not because I thought I could change the world, but because I intuited that it was important to demonstrate to my children the importance of acting on one's values. I needed to 'walk the talk', as they say. In silence, I recognised that the greatest mistakes in my life were made at times when I was trying to please others or fit in with the status quo, usually by either moulding my words to suit a situation or by holding my tongue altogether.

Spending time in silence has also allowed me to become familiar with the physical ways in which fear manifests in my body, and to recognise the thoughts and 'stories' that trigger those fears. It has revealed to me that I am terrified of financial insecurity. That I still think of myself as an ungainly, shy kid. That I habitually assume I will never be good enough. That I am unlovable. It has showed me that my perfectionism is just a desperate—and futile—attempt to control the world, and to prevent people from seeing the real person hiding behind the façade.

In silence, I recognised that if I didn't take action to contain and curtail the noise of my life, it would drown out the things that really matter to me. I realised quite suddenly that I alone had to make the decisions necessary to put my relationships and my values first. Otherwise, those decisions would be made by default, by whoever or whatever spoke loudest: work, peer pressure, status anxiety, financial insecurity, shame.

Silence showed me that it was time to stop living fearfully. It showed me that although living honestly is not completely comfortable, it is better than living a lie. It prompted me to forgive myself for not fitting the mould of the smart-suited communications executive. It lit the path that would lead me back home to my ailing father, to my estranged friends, to my family and, ultimately, to myself.

But silence also taught me that I didn't have to do all this in one big leap. Little by little is fine. You learn that when you spend time simply observing things as they rise and fall away: change is happening all the time, in small moments as well as large. They all mark a birth or a death in some way.

# EPILOGUE

*My father is dying.*
*He is dying.*
*My father is dying now.*

The words roll around my skull like marbles, crashing through nerves, bruising my brain. Sometimes they come to rest in the back of my throat, blocking breath and voice. I pull them forward into my mouth, these unfamiliar words, and move them around gingerly, probing for weaknesses, testing for crevasses where something more may hide.

*My father is dying.*

Sometimes I can even push them to my lips. But no further. These brittle words, so heavy in my skull, won't cross that boundary. What would happen? Would they fall like dead weights and shatter on the floor, sending jagged shards to pierce those around me? Would they burst on contact with the air, spewing something more noxious into the atmosphere? Or would they simply evaporate, become transparent, disappear? Perhaps that would be worst of all. To release those words—*My father is dying*—into the world, only for them to be left unheeded. Is that why I suck them back reflexively, deep into my gut, whenever they drift close to the tip of my tongue?

Sometimes in my sleep, or when I'm awake but distracted, my fingers seek out imaginary marbles to play with. It's almost sooth-ing, this brushing of the whorls of my fingertips against something unfamiliar, rolling and moving, seeking patterns and solidity. Vaguely, in the smoky recesses of my memory, I recognise this as a habit from my childhood. When I hid in the kindy cubbyhouse, whispering stories to myself, I would swirl my fingertips against each other. Grounding myself through touch, reminding myself I am here. I am solid too. I am still that child.

*And my father is dying.*

*He is dying.*

*Is he dying now?*

Nobody will answer that question. Not out loud.

I discovered many things in the months after silence whispered to me that it was time to be with my father in Brisbane. I discovered that I had harboured all sorts of preconceived notions about death. With the luxury of naivety, I had assumed it was an event, not a process. Such a big thing, death; I had expected it would reveal itself unambiguously. I was prepared for it to be traumatic, shattering, definitive. A sudden severing of life's bonds.

Instead, I found myself witnessing the fabric of a life wearing away in tiny increments. Sometimes a few threads frayed and snapped in resounding ways, as they had on the afternoon of Dad's stroke or when he had broken his thigh. But mostly it was a quiet thinning. A material once rich in detail and texture was now fading so slowly that it was impossible to detect the colour leaching away, until one day I looked and he was pale. And the next day I looked and he was translucent. And the day after that he had lost more colour again, even when I was certain there had been no more left to lose.

On those days, I had to fight the urge to snatch at the remaining fragments of his being, to gather and clutch them close. Driving to the hospital one morning, this vision came to me: that sometime soon, the fabric of my father would simply disintegrate, the last gossamer threads scattering to the wind.

But when? Nobody would tell me.

Another thing I discovered about death was that, in its thrall, time begins to behave unpredictably. 'When' becomes a foreign landscape, treacherous and tricky to navigate. There were times, sitting in the dim, close confines of a hospital room, listening to Dad's breath as he dozed or holding a teaspoon of ice cream up for him to eat, when the passage of minutes and hours felt like swimming through honey. But then something would happen—a new wave of pain, a doctor's request for more tests, a physio with a daunting new exercise regimen—and time would accelerate again, screeching away with me left scrabbling in its wake, trying to keep my balance.

When the latest urgent flurry settled again, I would feel almost grateful for the insatiable maws of the parking meters that lined the streets around the hospital, demanding to be fed. They imposed some order on an otherwise disordered experience; here was a task I could complete with some certainty of a positive outcome. Plus, it was an opportunity to break through the membrane that contained this grey, dense twilight like a noxious bubble, and pretend I was normal again, just strolling a suburban street. But often, as I stepped outside, the weight of the sun landing on my skin, the explosion of fresh air in my lungs, would take me by surprise. It was almost too much to bear. I would feel untethered, disoriented, as if I might actually step out of my body if I moved too fast, and fall away into nothingness. I had to hunker down on my haunches against a fence, clutching onto the grass itself.

My brain would go to war with itself in those moments. The rational part, the professional overachiever, would insist there was something more I could do—something I *should* do—to assert control.

An action plan would help. A to-do list. If I just used my problem-solving skills, built a spreadsheet, created some group chats, all the scattered and lost pieces could be put back together, just like a jigsaw. The old mantra shouted in my ear: *Just. Keep. Moving!* Any challenge could be surmounted with a mobile phone and the right attitude; wasn't that how it worked? These old habits were familiar. Comforting. Beguiling, like sirens singing from rocks in the dark.

But what was the challenge I was trying to address? To stop the world spinning? To slow down time? To block the path of death itself?

One day a high-pitched screech split the air as I slumped in the street. At first my sleep-deprived brain thought it might be human, but eventually I recognised the squealing protest of metal forced against metal. A little further down the hill, an older man had climbed out of his SUV, leaving it in the middle of the road. Following his gaze, I saw that he had sideswiped one, possibly two, cars as he had driven up the narrow thoroughfare, which was always tightly packed with vehicles left by hospital visitors.

Momentarily I was flooded with irritation, my nerves jangling with the sensory overload of another crisis. I had come to depend on these trudging journeys to the parking meter for a respite of sorts. Instead, this man, his car, the overcrowded street, the punitive parking restrictions, the creaking hospital infrastructure—all were conspiring to make my day even worse than it already was.

But then I caught a glimpse of his face as he trudged towards me. It had eroded, caved in on itself, the eyes pooling like darkness amid the fleshy rubble. I recognised that face with a clarity so stark and sudden I felt seasick: the cheeks creased by nights of sleeplessness, the mouth dragged down with heavy resignation. This face was just like mine. I knew in a heartbeat that someone in this man's life was dying too.

From nowhere, a gust of compassion swept away my resentment. It was surprising, even shocking, the arising of this instinct that confirmed

I had more care to give, even when I felt so utterly drained. Had you asked me moments before, I would have told you in tight, cracked syllables that the only human being for whom I had energy at this time was my father. But still it comes. We see ourselves in others and it comes.

I steadied the stricken man until a nurse, arriving for her shift, took over, with that special blend of competence and warmth that only very good nurses have. Just like that, our paths sprang apart again.

As I continued on my way to the meter, I pondered this sudden reflex to care. Normally, I needed to know that what I was offering was right, appropriate, before I approached someone—and that I wouldn't offend or be rejected. But that was a response from the head. Perhaps I was beginning to lead with the heart.

I discovered too, during this time, that nobody truly becomes an adult until they have lost a parent. And while I was intensely grateful that this was not a threshold I had to cross until I was almost 50 years old, I was also somewhat mortified to realise that I had only been pretending up until then. I had been conducting an elaborate pantomime at being an adult, with only half the wisdom required to be fully grown.

Death continued its approach, coming so close now that its presence became an ever-present soundtrack to the days as they passed; in my mind, I still hear a cello in D minor. I told myself then that it was ridiculous to keep fighting something that was natural. Like water, like wind, this force would eventually flow around me and away.

But then there were days when I would visit Dad and he would amaze me. Or make me laugh. Or do one of a hundred familiar things that I was not ready to let go. One day, I sat on the bed with my laptop balanced on my knees as he dictated an entire newspaper column, including the layout of a bridge hand, and the winning play to follow. As one of Australia's enduring champions of the bridge world, having won significant titles over several decades since the 1960s, Dad had been writing the column for *The Courier-Mail* for more than twenty years. Apparently, it hadn't occurred to him to stop now. Propped up in a hospital armchair, grumpy because I'd refused to drive him home for the day so that he could write the piece on his own enormous PC, Dad simply conjured several hundred words of perfect syntax, without prompts or references.

Funny how the mind works. Or was that the spirit? He could barely walk, could no longer hear without aids or see without a glaring spotlight, but there were corners of Dad's brain where his formidable intellect still shone radiant and sure. When he opened the doors to those rooms, he was young again, the gregarious Australian bridge champion with a stunning general knowledge, loving his sport, and loved by his bridge partners, his mates, his readers and students.

Maybe that moment comforted me too much. The next day I gave myself the day off, eager to attend my favourite writers' group, at the Queensland State Library. We worked in silence for 25 minutes at a time, the energy of ideas and words pulsing through the room like an electric current. When I noticed the missed calls from my mother, and then my brother, I knew before I knew. I knew I would pack up and drive to the hospital, grateful that it was so close. I think I knew, too, that there would be a doctor waiting there who would talk in long syllables about the latest test results. If the doctor was good, he or she would call my father by his name and listen to him too. If he or she was good, they would answer my questions in the hall outside. But those answers wouldn't really matter. Already, I knew.

That night, Dad had his lungs drained, and at some point it was confirmed that the multiple spots on his lungs and his liver, and elsewhere around his body, were cancer.

I arrived early the next morning with newspapers, to feed the current affairs habit he had so emphatically passed on to me, and cake, in the hope I might also feed his once avid sweet tooth. He had already lost another layer of himself. Was it possible he was collapsing into two dimensions only, framed by a stark white sheet? But Dad seemed so sanguine that I had a moment of uncertainty: perhaps he was addled by the painkillers, or had even forgotten the prognosis?

Since his stroke, he had always been very matter-of-fact about the possibility of his death. Possibility? That is my euphemism, a pallid attempt to hide my unwillingness—still!—to call it what it was: an inevitability. But Dad seemed at peace with it. The only urgency I had detected in the ensuing months was his need to have this inevitability recognised by others, and for us to listen to his wishes. I had listened. But always these requests had seemed safely hypothetical. Now we had a death sentence captured in crisp, clinical jargon on a single white page.

The air in Dad's room, usually so dense and warm, became liquid. I bobbed, unsteady in the ripples around me, as I tentatively reviewed those conclusions.

'Now,' I began, my eyes locked on the carrot cake between us, 'is the time to speak up and tell me if you want to revise any of your plans.'

Did he wish to rescind his desire to accept the outcome rather than seek more medical intervention? The child in me hovered close by, hoping he would say he is going to fight on. That kid who had hidden in the cubbyhouse—she wasn't going to leave his side. But the adult, the one so equipped to deal with crises in the world of noise and artificial busyness—she was ready to flee or fall.

Dad told me he was happy with the life he has led. He felt his children and grandchildren were now making their way in the world. He just didn't want to be in any pain. He gave the names of some friends he wanted me to call. Then he asked whether there had been any queries about the bridge column and what I thought about the next likely leadership battle in Canberra. And then he fell asleep.

I suspected the mischievous side of him was pleased he would no longer have to acquiesce to the upbeat physios and their ambitious exercise routines. And he probably knew the nurses would no longer confiscate the beer his mates liked to smuggle in. He was peaceful. It was good.

I went downstairs to buy another coffee. He was peaceful, I reminded myself. It was good. I made a few phone calls. It was good, I reassured people. He was peaceful. Then it was time to feed the meter.

I should have been prepared. When I stepped outside, the heft of the sunshine and the force of fresh air almost knocked me off my feet. Time went rubbery again. It wasn't good and I wasn't peaceful. I made it halfway to the car before my knees gave way and I curled over myself on the grassy verge.

I wanted desperately, angrily and, yes, selfishly, for anybody else to take charge and tell me what to do. I wanted to claw back time, like a mountain climber might claw for a rope after they lose their footing and begin sliding inexorably towards a ravine. I wanted a straight-forward series of steps that would achieve a concrete, clear objective. I wanted all of those busy routines that used to feel so effective to be enough again. Otherwise, I wanted to run.

Then, after a few minutes breathing in the grass, I opened my eyes. Silence was all around me. The ancient trees of the Hoh were there, waiting without judgement. The space of a meditation stool, too, and the quiet rhythms of a hall in the Tasmanian bush. The boom and sigh of the ocean leaning into the headland at Noosa National Park. The velvet air before sunrise on a clifftop in Big Sur. The songs of monks, their faces turned upwards in soft candlelight, at Tarrawarra Abbey. Gordon Hempton waiting to capture the dawn chorus in another hidden corner of the planet. Miriam-Rose Ungunmerr watching the birds rise from Daly River: 'To know me is to breathe with me. To breathe with me is to listen deeply.' They were all there. With me and inside me. In silence, there is space for everything.

I put some coins into the meter and made my way back to the hospital ward. Soon, Dad's family would arrive, in pairs and alone. But for now, things were quiet.

I sat down by my father's bed. I took his hand, and stroked his battered head, and I joined him in the silence. I stayed there with him as the silence expanded, until he was ready to walk on ahead alone.

# Appendix

# SILENCE: A HOW-TO GUIDE

I've heard runners talk about completing their first marathon on a high—only to come back to earth with a disappointing thud when their very next training run turns out to be just like every other training run they'd done before achieving their big goal: sometimes easy, sometimes tough, sometimes invigorating, sometimes soul-destroying. The same old challenges—of fitting in training sessions, regardless of the weather or their social activities or other demands—still apply.

So it is with silent practices. I felt transformed by my ten-day silent retreat in Tasmania—and in many ways I was. Just not how I expected. My frustrations and bad habits and triggers weren't magically erased, but I now had the ability to recognise them more clearly—and to recognise when I needed to 'top up' my silent time.

Since then, I've learned not to depend on a meditation practice alone. While it's great when I can meditate twice a day for 30 to 45 minutes (my current ideal), there are plenty of occasions when this is just impossible with two children, a partner who travels, unpredictable work deadlines of my own, and the obligations of caring for ageing parents.

Even when I can make it to my meditation stool for these sessions, I have found myself reaching for silence at other times during the day: sometimes because I simply feel the need for a pause, or because I am feeling overwhelmed by negativity, but also when I'm in the presence of something profoundly beautiful, like great music, a stunning view or an act of raw humanity.

Without realising it at first, I developed different practices for different situations—and I'm sharing them here. If I was still working in communications consultancy, I'd give them a fancy title, like 'a suite of silence tactics' or 'a toolbox for wellbeing'. But instead, I've catalogued them here by the time they take; after all, for most of us, when we're hustling through our days, that's the crucial factor.

*Slivers of silence* are the little fragments of time, often mere minutes, that present themselves throughout the day on an ad hoc basis: when we're waiting in a queue to order coffee, or caught in traffic, or between tasks at work or at home. (Since we're being honest here, let's acknowledge that they can even present themselves when we're in the loo.) These moments may be brief but they tend to be plentiful—and many of us have grown accustomed to filling them with distractions from our newsfeed or social media.

*Slices of silence* require more intention, in terms of planning time for them in a day or week, but they are still completely manageable. They're like gym sessions or yoga classes—you make the commitment and hold the space in your diary in order to feel better afterwards—while slivers are usually impromptu. In my experience, if you can commit to one regular daily slice of silence, at a minimum of about ten minutes, you'll quickly begin to build around it. It is the foundational tool.

*Slabs of silence* are just that: great dollops of the stuff, which require significant planning. For that reason, I don't think it's helpful to put an expectation on when or how many slabs of silence are ideal. Frankly, you'll know you're ready for a slab of silence when your existing silence practice tells you that you're ready to go further—and even then you may have to be patient. I became interested in Vipassana years before I attended my first ten-day retreat; it was frustrating, but I can see in retrospect that it happened when it was meant to. In the intervening years, I had been 'forced' to work on a more manageable meditation practice, which was actually more appropriate for my mindset at the time. Ten days in silence would have been too much for me then—but by the time I made it to Tasmania for my retreat, it was perfect . . . while still incredibly challenging!

Finally, be gentle with yourself. The modern world bombards us with messages about productivity and hyper-achievement—the idea that your worth is bound up with setting goals and then moving through them doggedly, even ferociously. But life's not linear like that. Sometimes we are diverted, even overwhelmed. Along the way, we may discover that the goals we set aren't the right ones for us, right now, and others are more appropriate.

In the spirit of full disclosure, here's a confession: while writing this book, I 'lost' my meditation practice completely. Ill health (mine and others), insomnia, moving house, the needs of my family, competing work deadlines—sometimes life just became too full.

But what has changed since my ten-day meditation retreat is my recognition that this is the norm. Instead of beating myself up and deciding that I'm never going to be 'good enough' at this, I simply start again. The practice of recognising thoughts and sensations as they arise, and then letting them go rather than attaching a story to them—this can work in daily life too. Just as thoughts will arise, so too will daily distractions and demands. It's not about resisting or judging them, but training ourselves to recognise them as something that will pass too.

The good news is that silence is always there waiting for you, when you're ready to return.

## Slivers of silence

### ❀ Half-smile meditation

Curve your mouth into a half-moon. (You can grin more widely, if you're comfortable—just be aware you might look like the Joker.) Close your eyes or hold your gaze softly on a steady point. Count three slow, deep breaths, staying aware of the air flowing in and out of your belly. That's it! The smile is key because it activates certain neurotransmitters, including dopamine (the one your brain is craving when it seeks out social media likes).

This sliver is ideal for moments of frustration or simply waiting. If you're stuck in traffic, just hold your gaze on the traffic lights to ensure you stay safe. I've used it in interminable work meetings, staring down at my notebook, and at school assemblies, where I assume everyone else thought I was smiling at the kids. (I learned of this practice in Vicki Mackenzie's book *Cave in the Snow*, where it was recommended by the Zen lay priest Yvonne Rand.)

### ❀ Hold space

When someone is speaking to you—colleague, partner, child—imagine you are creating a space for their words. Treat that space like a blank page or calm pool (it may help to envision a 'cone of silence' around you), into which they are adding their thoughts and emotions. Pay attention. This is about listening 'with the ear of the heart', as Benedict would say, not simply waiting for a pause into which you can insert your own words.

### ❀ Pause—and respond

When you're called upon to respond to the thoughts of another person (for example, after holding space for them), channel my former work colleague who took a few seconds in his job interview to absorb the question and prepare a considered reply. Count to three or give yourself three breaths—whatever works. If necessary, tell the other person you'd like to think for a moment, because what they have suggested is complex/challenging/interesting/promising and you want to give it the consideration it deserves.

(A confession: I'm not very good at this one. But I'm sure I could become a lot better if our elected leaders were wise enough to model it for the rest of us whenever they speak publicly.)

### ❀ Have esteem for silence

Whether you're responding to another person or considering speaking of your own volition, take a moment to consider Benedict's advice in Chapter 6 of *The Rule*: 'There are times when even good words are to be left unsaid out of esteem for silence.' In Buddhism, 'Right Speech' is one of the Five Precepts of Ethical Conduct. In the Hindu text, the *Bhagavad Gita*, followers are encouraged to observe 'austerity of speech'. The guiding principles are roughly the same in all three traditions, and are often summarised in secular terms thus: Is it true? Is it kind? Is it necessary? Only when you can answer 'yes' to all three should you consider opening your mouth.

### ❀ Nature break

If possible, position an attractive plant close to your workstation. Between tasks, use the plant as the focal point for a half-smile meditation. During phone calls, settle your gaze on it, then allow your eyes to follow its contours and study the range of colours and shades. Emerging research shows that even 40 seconds staring at green space can boost your concentration and productivity.[1]

## Slices of silence

### ❀ Meditation practice

Establish a meditation practice, preferably in the morning before you start the day, or at the end of the day, before you go to bed. If you have young children, give yourself permission to be more flexible about timing; perhaps tie it instead to an event like the baby's morning or afternoon nap.

If you are new to meditation, aim for five to ten minutes at first. Aim to build up to half an hour—or more, if you can. Remember, there is good science to show that your brain will enjoy benefits from even short sessions, provided they are regular.

Don't get hung up on a particular style or school of meditation. There are a range of good meditation apps that provide timers for silent meditation, as well as guided sessions and general lessons for those wanting to learn more. Check out Insight Timer, Calm, Headspace and 10 Percent Happier. Sam Harris's app Waking Up provides an excellent series of lessons for those particularly interested in Vipassana style. The important thing is to start and maintain a practice, remembering that the aim is not to erase or stop all thoughts, but simply to get used to watching them, and other sensations, come and go.

A final note about meditation: there are some schools and teachers that charge hundreds of dollars for meditation courses. You do *not* need to spend money to establish a practice. For some, paying for a teacher may be an appropriate additional step to help guide an advanced practice, but no one should make you feel it is necessary to pay large sums to get started.

### ❈ Tech-free bedtime

Make a rule of cutting digital noise at least an hour before bedtime. That means no phone, no tablet, no TV and no laptop/computer. Read a book, listen to calming music, meditate, do yoga. Remember what sex was like? That's permissible too, provided you don't need tech-related tools (no judgement!).

### ❈ Quiet quest

Set yourself a challenge to find a new, quiet place near your place of work, and aim to visit at least once a week; you could eat lunch there, or meditate, or simply sit—but treat it as a tech-free zone. If you don't work, you could do the same with somewhere else you visit often—near the school drop-off, the gym, your parents' house or the doctor's surgery. This can be a lovely way of exploring a neighbourhood. I've found sanctuaries of silence in churches (many are open to visitors all day, and you'll be left alone, provided you behave appropriately), parks, art galleries and libraries.

## ❊ Walk in nature

This is similar to a quiet quest, but this time you're seeking out a place to walk among trees for at least twenty minutes. Leave the earphones at home. If you carry a phone, put it in your pocket on silent and aim to leave it there.

It's quite possible you'll feel bored or even slightly panicky at first; this is the brain registering that it doesn't have its normal distractions. Choose a sense to focus on, and explore what you can see, smell, hear, feel or even taste as you slowly walk. Once you've found a trail or walking spot that suits you, try to visit it regularly, at different times of the day. Allow yourself to get to know it, as you would a new friend, noting its different 'moods' at different times.

Many women feel vulnerable being alone on bush trails or even on paths through parkland or suburban streets. That's understandable, but don't allow it to stop you, if possible. Find a walking group in your area (a positive use for social media!); many are happy to have members participate without chatting avidly to others. Some even encourage quiet activity.

Alternatively, consider finding a dog to walk (either your own, a friend or neighbour's, or even through a pet walking service). Not only are you likely to feel safer, but most dogs are brilliant at showing how to be in the moment. If I could be as present as our labrador is when we're exploring the sights and smells of our local fauna reserve, I'd be one step closer to enlightenment.

## ❊ Reset between tasks

Ideally, it would be great to be able to control our days to ensure there were no interruptions until we have finished a set task. But in the real world, most of us must divide our time between several ongoing projects, while also juggling unscheduled interruptions.

In that case, it makes sense to have a plan for how we deal with competing demands on our attention. Key to this process is helping our brains reset between tasks. Otherwise, we're likely to carry what Sophie Leroy, an associate professor at the University of Washington, calls 'attention residue' from one task into the next meeting or project, gradually draining our energy.

'It's like windows staying open in our brains, and it makes it hard to focus on the intervening work,' Leroy says. 'As I am still thinking about Task A while trying to do Task B, I don't have the cognitive capacity to process those two tasks at the same time and do a perfect job on both tasks. It's not cognitively possible.'[2]

She recommends getting into the habit of pausing briefly before moving from one uncompleted task to the next, and jotting down a 'ready-to-resume plan'. It may be as simple as noting where you have finished for the moment, what actions you will tackle next and whether there are unresolved issues you need to consider. This might only take a minute, so feel free to consider this a sliver of silence. If the task is more complex, you might alert your colleagues that you'll routinely take five minutes to do this. Either way, research by Leroy and the University of Minnesota's Theresa Glomb indicates that this 'brain reset' exercise will improve your performance on the next piece of work demanding your attention.

## ❀ Media diet

Some people refer to this as an 'attention diet', but the principle is the same: we should address 'feeding' our attention in the same way we approach feeding our body. Like junk food, too much junk media is bad for our wellbeing.

There are now plenty of books and articles devoted to this topic but here are some basic steps that will help you increase the amount of quiet time available to you during your day:

- Remove all social media apps from your phone, and schedule a regular time or times during the day when you check your accounts on your laptop or PC instead. This ensures your use becomes mindful, rather than as a default distraction.

- Cull/unfollow your news media. Just because it purports to be 'news' doesn't make it good for you! Replace these with a small selection of news outlets, preferably representing a range of views (or aim to balance a conservative outlet with a liberal outlet), and schedule a specific time during the day when you deliberately update yourself. As we've seen, following rolling news coverage during the day only stokes anxiety and outrage—with the aim of holding your attention—rather than providing you with thoughtful new material.

o  Where possible, choose long-form material like podcasts, documentaries, books or feature articles. Like food, media that takes longer to create is usually of higher quality.

o  'Greyscale' your phone. Like black-and-white TV, a greyscaled phone is less appealing to the eye and therefore less of a distraction. It is relatively easy to greyscale most modern smartphones (my iPhone takes three clicks on the right side button to toggle between grey and colour), but the tech companies are in no hurry to help you learn! Yet Google can be your friend: use the search terms 'greyscale', 'phone' and your particular operating system.

o  Turn off notifications on your devices.

o  Install a productivity app on your laptop or desktop. I use Freedom, but there are a range available. The best will allow you to schedule times when you cannot access websites or apps, ranging from a total blackout of all digital content (transforming your laptop into a basic word processor) to a partial blackout on selected apps (like social media or news).

## ❋ Cone of car silence

This is an unexpected favourite of mine, and can also be done in slivers. Most of us are creatures of habit in the car; after all, the act of driving is a series of reflexes and habits. Often we introduce more noise in the car, putting on the radio, listening to podcasts or music, or returning calls. Instead, consciously create a space in the car that is quiet, at least when you're driving alone. Turn all devices off (or put them on silent); if you use an iPhone, you can even set it to inform callers or those sending texts that you are driving and will not receive their message until you have stopped.

Then . . . just drive. Recognise that this is an opportunity to let your brain rest and focus on one activity alone. If you're like me, you'll be surprised to discover that you start looking forward to this time.

## ✸ Library rules

This is an idea I have happily borrowed from Basecamp's Jason Fried, who I introduced in Chapter 10. Not everyone has a say over how their workplace is organised, but for those who do—or who are prepared to suggest it at the next staff meeting—the productivity and morale benefits make it worth considering.

On the Basecamp blog, Fried explains it this way: 'Open offices work all around the world every day. They're called libraries! And the more you treat your office as a *library of work*—rather than a chaotic kitchen of work—the better an open floor plan is going to work.' Library rules, according to Fried, 'means keeping to yourself, keeping your voice down in hushed tones, not distracting one another'.[3] Basecamp's open-plan office also has a number of enclosed rooms available in which staff can have proper discussions.

If the idea of running your workspace like a library full-time is too onerous, or not feasible because there are no rooms available for team discussions, an alternative may be to nominate one day a week when library rules apply. On that day, no meetings are scheduled and phone discussions are kept to a minimum. This is the day for quiet work, research, creative thinking and planning.

## ✸ Digital Sabbath

Like tech-free bedtime, but for 24 hours. Enjoying a day of rest from technology is not a new idea—I've found reports of the concept dating back to 2001, long before mobile devices were on the market[4]—but it has gained popularity in recent years. If I was a stickler, I would not include it here, as the emphasis is on spending a day doing anything that does not involve technology, and that could include going to a heavy metal concert, playing in a brass band and plenty of other very noisy alternatives. However, the value is so great—in terms of refocusing on digital-free interaction with each other and the world—that I endorse it regardless.

## Slabs of silence

### ❀ Digital holiday

Much like the Digital Sabbath, but for longer. Plan at least one holiday a year at a destination without wi-fi or TV (or at least no multichannel pay TV). Take books. Play board games. Talk to your children. Go to the movies. Cook together.

Again, there is the possibility that plenty of analogue activities will involve substantial noise. For example, I wouldn't rule out a holiday for the family at a music festival, particularly one with plenty of cultural and creative activities for all ages, like the Woodford Folk Festival. Even with plenty of music or other rowdy entertainment, the absence of digital devices ensures there will be plenty of quiet spaces where there was once digital 'wallpaper' and white noise.

### ❀ Formal silent retreat

Once you have established a meditation routine and sustained it for several months, you may choose to attend a longer silent retreat. Several contemplative traditions offer supervised retreats ranging from a weekend to ten days (or longer, if you have more experience).

Another option is to stay with a silent order, outside of a formal retreat. As I discovered, the Benedictines extend hospitality where possible to any visitor, provided they are respectful of the monks' daily routine. Spiritual guidance—or just a good chat—is usually available, should you request it; otherwise, guests are not required to attend meditation or prayer sessions, as they might be in a formal retreat. Many Buddhist monasteries and centres offer similar hospitality, but often expect guests to help with chores for part of the day.

## ❈ Secular silent retreat

Many, if not most, health and wellness retreats will support guests who ask to conduct some or even all of their stay in silence. Indeed, an increasing number now offer silent retreats that are not attached to any religious tradition or rigorous meditation practice (like Vipassana).

Alternatively, it might be possible to conduct a silent retreat at home, particularly if you live alone or don't have children, or at a holiday house or apartment. This is another opportunity to use the internet in a positive way: google something like 'silent retreat at home' and you will find plenty of tips and suggestions, some involving formal meditation or prayer, and others that are completely secular, and even include pampering options as well.

The magic here is not in how strict you are with yourself—silence does not have to be synonymous with suffering—but, rather, in establishing your own rules in advance and sticking to them mindfully. Consider things like how comprehensively you will ban screens (which devices will you forgo, and for what time periods?), whether you will allow yourself to read, and if so, which material (some people prepare a themed reading list appropriate to the purpose of their retreat), and whether you will participate in activities outside your home or accommodation, like yoga classes or gym sessions (and how you will manage communication in those settings).

# ACKNOWLEDGEMENTS

Books are like babies. Some are the result of months, even years, of careful planning. Others take you by surprise. Either way, from the moment when a writer first detects the delicate flutterings of something new taking form inside them, it's tempting to assume this entity will be your creation, and yours alone.

But babies and books have their ways of humbling us. The journey to delivery rarely goes entirely to plan. They arrive in their own time, and it's folly to expect that you can control how the labour will progress or exactly how the final product will look when it enters the world.

Ultimately, all we can do is work hard to help this unique little thing be the best it can be. At some point, you present it to the world and hope everyone else will appreciate it—and maybe even love it—as much as you do.

And by then, if you're very lucky, you will have enjoyed the support of many amazing and talented people.

Very early in this book's gestation, when I was uncertain about whether I should persevere, Louise Adler's enthusiasm convinced me. (Anyone who has experienced the force of nature that is Adler enthusiasm will understand it is very hard to resist.) Sally Heath was a patient, skilled and caring midwife, to whom I owe more than I can express here. Thanks to both women for being so utterly gracious when circumstances changed and this book was ultimately birthed elsewhere.

I am yet to meet a writer who doesn't value quiet places. But when you are writing about silence, they become essential—as are the people who tend, protect and advocate for them.

Thank you to Gordon Hempton: for being a compelling voice in the diminishing wilderness, for pointing me in the direction of a certain Sitka spruce, and for believing I could find my own way to my own answers, even when I wanted him to tell me his instead.

Also to David George Haskell: your writing on this topic is so beautiful and brilliant, I am rendered almost mute. (Not the sort of silence I'm aiming for!) Your generosity of spirit and curiosity about the world and its humans remain an inspiration. Thanks to you and to Katie for sharing your limited time in Brisbane.

As both a reader and a writer, I have boundless gratitude for Fiona Stager, who has built a remarkable community around her bookshop, Avid Reader, in Brisbane. Thanks, Fiona, for providing a supportive space for writers to work—and for employing so many of them! (Shout out to Krissy Kneen, whose words of advice and encouragement are always invaluable.)

Thanks, too, to the Queensland Writers Centre, and particularly to Connor and the team who host Writing Fridays. Imagine a room full of people, all united in their commitment to writing in silent, 25-minute bursts. Thousands of the words between these covers were born that way.

And to all the libraries I've loved . . . One of the joys of writing this book was rediscovering them, to tap into their gentle rhythms and be reminded that this is where real Australian life unfolds, far from the noise and self-importance of politics and big media. The State Library of Queensland, with its sunlit spaces and expansive river views, is a glorious place to write or read. But I have also been a regular visitor to Chermside, Grange and Ashgrove libraries in Brisbane, and Stanton and Mosman libraries in Sydney. I name them all here because if we don't use them, we may lose them—and the staff in each deserve recognition for the role they play in our communities.

I remain amazed by the myriad small miracles that emerge when one is on a quest like mine. A radio interview overheard in a cab, a chance encounter in a café queue, a conversation with the person who is organising the meeting with the person you actually want to interview—answers and inspiration are waiting everywhere, but often not where you've decided they will be.

Love and gratitude to: Janella Purcell, for telling me I was becoming a crone—and why that's a good thing; Sharon Kolkka, for understanding me before I said a word; Yvonne Shepherd and the group at Women's Fitness Adventures, for quiet company when I needed it; Brother Bernard, for conversations in the Tarrawarra kitchen; and the Langri Tangpa Buddhist Centre, for solace and solidarity.

I'm indebted to Corrine, Julie, Carol and the team at Murdoch Books for their enthusiasm and commitment to all that this book represents. Most of all, thanks for your grace and indefatigability when confronted by the game-changer that was, and is, COVID-19. You are warrior women of the best sort.

Julian Welch, you are a wizard with words. I can't thank you enough for your masterful edits and the wisdom, patience and good humour you brought to every one of our conversations.

Alex Adsett, you are my fairy godmother masquerading as an agent. Wisdom, cake and lawyerly smarts, served up as required; what more could a writer ask for? Oh, that's right, an agent who loves Pub Choir as much as I do. I guess you're perfect.

Thank you to my oldest friend, Alexis Beebe, for sharing history and histrionics. And to Jared, Pero and Jacqui for providing me with gossip and GIFs when I was supposed to be working.

To Riley and Luke: I owe you big-time, for keeping the secret that Mum is not always as quiet as she pretends to be, and for loving me regardless. I wish I was a better writer, so I could describe just how big and profound my love for you both is.

Finally, to Peter, who believed in me more than I believed in myself. Thank you for sending me to the other side of the world to chase silence on my own, and then travelling to Tasmania so we could discover it together. Not a day goes by when I don't marvel at the uncommon grace that gave us a chance to be together. I love you.

# NOTES

## Chapter 2. Into Silence

1.  Sarah Wilson, 'One month without exercise, soap and loo paper . . .', 29 July 2015, <www.sarahwilson.com/2015/07/one-month-without-exercise-soap-and-loo-paper>.
2.  Mike Wass, 'Sheppard talk breakthrough hit "Geronimo", cracking America & their next single: Idolator Interview', *Idolator*, 14 November 2014, <www.idolator.com/7570487/sheppard-geronimo-cracking-america-next-single-interview>.

## Chapter 3. The Rule

1.  Benedicta Ward (translator), *The Sayings of the Desert Fathers: The alphabetical collection*, Mowbray: Cistercian Publications, 1984.
2.  *The Rule of Saint Benedict*, chapter 48.
3.  Pico Iyer, 'Vacationing with Big Sur's monks', *Reuters*, 26 February 2011, <www.reuters.com/article/idUS3421279875201102218>.
4.  Pico Iyer, 'Unsurpassed contemplation at Big Sur's New Camaldoli hermitage', *The Orange County Register*, 30 October 2015, <www.ocregister.com/2015/10/30/pico-iyer-unsurpassed-contemplation-at-big-surs-new-camaldoli-hermitage>.
5.  Michael Casey, *Strangers to the City: Reflections on the beliefs and values of the Rule of Saint Benedict*, Orleans, MA: Paraclete Press, 2005.

## Chapter 4. Contemplation

1.  Peter A. Cameron et al., 'Black Saturday: The immediate impact of the February 2009 bushfires in Victoria, Australia', *The Medical Journal*

*of Australia*, vol. 191, no. 1, 2009, pp. 11–16, <www.mja.com.au/
journal/2009/191/1/black-saturday-immediate-impact-february-2009-
bushfires-victoria-australia>.

2.  Michael Casey, *Toward God: The ancient wisdom of Western prayer*,
    Liguori, MO: Triumph Books, 1996.

3.  Translation by Coleman Barks with Reynold Nicholson, A.J. Arberry
    and John Moyne, *The Essential Rumi: New expanded edition*, New York,
    NY: HarperOne, 2004, p. 22.

4.  See Melanoma Institute Australia, 'Melanoma facts and statistics',
    <www.melanoma.org.au/understanding-melanoma/melanoma-facts-
    and-statistics>.

## Chapter 5: Vipassana

1.  Sam Harris, *Waking Up: Searching for spirituality without religion*,
    London: Bantam Press, 2014, p. 34.

2.  Harris, *Waking Up*, p. 35.

## Chapter 6. Equanimity

1.  Joseph Goldstein, 'Mindfulness, compassion & wisdom: Three means to
    peace', *PBS.org*, 11 May 2010, <www.pbs.org/thebuddha/blog/2010/
    may/11/mindfulness-compassion-wisdom-three-means-peace-jo>.

2.  See *10% Happier with Dan Harris: Tim Ferriss*, 2 February 2018,
    <https://podcastnotes.org/tim-ferris-show/10-happier-with-dan-harris-
    tim-ferriss>.

## Chapter 7. Noise

1.  Marion Burgess, 'Quiet please! Fighting noise pollution', Australian
    Academy of Science, 2015, <www.science.org.au/curious/people-
    medicine/noise-pollution>.

2.  World Health Organization, *Burden of Disease from Environmental
    Noise: Quantification of healthy life years lost in Europe*, Copenhagen,
    WHO Regional Office for Europe, 2011, <www.euro.who.int/__data/
    assets/pdf_file/0008/136466/e94888.pdf>, p. 105.

3.  World Health Organization, *Burden of Disease from Environmental
    Noise*, p. 102.

4.  European Environment Agency, *Noise in Europe 2014*, EEA Report
    no. 10/2014, Luxembourg, Publications Office of the European
    Union, 2014, <www.eea.europa.eu/publications/noise-in-europe-2014>,
    p. 5.

5.  Claire Richardson, 'The historical and current challenge of
    environmental noise nuisance', *Proceedings of Acoustics2016—The
    Second Australasian Acoustical Societies Conference*, Brisbane,
    9–11 November 2016, <www.acoustics.asn.au/conference_proceedings/
    AASNZ2016>.

6.  enHealth, *The Health Effects of Environmental Noise*, Canberra,
    Department of Health, 2018, <www1.health.gov.au/internet/main/
    publishing.nsf/Content/A12B57E41EC9F326CA257BF0001F9
    E7D/$File/health-effects-Environmental-Noise-2018.pdf>, p. 9.

7.  enHealth, *The Health Effects of Environmental Noise*, p. vi.

8.  Orfeu M. Buxton et al., 'Sleep disruption due to hospital noises:
    A prospective evaluation', *Annals of Internal Medicine*, vol. 157, no. 3,
    2012, pp. 170–79.

9.  Dorian Rolston, 'Night noise: What a sleeping brain hears', MIND
    Guest Blog, *Scientific American*, 17 June 2013, <https://blogs.scientific
    american.com/mind-guest-blog/night-noise-what-a-sleeping-brain-
    hears>.

10. L. Bernardi, C. Porta & P. Sleight, 'Cardiovascular, cerebrovascular, and
    respiratory changes induced by different types of music in musicians
    and non-musicians: The importance of silence', *Heart*, vol. 92, no. 4,
    2006, pp. 445–52.

11. Queensland Brain Institute, 'Adult neurogenesis', <https://qbi.uq.edu.
    au/brain-basics/brain-physiology/adult-neurogenesis>.

12. I. Kirste et al., 'Is silence golden? Effects of auditory stimuli and their
    absence on adult hippocampal neurogenesis', *Brain Structure & Function*,
    vol. 220, no. 2, 2015, pp. 1221–28.

## Chapter 8. Overload

1.  Andrew Sullivan, 'I used to be a human being', *New York Magazine*,
    19 September 2016, <https://nymag.com/intelligencer/2016/09/
    andrew-sullivan-my-distraction-sickness-and-yours.html>.

2. B.J. Fogg, 'Thoughts on persuasive technology', Stanford Persuasive Technology Lab, 2010, <http://captology.stanford.edu/resources/thoughts-on-persuasive-technology.html>.

3. Dominic Rushe, '$1b deal: Facebook buys Instagram mobile photo sharing app', *The Sydney Morning Herald*, 10 April 2012, <www.smh.com.au/technology/1b-deal-facebook-buys-instagram-mobile-photo-sharing-app-20120410-1wllb.html>.

4. Tristan Harris, 'Humane: A new agenda for tech', <https://vimeo.com/332532972>.

5. Tristan Harris, 'A call to minimize distraction & respect users' attention by Tristan Harris', <www.scribd.com/document/378841682/A-Call-to-Minimize-Distraction-Respect-Users-Attention-by-Tristan-Harris>.

6. Center for Humane Technology, <https://humanetech.com>.

7. Stanford Graduate School of Business, 'Chamath Palihapitiya, Founder and CEO Social Capital, on money as an instrument of change', 13 November 2017, <www.youtube.com/watch?v=PMotykw0SIk>.

8. Peter Kafka, 'Amazon? HBO? Netflix thinks its real competitor is . . . sleep', *Vox*, 17 April 2017, <https://www.vox.com/2017/4/17/15334122/netflix-sleep-competitor-amazon-hbo>.

9. Harry McCracken, 'Netflix's Reed Hastings: "We're tiny!"', *Fast Company*, 24 October 2016, <www.fastcompany.com/4022814/netflixs-reed-hastings-were-tiny>.

10. Timothy D. Wilson et al., 'Just think: The challenges of the disengaged mind', *Science*, vol. 345, no. 6192, 2014, pp. 75–77.

11. Fariss Samarrai, 'Study: Smartphone alerts increase inattention—and hyperactivity', *UVAToday*, 9 May 2016, <https://news.virginia.edu/content/study-smartphone-alerts-increase-inattention-and-hyperactivity>; Michael Blaustein, 'Study: 62 per cent of women "check phones during sex"', *News.com.au*, 25 July 2013, <www.news.com.au/lifestyle/relationships/study-62-per-cent-of-women-check-phones-during-sex/news-story/4f067881c8d45a4c13cd8702e897fcae>.

12. Ashley Rodriguez, 'YouTube's recommendations drive 70% of what we watch', *Quartz*, 13 January 2018, <https://qz.com/1178125/youtubes-recommendations-drive-70-of-what-we-watch>.

13. Emily Bell, 'The end of the news as we know it: How Facebook swallowed journalism', Tow Center, 8 March 2016, <https://medium.com/tow-center/the-end-of-the-news-as-we-know-it-how-facebook-swallowed-journalism-60344fa50962#.pqtvqzrfi>.

14. Steve Rayson, 'We analyzed 100 million headlines. Here's what we learned (new research)', *BuzzSumo*, 26 June 2017, <https://buzzsumo.com/blog/most-shared-headlines-study>.

15. Amanda Meade, 'News Corp tabloid the Herald Sun offers journalists cash bonuses for clicks', *The Guardian*, 24 June 2019, <www.theguardian.com/media/2019/jun/24/news-corp-tabloid-the-herald-sun-offers-journalists-cash-bonuses-for-clicks>.

16. See www.edelman.com/trustbarometer.

17. Adrian F. Ward et al., 'Brain drain: The mere presence of one's own smartphone reduces available cognitive capacity', *Journal of the Association for Consumer Research*, vol. 2, no. 2, 2017, pp. 140–54.

18. Matt Richtel, 'In study, texting lifts crash risk by large margin', *The New York Times*, 27 July 2009, <www.nytimes.com/2009/07/28/technology/28texting.html>.

19. Andrew K. Przybylski & Netta Weinstein, 'Can you connect with me now? How the presence of mobile communication technology influences face-to-face conversation quality', *Journal of Social and Personal Relationships*, vol. 30, no. 3, 2012, pp. 237–46.

20. Pekka Räsänen et al., 'Targets of online hate: Examining determinants of victimization among young Finnish Facebook users', *Violence and Victims*, vol. 31, no. 4, 2016, pp. 708–25.

21. B. Carter et al., 'Association between portable screen-based media device access or use and sleep outcomes: A systematic review and meta-analysis', *JAMA Pediatrics*, vol. 170, no. 12, 2016, pp. 1202–08.

22. Mitch van Geel et al., 'Relationship between peer victimization, cyberbullying, and suicide in children and adolescents: A meta-analysis', *JAMA Pediatrics*, vol. 168, no. 5, 2014, pp. 435–42.

23. Jean M. Twenge et al., 'Age, period, and cohort trends in mood disorder indicators and suicide-related outcomes in a nationally representative dataset, 2005–2017', *Journal of Abnormal Psychology*, vol. 128, no. 3, 2019, pp. 185–99.

24. Jean M. Twenge, 'Have smartphones destroyed a generation?', *The Atlantic*, September 2017, <www.theatlantic.com/magazine/archive/2017/09/has-the-smartphone-destroyed-a-generation/534198>.

25. Melinda Gates, 'Melinda Gates: I spent my career in technology. I wasn't prepared for its effect on my kids', *The Washington Post*, 24 August 2017, <www.washingtonpost.com/news/parenting/wp/2017/08/24/melinda-gates-i-spent-my-career-in-technology-i-wasnt-prepared-for-its-effect-on-my-kids>.

26. Nick Bilton, 'Steve Jobs was a low-tech parent', *The New York Times*, 11 September 2014, <www.nytimes.com/2014/09/11/fashion/steve-jobs-apple-was-a-low-tech-parent.html>.

27. Tony Fadell, 'The iPhone changed our lives. Now Apple needs to tackle addiction', *Wired*, 14 April 2018, <www.wired.co.uk/article/tony-fadell-apple-iphone-addiction-control-design>.

28. Paul Lewis, '"Our minds can be hijacked": The tech insiders who fear a smartphone dystopia', *The Guardian*, 6 October 2017, <www.theguardian.com/technology/2017/oct/05/smartphone-addiction-silicon-valley-dystopia>.

29. Mike Allen, 'Sean Parker unloads on Facebook: "God only knows what it's doing to our children's brains"', *Axios*, 9 November 2017, <www.axios.com/sean-parker-unloads-on-facebook-god-only-knows-what-its-doing-to-our-childrens-brains-1513306792-f855e7b4-4e99-4d60-8d51-2775559c2671.html>.

30. Tim Hains, 'Former Facebook exec: Social media is ripping our social fabric apart', *RealClear Politics*, 11 December 2017, <www.realclearpolitics.com/video/2017/12/11/fmr_facebook_exec_social_media_is_ripping_our_social_fabric_apart.html>.

31. Yongey Mingyur Rinpoche with Helen Tworkov, *In Love with the World: A Monk's journey through the bardos of living and dying*, New York, NY: Pan Macmillan, 2019.

32. Daniel Goleman & Richard J. Davidson, *The Science of Meditation: How to change your brain, mind and body*, London: Viking, 2017.

33. National Center for Complementary and Integrative Health, 'National Health Interview Survey 2017', <https://nccih.nih.gov/research/statistics/NHIS/2017>.

34. Rebecca Muller, 'The 2018 app trend of the year will make you rethink how you're using your phone', *Thrive Global*, 6 December 2018, <https://thriveglobal.com/stories/apple-self-care-sleep-trend-app>.

35. Beth McGroarty, 'Meditation goes plural', Global Wellness Summit, <www.globalwellnesssummit.com/2019-global-wellness-trends/meditation-goes-plural>.

36. J.A. Grant, J. Courtemanche & P. Rainville, 'A non-elaborative mental stance and decoupling of executive and pain-related cortices predicts low pain sensitivity in Zen meditators', *Pain*, vol. 152, no. 1, 2011, pp. 150–56; Joshua A. Grant & Pierre Rainville, 'Pain sensitivity and analgesic effects of mindful states in Zen meditators: A cross-sectional study', *Psychosomatic Medicine*, vol. 71, no. 1, 2009, pp. 106–14.

37. Richard J. Davidson et al., 'Mental training affects distribution of limited brain resources', *PLOS Biology*, 8 May 2007, <https://journals.plos.org/plosbiology/article?id=10.1371/journal.pbio.0050138>.

38. Sara van Leeuwen, Notger G. Müller & Lucia Melloni, 'Age effects on attentional blink performance in meditation', *Consciousness and Cognition*, vol. 18, no. 3, 2009, pp. 593–99.

39. Lorenzo S. Colzato et al., 'Meditation-induced states predict attentional control over time', *Consciousness and Cognition*, vol. 37, 2015, pp. 57–62.

40. Michael Mrazek, Jonathan Smallwood & Jonathan Schooler, 'Mindfulness and mind-wandering: Finding convergence through opposing constructs', *Emotion*, vol. 12, 2012, pp. 442–48.

41. Michael Mrazek et al., 'Mindfulness training improves working memory capacity and GRE performance while reducing mind wandering', *Psychological Science*, vol. 24, no. 5, 2013, pp. 776–81.

42. Helen Y. Weng et al., 'Visual attention to suffering after compassion training is associated with decreased amygdala responses', *Frontiers in Psychology*, vol. 9, 2018, p. 771.

43. Nobel Media AB, 'Summary', NobelPrize.org, 10 May 2009, <www.nobelprize.org/prizes/medicine/2009/press-release>.

44. Cameron Stewart, 'Elizabeth Blackburn's latest quest: To save scientific research', *The Australian*, 10 August 2019.

## Chapter 9. Nature

1. 'Gordon Hempton: Silence and the presence of everything', *On Being*, 10 May 2012, <https://onbeing.org/programs/gordon-hempton-silence-and-the-presence-of-everything>.

2. Gordon Hempton, *Earth Is a Solar Powered Jukebox*, Sound Tracker, 2016.

3. Lama Yeshe, *The Peaceful Stillness of the Silent Mind*, Boston: Lama Yeshe Wisdom Archive, 2004.

4. Hempton, *Earth Is a Solar Powered Jukebox*.

5. Miriam-Rose Foundation, *Dadirri: Official Miriam-Rose Ungunmerr video: 3 minute promo*, <https://youtu.be/tow2tR_ezL8>.

6. Miriam-Rose Ungunmerr, *Dadirri: Inner deep listening and quiet still awareness*, <www.erea.edu.au/docs/default-source/justice-peace/dadirri---a-reflection-by-miriam---rose-ungunmerr--baumann.pdf?sfvrsn=1ea17f68_2>.

7. Leonardo Correa, 'Watch a conversation on The Art of Meditation and Dadirri', *Meditatio*, 3 August 2017, <www.meditatio.co.uk/watch-a-conversation-on-the-art-of-meditation-and-dadirri>.

8. Ungunmerr, *Dadirri*.

9. Ungunmerr, *Dadirri*.

10. Miriam-Rose Foundation, *Dadirri*.

11. Forest Therapy Society, '62 forests across Japan', *Forest Therapy*, n.d., <www.fo-society.jp/quarter/cn49/62forest_across_japan.html>.

12. Yoshifumi Miyazaki, *Shinrin-yoku: The Japanese way of forest bathing for health and relaxation*, London: Aster, 2018.

13. Qing Li et al., 'Forest bathing enhances human natural killer activity and expression of anti-cancer proteins', *International Journal of Immunopathology and Pharmacology*, vol. 20, no. 2, supp. 2, 2007, pp. 3–8.

14. Qing Li et al., 'Visiting a forest, but not a city, increases human natural killer activity and expression of anti-cancer proteins', *International Journal of Immunopathology and Pharmacology*, vol. 21, no. 1, 2008, pp. 117–27.

15. Qing Li et al., 'Effect of phytoncide from trees on human natural killer cell function', *International Journal of Immunopathology and Pharmacology*, vol. 22, no. 4, 2009, pp. 951–59.

16. Hyunju Jo et al., 'Physiological benefits of viewing nature: A systematic review of indoor experiments', *International Journal of Environmental Research and Public Health*, vol. 16, no. 23, 2019, p. 4739.

17. George MacKerron & Susana Mourato, 'Happiness is greater in natural environments', *Global Environmental Change*, vol. 23, no. 5, 2013, pp. 992–1000.

18. See www.mappinessapp.com.

19. Elle Hunt, 'Blue spaces: Why time spent near water is the secret of happiness', *The Guardian*, 3 November 2019, <www.theguardian.com/lifeandstyle/2019/nov/03/blue-space-living-near-water-good-secret-of-happiness>.

20. Mireia Gascon et al., 'Outdoor blue spaces, human health and well-being: A systematic review of quantitative studies', *International Journal of Hygiene and Environmental Health*, vol. 220, no. 8, 2017, pp. 1207–21.

21. BlueHealth, 'About BlueHealth', <https://bluehealth2020.eu/about>.

22. Marc Berman et al., 'The cognitive benefits of interacting with nature', *Psychological Science*, vol. 19, no. 12, 2009, pp. 1207–12.

## Chapter 10. Work

1. Paul Armstrong, 'Neuroscience, narrative, and narratology', *Poetics Today*, vol. 40, no. 3, 2019, pp. 395–428.

2. Safe Work Australia, 'Mental health: Overview', 2019, <www.safework australia.gov.au/topic/mental-health#overview>.

3. An obvious exception to this would be in sporting environments, where performance depends on superior teamwork.

4. Katharine Schwab, 'Everyone hates open offices. Here's why they still exist', *Fast Company*, 15 January 2019, <www.fastcompany.com/90285582/everyone-hates-open-plan-offices-heres-why-they-still-exist>.

5. Eric Savitz, 'Jack Dorsey: Leadership secrets of Twitter and Square', *Forbes*, 17 October 2012, <www.forbes.com/sites/ericsavitz/2012/10/17/jack-dorsey-the-leadership-secrets-of-twitter-and-square>.

6. Mark Zuckerberg, Facebook post on 30 March 2015, <www.facebook.com/photo. php?fbid=10101999874192881&set=a.612287952871&type=3&theater>.

7.  Jungsoo Kim & Richard de Dear, 'Workspace satisfaction: The privacy–communication trade-off in open-plan offices', *Journal of Environmental Psychology*, vol. 36, 2013, pp. 18–26; The University of Sydney, 'Workers dissatisfied with open plan offices', 17 September 2013, <www.sydney.edu.au/news-opinion/news/2013/09/17/workers-dissatisfied-with-open-plan-offices.html>.

8.  Christian Camerota, 'The unintended effects of open office space', *Harvard Business School Newsroom*, 9 July 2018, <www.hbs.edu/news/articles/Pages/bernstein-open-offices.aspx>.

9.  Ethan Bernstein & Ben Waber, 'The truth about open offices', *Harvard Business Review*, November–December 2019, <https://hbr.org/2019/11/the-truth-about-open-offices>.

10. Alex Heber, 'Australians are spending more time in meetings than ever but most are a waste of time', *Business Insider Australia*, 28 October 2014, <www.businessinsider.com.au/australians-are-spending-more-time-in-meetings-than-ever-but-most-are-a-waste-of-time-2014-10>.

11. LogMeIn, 'Ovum & LogMeIn study finds late meetings cost executives 5 1/2 days per year', press release, 7 August 2014, <https://s2.q4cdn.com/247461878/files/doc_news/LOGM_News_2014_8_7_General_Releases.pdf>.

12. Jason Fried, 'Status meetings are the scourge', *SvN*, 31 October 2016, <https://m.signalvnoise.com/status-meetings-are-the-scourge>.

13. Dominic Price, 'That time I deleted all my meetings (on purpose)', 1 January 2019, <www.atlassian.com/blog/teamwork/time-deleted-meetings-purpose>.

14. Rebecca Hinds & Bob Sutton, 'Dropbox's secret for saving time in meetings', *Inc.*, 11 May 2015, <www.inc.com/rebecca-hinds-and-bob-sutton/dropbox-secret-for-saving-time-in-meetings.html>.

15. The Radicati Group, 'Email statistics report, 2015–2019', <www.radicati.com/wp/wp-content/uploads/2015/02/Email-Statistics-Report-2015-2019-Executive-Summary.pdf>.

16. Collins Dictionary, <www.collinsdictionary.com/dictionary/english/knowledge-worker>; Michael Chui et al., *The Social Economy: Unlocking value and productivity through social technologies*, McKinsey Global Institute, July 2012, <www.mckinsey.com/~/media/McKinsey/

Industries/Technology%20Media%20and%20Telecommunications/
High%20Tech/Our%20Insights/The%20social%20economy/MGI_
The_social_economy_Executive_Summary.ashx>.

17. Matt Plummer, 'How to spend way less time on email every day',
    *Harvard Business Review*, 22 January 2019, <https://hbr.org/2019/01/
    how-to-spend-way-less-time-on-email-every-day>.

18. Kantar Media & OFCOM, *Digital Day 2016: Media and
    communications diary*, <www.digitaldayresearch.co.uk/media/1083/
    digital-day-2016-chart-deck-adults-aged-16plusin-the-uk.pdf>.

19. 'Too many interruptions at work?', *Business Journal*, 8 June 2006,
    <https://news.gallup.com/businessjournal/23146/Too-Many-
    Interruptions-Work.aspx>.

20. Victor González & Gloria Mark, '"Constant, constant, multi-tasking
    craziness": Managing multiple working spheres', *Proceedings of ACM
    CHI 2004 Conference on Human Factors in Computing Systems April
    24–29, 2004, Vienna, Austria*, 2004, pp. 113–20.

21. Karen Renaud et al., 'You've got e-mail! . . . Shall I deal with it now?
    Electronic mail from the recipient's perspective', *International Journal of
    Human-Computer Interaction*, vol. 21, no. 3, 2006, pp. 313–32.

22. See www.profjackson.com/email_cost_calculator.html.

23. Loughborough University Media Centre, 'Email: Yet more stress at the
    office?', press release, 4 June 2013, <www.lboro.ac.uk/media-centre/
    press-releases/2013/june/email--yet-more-stress-at-the-office.html>.

24. 'Too many interruptions at work?', *Business Journal*, 8 June 2006,
    <https://news.gallup.com/businessjournal/23146/too-many-
    interruptions-work.aspx>.

25. PBS, 'Interview: Clifford Nass', *Frontline*, 1 December 2009,
    <www.pbs.org/wgbh/pages/frontline/digitalnation/interviews/
    nass.html>.

26. Melina R. Uncapher & Anthony D. Wagner, 'Minds and brains of
    media multitaskers: Current findings and future directions', *PNAS*,
    vol. 115, no. 40, 2018, pp. 9889–96.

27. Shankar Vedantam, 'You 2.0: Deep work', *Hidden Brain*, NPR,
    26 August 2019, <www.npr.org/2019/08/26/754336716/
    you-2-0-deep-work>.

28. Australian Bureau of Statistics, '4364.0.55.001 – National Health Survey: First results, 2017-18', ABS, Canberra, 28 May 2019, <www.abs.gov.au/ AUSSTATS/abs@.nsf/Lookup/4364.0.55.001Main+Features 702017-18>; Peter Dockrill, 'America really is in the midst of a rising anxiety epidemic', *Science Alert*, 9 May 2018, <www.sciencealert.com/ americans-are-in-the-midst-of-an-anxiety-epidemic-stress-increase>; Medibank, 'Anxious Australia: Mental health conditions continue to increase', 14 June 2019, <www.medibank.com.au/livebetter/health-brief/ health-updates/anxious-australia-mental-health-conditions-continue-to-increase>; A.J. Baxter et al., 'Challenging the myth of an "epidemic" of common mental disorders: Trends in the global prevalence of anxiety and depression between 1990 and 2010', *Depression and Anxiety*, vol. 31, no. 6, 2014, pp. 506–16.

## Chapter II. Action

1. Graham Lloyd, 'Great Barrier Reef is better than expected', *The Weekend Australian*, 14 August 2019.

2. Great Barrier Reef Marine Park Authority, 'Statement: Coral bleaching on the Great Barrier Reef', 26 March 2020, <www.gbrmpa. gov.au/news-room/latest-news/latest-news/coral-bleaching/2020/ statement-coral-bleaching-on-the-great-barrier-reef>.

3. Audre Lorde, *Your Silence Will Not Protect You*, London: Silver Press, 2017.

4. Greta Thunberg, *No One Is Too Small to Make a Difference*, London: Penguin Books, 2019.

5. Lorde, *Your Silence Will Not Protect You*.

6. Thomas Merton, *Seeds of Destruction*, New York: Farrar, Strauss & Giroux, 1980 [1964].

7. Morgan Atkinson, 'Dalai Lama reminisces about meeting kindred spirit Thomas Merton', *HuffPost*, 5 November 2015, <www.huffpost.com/ entry/dalai-lama-reminisces-about-meeting-kindred-spirit-thomas-merton_b_8481898>.

8. Thomas Merton, 'Is the world a problem? Ambiguities in the secular', *Commonweal*, 3 June 1966, <www.commonwealmagazine.org/ world-problem>.

9.  Vicki Mackenzie, *Cave in the Snow*, New York, NY, and London: Bloomsbury, 1998, p. 197.
10. Mackenzie, *Cave in the Snow*, pp. 197–98.
11. Henri Nouwen, *The Way of the Heart*, New York, NY: Ballantine Books, 1981.

## Appendix. Silence: A How-To Guide

1.  Kate Lee et al., '40-second green roof views sustain attention: The role of micro-breaks in attention restoration', *Journal of Environmental Psychology*, vol. 42, 2015, pp. 182–89.
2.  Peter Kelley, 'Task interrupted: A plan for returning helps you move on', *UW News*, 16 January 2018, <www.washington.edu/news/2018/01/16/task-interrupted-a-plan-for-returning-helps-you-move-on>.
3.  Jason Fried, 'Library rules: How to make an open office plan work', *SvN*, 23 July 2018, <https://m.signalvnoise.com/library-rules-how-to-make-an-open-office-plan-work>.
4.  Sally Macdonald, 'SPU students take a break from technology', *The Seattle Times*, 8 February 2001, <https://archive.seattletimes.com/archive/?date=20010208&slug=notech08m>.

# FURTHER READING

There is no definitive guidebook for silence. If I learned anything from my own quest, it's that silence is something you have to experience rather than read or think about.

That said, it sometimes helps to be assured that you're not alone, and to learn from the experiences of the very broad and diverse community who also appreciate this beautiful quality. My only advice would be to embark on your own voyage with an open mind. Rather than beginning with the idea that you would *never* meditate, or sit in a church, or go for a long hike on your own, perhaps start out with the words: *Why not?* One of the best ways to strip away noise is to step out of your comfort zone. Time and again, that is exactly where I came face to face with silence.

## General

Anything written by Pico Iyer is worth reading, in my opinion, but *The Art of Stillness* (TED Books, London, 2014) is a deliciously light introduction to the topic. Or you can watch the TED talk on which it is based. Similarly, Norwegian explorer Erling Kagge says a lot in a few, well-crafted words in *Silence in the Age of Noise* (Viking, Melbourne, 2017).

Eventually, you will have to read *Walden* (Vintage, London, 2017). He can be a crotchety old grinch, Henry David Thoreau, but you'll forgive him because he was clearly ahead of his time. Still is, I suspect. More than a century after Thoreau wandered into the woods to live by himself, Sara Maitland tried the same, albeit on the Isle of Skye. Her *A Book of Silence* (Granta, London, 2009) is considered a seminal text on the topic, as is George Prochnik's *In Pursuit of Silence* (Anchor Books, New York, 2011).

*In Pursuit of Silence* is also the name of a compellingly beautiful film exploring the topic, directed by Patrick Shen. If you can find it somewhere online, it's worth sitting down somewhere very still and watching. The accompanying book, *Notes on Silence*, by Patrick Shen and Cassidy Hall, is full of evocative photos, interviews and essays related to the film.

And I am about to start Ryan Holiday's *Stillness Is the Key* (Profile Books, London, 2019), because stillness and silence tend to go hand in hand.

## Contemplative traditions

I will not even try to do justice to centuries of religious tradition within a simple reading list. And I'm certainly no expert in this area. If a particular religious tradition appeals to you, it's highly likely you'll be able to find contemplatives within it somewhere. So googling 'contemplatives' or 'mystics' with that particular tradition may be your best bet.

The podcast *Encountering Silence* is an excellent guide and companion. The three hosts all share Christian backgrounds, but they are committed to exploring silence in all its forms, including its role in politics, education and the arts, as well as the psychology of silence.

Like me, the American writer Judith Valente was living a very hectic life as a journalist and poet when she felt drawn to silence. She was also drawn to life at a Benedictine monastery, although her teachers were the sisters of Mount Saint Scholastica in Atchison, Kansas. Her books, *Atchison Blue* (Sorin Books, Notre Dame, 2013) and *How to Live* (Hampton Roads, Charlottesville, 2018), are full of wit, warmth and advice about how to apply the Rule of Saint Benedict in modern life.

Thomas Merton was prolific, but I prefer his later writing, as he became more vocal on social issues and explored Eastern philosophies in the 1960s. *New Seeds of Contemplation* (New Directions, New York, 2007) and *Mystics and Zen Masters* (Farrar, Straus & Giroux, New York, 1999) spring to mind.

Tarrawarra's Father Michael Casey is just as prolific, and writes with a wry humour, which is endearing. As documented in this book, I was captivated by *Strangers in the City* (Paraclete Press, Orleans, 2013). For those interested in diving deeper into Christian contemplative practice, he has written extensively on the topic in other volumes.

*Prayer in the Cave of the Heart*, by New Camaldoli's Father Cyprian Consiglio (Liturgical Press, Collegeville, 2010), helped me join the dots between the Eastern and Western contemplative traditions. Thich Nhat Hanh took over at that point; he has written many books, but *Silence* (Rider, London, 2015) is a wonderful introduction to the Buddhist approach to the topic.

For an intense Buddhist adventure, I highly recommend *In Love with the World*, by Yongey Mingyur Rinpoche (with Helen Tworkov) (Pan Macmillan, New York, 2019), the Tibetan lama who was the focus of many of neuroscientist Richie Davidson's early meditation experiments.

And I dived in and out of Coleman Barks' translations of *The Essential Rumi* (HarperOne, New York, 2004) whenever I felt that silence needed some poetry.

## Nature

My advice: seek out men and women who listen to trees, and listen in turn to them. They are our modern mystics.

David George Haskell's *The Songs of Trees* (Penguin, New York, 2017) is an ethereal blend of science and philosophy. But if you prefer fiction, *The Overstory*, the Pulitzer Prize–winning novel by Richard Powers (William Heinemann, New York, 2018), explores many of the same themes.

And I defy you to read *One Square Inch of Silence* by Gordon Hempton and John Grossman (Free Press, New York, 2009) and *not* want to book a hiking trip to Olympic National Park immediately afterwards. If that's not possible, hunt down *Sound Escapes*, a podcast collaboration Hempton did with BirdNote, in which Hempton guides listeners on aural journeys through diverse soundscapes, such as the Amazon and Hawaii's Big Island.

## Neuroscience

In my view, *The Science of Meditation* by Daniel Goleman and Richard Davidson (Viking, London, 2017) is the definitive text on this topic—although the science continues to advance apace.

*Beyond the Self* by Matthieu Ricard and Wolf Singer (MIT Press, Cambridge, MA, 2017) is a great accompaniment for those who would like to weave Buddhism and neuroscience together, while Sam Harris's *Waking Up* (Bantam, London, 2014) is essential reading for those who would like to understand and explore meditation without religious overtones. His podcast *Making Sense* is also excellent, although its interests and topics range much further than what is covered here.

If you are keen to learn more about how Big Tech is using neuroscience to mine your attention, subscribe to *Your Undivided Attention*, an excellent podcast by Tristan Harris and Aza Raskin from the Center for Humane Technology, and keep an eye on the excellent work they continue to do via their website.

## Work

Related to the above, Cal Newport's *Deep Work* (Grand Central Publishing, New York, 2016) examines how distractions undermine our ability to do strategic and creative thinking, and in *Digital Minimalism* (Penguin Business, Melbourne, 2019) he offers more practical advice about reducing the digital noise in your life.

The Benedictine monk Father Laurence Freeman has written a number of books about how meditation and contemplative practices can improve our performance at work and in life, including *Good Work* (Meditatio, Singapore, 2019). Similarly, Sharon Salzberg applies the principles of her Buddhist practice and teachings in *Real Happiness at Work* (Workman Publishing, New York, 2014).

## Meditation

These days there are plenty of options for those wanting to learn to meditate. I can only reiterate my advice that you do not need to pay enormous amounts of money to do so. Indeed, in many traditions it is considered inappropriate (or worse) to ask for money beyond a donation.

There are plenty of amazing teachers and courses now available free of charge via apps, with others charging a fee for some lessons. Sam Harris offers a solid foundation course in Vipassana techniques on his Waking Up app (which has some paid content), while I am also a fan of Insight Timer. Other well-reviewed apps include Calm and Headspace.

Enough words. More silence. Over to you.

# INDEX